JEALOUSY

The American Social Experience Series
GENERAL EDITOR: JAMES KIRBY MARTIN
EDITORS: PAULA S. FASS, STEVEN H. MINTZ,
CARL PRINCE, JAMES W. REED & PETER N. STEARNS

JEALOUSY

The Evolution of an
Emotion in American History

PETER N. STEARNS

NEW YORK UNIVERSITY PRESS
NEW YORK AND LONDON
1989

Library of Congress Cataloging-in-Publication Data
Stearns, Peter N.
Jealousy : the evolution of an emotion in american history / Peter
N. Stearns.
p.   cm.—(The American social experience series ; 14)
Bibliography: p.
Includes index.
ISBN 0-8147-7888-7 (alk. paper)
1. Jealousy—United States—History—19th century.   2. Jealousy—
United States—History—20th century.   I. Title.   II. Series.
BF575.J4S74   1989   89-34055
152.4—dc20   CIP

New York University Press books are printed on acid-free paper,
and their binding materials are chosen for strength and durability.

Book design by Ken Venezio

For Carol, green eyes and all

Contents

Preface

Jealousy is a natural topic in modern social history, particularly that kind of social history which focuses on basic attitudes and family relationships. Notwithstanding the flowering of these facets of social history, jealousy has never been subjected to systematic historical scrutiny. Despite much work on the rise of romantic love in Western civilization, including the United States, despite a number of good treatments of courtship, many of them vital contributions toward a study of jealousy, green eyes have yet to open in historical scholarship. The same holds true, again despite important and compelling treatments, for the history of children, where not only jealousy but sibling relationships more generally have been oddly ignored.

Yet approaches to jealousy, and key changes in these approaches, form an important chapter in the development of emotional styles and therefore in a variety of personal and social relationships, particularly in the nineteenth and twentieth centuries. Jealousy is to a substantial degree a social emotion. Animals may display some forms of jealousy—there is dispute on this, though Darwinians were convinced of it. Male animals, in particular, may experience something like jealousy as a spur to establishing or defending sexual access to females. Yet most students of human jealousy have argued that jealousy is an amalgam of more basic emotions—fear of impending loss, grief, and anger at the source of loss. As an amalgam, jealousy is open to various socially determined combinations. Different cultures certainly distinguish widely varied occasions for jealousy; some accept, even welcome, a sharing of sexual favors that in other settings would trigger a violently jealous response. Cultural distinctions raise the strong probability of changes over time within the same culture, although, a few French literary studies aside, the historical vantage point has yet to be explored.

Within the more specific context of American history, and in terms of what is already known about the history of emotions, jealousy focuses a fascinating clash among evolving standards. This potential conflict was indeed a principal spur to the present study. Insofar as jealousy entails anger, American emotional standards have increasingly urged antipathy: anger in family relationships and other contexts is seen as wrong. Yet jealousy is not just anger: in many expressions, it also entails an attachment to loving relationships and a need for affection that Americans have been increasingly schooled to see as desirable and natural.[1] As a blend of emotional ingredients whose approval ratings have moved in opposite directions, jealousy inherently compels complex assessments and strategies—not only in theory, but in the actual working out of the emotion in dealing with children, suitors, spouses, and rivals. This study traces the several major stages in coming to terms with this complexity in American history, and it argues for the importance of the result in understanding certain facets of American life.

Jealousy has of course been examined by researchers from other disciplines, though even here, in recent decades, it has not commanded overwhelming attention, in part, as we shall see, because the emotion is judged so messy by scholars as well as those contemporaries whom scholars might study. Nevertheless, we know a good bit about the types of situations that make people jealous (known rivals thus stimulate more emotion than unknowns), about divisions among contemporary Americans in proneness to jealousy—including ongoing efforts to capture any gender distinctions accurately, and about jealousy-inducing sibling relationships (now held to be scant problem save where an oldest male child may be target). A few of the more elaborate studies have some historical dimension. A significant 1970s collection on the sociology of jealousy stressed (and, its editors would probably today agree, exaggerated) trends toward the reduction and control of jealousy.[2] In the same vein, an impressive social-psychological study argued that by the 1960s middle-class Americans (in apparent contrast to their predecessors in the 1950s) had abandoned traditional beliefs in the inevitable and desirable linkage of jealousy with true love.[3]

Research of this sort is important, and methods applied to jealousy research are, happily, beginning to diversify.[4] Still, much recent work on jealousy has a diffuse quality (romantic jealousy thus kept rigorously separate from sibling studies save for somewhat loose assumptions about inadequate socialization). Historical impressions, though by no means totally wrong, are only that: they misdate major change, oversimplify it, and fail to deal with causation or impact. A historical approach to American jealousy, in other words, has a central place in emotions research, given the need for synthesis and for more than descriptive assessments of the results of current jealousy patterns; the approach is all the more relevant because of the realization, yet to strike historians themselves, that recent change is a vital factor in the emotion's presentation.

Precisely because the emotion became problematic, in the contemporary American emotional arsenal and even in the nineteenth century, jealousy research is not a simple matter. Most recent studies have focused on interview schedules with college students or on examination of special contexts like 1960s communes. These are useful but hardly comprehensive in their implications. The historian of jealousy has particular problems, given the vagueness of evidence about actual emotional experience in the past and, with a disapproved emotion, some reticence even in discussing emotionology or the rules by which feelings are judged. Silence must sometimes be interpreted, and much remains unknown. Nevertheless, a central trajectory is clear, as control over jealousy becomes a more urgent ingredient in American emotional life. While the central dilemma in dealing with jealousy was anticipated in the framing of this project, from what was already known about reactions to love and anger, the significance of the dilemma, and its ramifications into various emotion-driven behaviors, proved surprisingly great.

A number of people have assisted me in this study, and I owe them considerable thanks. Judy Kane and Gail Dickey oversaw manuscript preparation. John Modell, Steven Gordon, James K. Martin, Herrick Chapman, Lizabeth Cohen, Judy Grumet, Steven Mintz, and Richard Schoenwald commented on major portions of this work and provided very useful suggestions. John Spurlock, Jan Lewis, Robert Ireland, Ellen Rothman, and Linda Rosenzweig guided me to materials, derived from their own research, that I would not otherwise have encountered: this study benefited greatly from their generosity. Research assistance from Amy deCamp, Barry O'Rorke, and Lori Cole was invaluable, and Steve Tripp provided even more systematic contributions during an early phase of the project. Several of my children aided in dealing with sibling materials both recent and past, and all of them (along with my own convoluted jealousy experiences) helped me think about how the emotion works out in real life. Finally, my wife, Carol, provided insight as well as intelligent reading of the work, even as she stimulates good management of the emotion in our marriage. I feel an unusual debt to her and to all who have contributed to shaping this work.

CHAPTER I

Introduction:
Traditions of Jealousy

Jealousy has long been a disputed emotion. It can be compulsive, seizing the judgment and motivating acts of extreme violence or self-degradation. Even in milder forms it can lead to nagging attempts to control others, or endless bickering over claims to attention and affection. Yet, in the judgment of some, jealousy can also motivate: the word comes from the same Greek stem as does *zeal* and was originally used (until the eighteenth century, to be precise) almost interchangeably with that more enthusiastic term. A jealous defense of rights was once, before the adjective came into more modern disfavor, a good and legitimate defense. Jealousy may also intensify certain relationships, helping people decide that attraction is really love, and a love worth converting into a more stable relationship. Making someone jealous risks appearing, again to contemporary eyes schooled to view the emotion a certain way, like a last-ditch defense, a distasteful stratagem to be tried, if at all, when everything else has failed; but in other cultures, and for some individuals today, a certain amount of jealous game playing adds spice to romance. Jealousy unquestionably causes discomfort, and sometimes even worse, but one can argue it also vivifies, and that it has some utility, properly targeted, precisely because it can be painful.

A key reason to study jealousy lies in its very complexity, in the diverse and even contradictory qualities that can be assigned to the emotion. Furthermore, jealousy plays a role in a range of significant relationships—in family, friendship, school, work, and neighborhood —and may indeed affect institutional arrangements designed to bring these relationships in line with desired emotional levels. Jealousy thus can affect law, domesticity, consumer behavior and advertising, grading, perhaps even politics. Jealousy stands, then, as an intriguing social emotion, with considerable potential impact beyond the strictly emotional sphere.

Yet it has not been widely or systematically studied of late—even when due recognition is paid to the important research findings from psychology and sociology. We know that Americans report diverse reactions to jealousy, depending on larger views about romance and self. Gender has also been explored, with an eye to countering older behavioral-science beliefs that women are more jealous than men. Some indications of social-class distinctions have been raised, with workers considered more jealous in family than middle-class adults, though here further, more concentrated study on jealousy remains urgent.[1] We know that siblings can be jealous but (according to the most recent findings) that the incidence is neither inevitable nor random.[2] We know that, despite important diversities, Americans in general profess dislike of jealousy and manifest a desire to conceal it, at least when quizzed by emotions researchers, scoring high in these areas in comparison with a number of other cultures. Thus Americans are more likely to disapprove of jealousy than are Chinese (hardly a stereotypically passionate people), but their interest in hiding it reflects a tension that can be further explored. The role of social disapproval in inhibiting communication about jealousy for individual couples has also been noted, and with it the complex impact that unacknowledged jealousy can have on a relationship—another point that can be fleshed out in historical context.[3] We know, finally, that evidence both from sociologically fascinating groups—like late-1960s communes[4]—and from still more recent social-psychological opinion studies suggest an important twentieth-century (some would claim, postwar) change in our outlook on jealousy, a growing desire to separate proper love from the green-eyed emotion and a belief that jealousy reflects immature insecurities.[5]

This knowledge is extremely valuable, and it gives direction and substance to any larger study, including a historical one. Still, jealousy sits at the margins of most larger inquiry into emotional styles. Despite widespread popular belief and ongoing expert opinion that poor management of children's jealousy and later romantic jealousy are linked, there have been no comprehensive studies of the subject since the 1930s (and the results of the research conducted then are now disputed). Comparative insights have not been closely matched with the diversity studies, if only because the former rest on generalized characterizations about American jealousy, which the latter implicitly dispute. Furthermore, both kinds of research rest too exclusively on polling data, rather than on wider inquiries into attitudes and attendant behavior, to be fully satisfactory. Beyond the fragmentation of much available work is sheer neglect. A number of excellent studies of love, both historical and other, thus pass jealousy by. Anthropologists, despite extensive interest in kinship, competition, and property, have not evoked jealousy since interwar studies by Margaret Mead and a fine overview article by Kingsley Davis.[6] And there is no history of jealousy at all, despite growing attention to past patterns of love, grief, anger, and fear, of marriage and childhood, and despite the sense in other expert camps that jealousy has recently changed—becoming, that is, an obvious topic for contemporary history.

Why the neglect? Emotions research in general has only lately revived, after a several-decades doldrums—witness the foundings since 1984 of a new International Society for Research on Emotion and an emotions section of the American Sociological Association. Historical work on emotion, of any explicit sort, remains also a novel field. Because not everything can be covered at once in a new or reviving field, some shortchanging of jealousy may warrant only practical explanation. Yet, since other emotions have been privileged, additional factors can be sketched. Some researchers may find jealousy essentially a constant, not worth folding into a serious study of cultural diversity in emotion or change over time; this view, we will hope to show, is wrong, but it may be pervasive. Historical studies of childhood and childrearing thus may have assumed sibling jealousy as a fact of nature and hence not explored it with the same sophistication they applied to other emotional attributes.[7] Other researchers—and obviously there are important exceptions here[8]—may turn from jealousy because it is so unpleasant; thus one psychological synthesis that does refer to jealousy is unusually terse and includes revealing comments on jealousy's nastily antisocial qualities.[9] Jealousy may have been unduly neglected, then, because of pervasive assumptions that took on new force in the twentieth century: that jealousy is inevitable (though open to management) and/or extremely noxious. These assumptions can be studied as part of a larger emotional picture.

It is also possible—and this view too would incorporate some popular thinking—that jealousy has been neglected because it is viewed as trite. Few Americans explicitly see their own jealousy as a problem, either because they profess to have little of it or because they claim to be comfortable with what they have. The complacency can be questioned, but on the face it reduces jealousy as a problematic emotion that demands inquiry. More common still is a view that jealousy should be so smoothly handled in childhood socialization that it will not spill over into adult relationships or activities; manifestations of jealousy here become mere individual aberrancies, not spurs to wider behaviors. This is one reason why many adults prefer to look back on a jealous adolescence, when jealousy is called to their attention (forgetting that as adolescents they had usually tried to deny jealousy as well), instead of giving the emotion any ongoing force or seeing its social ramifications. This book challenges these views, in arguing that jealousy arrangements have—though usually somewhat unwittingly, not graced by precise labels—played a significant role in American history, particularly on its personal side but in institutional expressions as well. There is no need to claim transcendent importance for jealousy —and this study does not attempt a precise comparison of jealousy issues with other emotional currents over time; but in fact judgments of jealousy, and strategies to implement these judgments, provide a revealing entry to a number of facets of American social history more generally.

Analysis of the modern history of American jealousy offers an opportunity not only to place the emotion in some perspective but also to interrelate currently disparate approaches to the emotion. The claim is, as with any self-conscious history, that jealousy has changed significantly over time (against any beliefs in its invariability) and also that the changes have a somewhat different and more interesting timing than historically sensitive researchers have thus far believed. The modern history of jealousy does not entail simply a 1960s rebellion against centuries of traditional attachment to the emotion, though the 1960s do play a role. The historical approach can also grapple with causation of change—largely omitted from sociological and psychological inquiries, which tend to assume some sudden enlightenment and leave it at that. And the approach can begin an exploration of the impact of this same change, beyond purely personal relationships. Too many emotions studies treat their topic as a black box, without inquiring about outreach into public arenas such as law or school. Here, historical research can even challenge some widely held beliefs, as in the area of jealousy's current role as a cause of crime, though at points the challenge must be slightly tentative.

The absence of historical consideration of jealousy—for historians and other emotions researchers alike—particularly invites remedy because of the emotion's precarious poise between anger at loss and invitation to love, between disapproved and hallowed emotional currents. More specifically still, a common-sense review of recent history would suggest that the opportunities for jealousy have increased substantially, with looser sexual behavior, more frequent marital dissolution, less rigid public roles for women. At the least, it is useful to inquire how adolescent and adult jealousies have been managed or mismanaged in the altered context of the twentieth century. Furthermore, the standards of jealousy have also shifted, for the most part toward greater disapproval of any effort to mix jealousy and love, green eyes and calf eye. Both shifts—in setting and in emotionology or feeling rules—require historical perspective, and their interrelationship can be probed over time as well.

Jealousy has become a more troubling emotion in American personal and family life during the twentieth century because of the combination of new opportunities for experiencing the emotion and increasing disapproval of this very experience. Charting this evolution opens new insights on various private behaviors and widens an understanding of jealousy itself, as an emotion. For jealousy, though it seems to have animal roots at least in male reactions designed to defend territoriality and sexual access, is in humans a supremely social emotion. It is capable of varied definitions depending on cultural context. Whatever the instinctual elements in jealousy, in other words, the emotion follows definite social rules, which can vary and also shift over time.[10] As one recent study notes, romantic jealousy seems to be a "complex of interrelated emotional, cognitive and behavioral processes,"[11] which means that it is abundantly open to study from a variety of disciplinary vantage points, including the historical. In examining important changes in the cultural context for romantic jealousy in the United States over the past century and a half, we grasp more fully what the emotional experience of what jealousy has meant, how it has been intended and what consequence it has had—and continues to have.

Jealousy in fact feeds into some of the larger themes of American personality study, sometimes adding emotional depth to findings already available but at points suggesting some unexpected twists. Grasp of the nature and causes of new approaches to jealousy touches base with an understanding of shifts in the family's emotional range around 1900 and with exploration of the tension between individualism and commitment in American life.[12] It feeds a wider inquiry into the decline of the nineteenth-century personality type—indeed, it has already been briefly evoked in Christopher Lasch's tantalizing survey —and into more specific topics such as the deterioration in the valuation of children in the later twentieth century or the series of articulations of the battle between the sexes over an even longer time span.[13] Above all, an understanding of the handling of jealousy over the past century and a half opens the way to a firmer definition of a new emotional control style taking shape from the 1920s onward—a style that embraces more than jealousy itself, but in which jealousy issues played a vital role.

This book, in sum, without trying to privilege jealousy as a disproportionately interesting or significant emotion, argues that an understanding of jealousy adds substantially to our understanding of nineteenth- and twentieth-century history and that an understanding of relevant history improves our grasp of jealousy even today.

Methods and Procedures

Historical study of emotion is sufficiently novel that a clear indication of approach, and its several limitations, is essential. We must briefly

discuss some standard historical issues, including relationship to e
ing work and periodization, but then turn to problems more specifi...
the emotions field.

1. Periodization. The heart of this study involves tracing a nineteenth-century reformulation of jealousy, based on changes in emotional standards and family context, then turning to a contextual transition in the decades around 1900, followed by an exploration of
various facets of the larger shift that resulted from the 1920s onward.
We will argue that the resultant new period persists essentially to the
present time, though with a differentiation between a missionary era
—when the new standards were being urgently disseminated, complete with scare tactics—and the decades of fuller integration after
about 1960. To set all this in motion, we must first gain some sense of
older traditions of jealousy in the West, without pretense of full exploration; this topic will end the present introduction.

2. Target population. Like most historians of emotion thus far, I
focus in this study primarily on the middle class. Unlike anger or even
love, jealousy standards have not cried out for application across class
lines, because the emotion is regarded as primarily personal; it is
unusually hard, even through indirection, to get a sense of what
working-class standards were, since (in contrast to behaviors regarding
sex, love, or anger) few middle-class pundits were explicitly telling
their inferiors what they were doing wrong. Middle-class emotional
standards do have influence beyond the class at least by the twentieth
century, which gives the topic a larger importance, but this is not a
history from the bottom up. The fascinating problem of how workers
fit in, though raised both by evidence that many workers differed in
their evaluation of jealousy and by my own claims about some generalized emotional-control strategies, is in no sense carefully resolved. I
hope it can be in future, but it is vital to realize the limits of coverage
here.

3. Historiography. The absence of historical treatment of jealousy
has already been noted. The claim is accurate, and not designed to
drive colleagues and reviewers to professional outbursts of the emotion
under study. Nevertheless, this analysis touches base with important
prior research in a number of respects. What we already understand
about changes in love and other emotions, and about causation and

impact of emotional transformations, vitally informs any assessment of
the history of jealousy. We already know that emotions history is
possible and useful, and this study is intended as a new application of
an established approach. It differs from some of the leading models in
one respect, beyond the specific emotion under examination. Most
leading emotions histories have focused on the seventeenth and eighteenth centuries as the period of key change, in which traditional
Western styles gave way to more modern ones.[14] It is not, to be sure,
unprecedented to point to subsequent change,[15] but it remains unusual. For jealousy, the redefinition of romantic and parental love in
the eighteenth century played a significant role in setting a new stage
for relevant standards in the nineteenth century, and this is an important part of the larger modern story. But even more decisive changes
in context and strategies occurred in the twentieth century, an insight
that calls attention to the subject of emotions history as an ongoing
process, at least in modern history, and not a handful of once-and-for-
almost-all transformations.

In addition to extensive reliance on earlier emotions histories, the
present study leans heavily on what historians have already uncovered
about families, marriage, law, and general culture over the past 150
years. Even though most of the relevant treatments do not explicitly
cover jealousy, and though some key topics like the "invention" of
sibling rivalry have been oddly ignored altogether, many established
findings are directly applicable to a history of jealousy, and at key
points it will be clear that I am putting familiar eggs in a slightly
different basket. The study claims to be innovative, but not icono-
clastic.

4. Data. In addition to reliance on important literature in history
and in nonhistorical emotions research, this study rests on a variety of
source materials. Evidence for emotional standards comes from advice
manuals (directed to parents, teenagers, and courting and married
couples), supplemented by some use of popular literature and other
data including legal cases. A large sample of advice literature has been
studied, grounded where possible on identifications of popularity and
impact by other researchers, otherwise on other evidence of popularity
supplemented by consultation of a wider-than-usual range of materials
and relevant popular magazines.[16] Representativeness was also tested

by the use of materials issued by major child-guidance or marriage groups and through analysis of internal consistency on key points within each period. Because disputes over jealousy were usually limited within any given period, the summary of principal approaches requires no liberties with the evidence. Claims about the impact of advice must be more tentative, but polling data and behavioral evidence—as, for example, on dating practices—allow some conclusions about the actual evaluation of jealousy within the American middle class. The materials available for emotions history are never as good as one would wish, even for relatively articulate groups, and some best-guessing, clearly labeled, becomes essential. But widely shared emotional standards can be established, their changes explored and explained; additional evidence, plus general findings in psychology that standards do have more than theoretical impact,[17] allow some extensions to actual emotional experience.

5. Emotionology and outreach. Differential quality of available data leads naturally to the essential categories within emotions history, already established in other work but vital to the present study. Historians (and some other kinds of emotions researchers, focused on social context) have easier access to emotional standards, or emotionology,[18] than to actual emotional experience. Emotionology is important in its own right: it affects one's perceptions of one's own emotions and (crucial, as we will see, where modern jealousy is involved) judgments of those of others, and it can determine institutional arrangements for emotional expression—clearly so, for example, with regard to jealousy and law. Yet it is possible also to discuss emotional experience to a degree, particularly because it has a distinct cognitive component heavily influenced by prevailing rules of feeling. The distinctions involved between emotionology and experience have already been defined and require only careful labeling to make it clear when a transition is being made from emotionology (and the evidence that suggests it was substantially accepted by a relevant public) to the more impressionistic signs of interaction between standards and behavior or experience.

The study of jealousy requires one other distinction, though in this case one that can be explored in the process of exposition. Jealousy is most obviously an emotion applied to personal relationships, particularly according to modern American emotionology. The bulk of this study, correspondingly, deals with jealousy among children, lovers, and spouses, and then in conclusion turns to the broader but still essentially emotional topic of control and suppression as these moved from nineteenth- to twentieth-century styles. Yet jealousy does have some outreach, and the penultimate chapter deals with relationships between jealousy standards and outlet needs, on the one hand, and wider public behaviors in work, school, law, and consumption. Labeling jealousy in these spheres must be tentative, which in turn is why a discrete chapter is devoted to the wider connections. The connections exist, however, and they link both emotionology and emotional experience to broader themes in American society.

The extent of the interaction between an emotion and other more familiar historical currents, both as cause and as effect, is a key challenge to emotions research historically construed. (The same challenge exists in linking emotions with social behaviors and institutions, in sociology.) The challenge is difficult, given problems of evidence, and particularly so with a less public emotion such as jealousy. Still, with due caution and recognition of the need for some speculation, the challenge can be addressed. Changes in jealousy have been significant outside the personal orbit.

6. Theory. The final issue in emotions history involves utilization of psychological theory. Theory remains relevant even when standards and experience are clearly differentiated, so that there is no pretense of fathoming all the depths of psyche. Consumers of emotion-oriented history, more than many other emotions researchers, may expect a wedding between past data and a precise model of the emergence of jealousy in the human personality, akin to much psychohistorical work in the Freudian vein. This study is less theoretically confined (some might claim, less theoretically informed), seeking rather to approach emotion from a social as well as individual vantage point and attempting to convey a distinctive understanding of emotional dynamics, infused above all by an appreciation of change over time, the sum total different from that which traditional psychoanalytical constructs provide.

Various theorists have, to be sure, attempted to find an inevitable basis for jealousy in the experience of human childhood. Freud posited natural sexual jealousy of the other-gendered parent and also inherent sibling rivalries for maternal affection. More recently, Melanie Klein has described a still earlier but if anything more fundamental envy of dependence on the breast—on mother as feeder—from which later manifestations of jealousy spring.[19]

A historical and essentially social approach to jealousy does not directly grapple with these theories, but it does raise questions about their utility in capturing the central meaning of jealousy. An inevitable childhood base for jealousy does little to explain the marked individual variations in jealous reactions that are so vivid in our own society, or the cultural variations in the targets and intensity of jealousy, or the kinds of changes in romantic jealousy that have occurred in the United States over the past century or so. We must indeed deal with certain relationships between childhood (and adult anxieties about childhood) and romantic jealousy. These are not incompatible with some notion of a linkage between infant tensions and adult experience, modified to allow for some real change over time, but the argument does not depend on a set theory and is not directed toward its test. It is possible that little connection exists between childhood personality and some facets of adult emotional range. Certainly traditional Western society cushioned young sibling relationships with a great deal of hierarchy, a sense of bonding among siblings that might modify rivalry, and (sometimes) relatively little intense mother-child focus of the classic sort that could spur jealous attachments. Yet this same society could produce immensely jealous adults, eager to use the emotion as a basis for defenses of honor and female fidelity alike. Contemporary culture, which sees the possibility of more overt jealousy among young siblings but also more deliberate strategies to prevent or alleviate the emotion, produces new kinds of concern about adult jealousy but also more proudly jealousy-free adults.

The modern history of jealousy, in sum, expands knowledge of the emotion's range and complexity and suggests some probable, but mutual rather than monocausal, interaction with emotional socialization in childhood. It does not depend, however, on any particular personality theory and may, as far as jealousy is concerned, partially substitute for this approach.

Save for the committed Freudian, there is not a great deal of sweeping theory about jealousy sufficiently well grounded to be useful for a different disciplinary approach to the subject. Even findings about siblings, because they have oscillated so often over the past fifty years, remain slightly suspect—quite apart from their resolute neglect of the possibility of change. At various points it will be clear that a valid, tested theory would be very useful: if sibling jealousy increases in volume, for example, does this predict a comparable increase in adult jealousy unless countered by other factors? It would be good to have an equation, in discussing the early part of the twentieth century, but there is none. More specific findings from psychology, a grasp of the more general dynamics of emotional development in childhood—these are vital to the present effort. Theory use in the more traditional sense, however, does not describe the framework of this study. Classic theoretical concerns are not jettisoned, and may indeed be further pursued once an understanding of jealousy's evolution is assimilated. We will see, for example, an important potential link between twentieth-century changes and psychoanalytic discussions of narcissism.

One theoretical issue of a different, more definitional sort does warrant attention. Some emotions researchers have devoted laudable efforts, as a means of relaunching analysis in the subject area, to defining discrete emotions, often using the legacy of past categorizing approaches, philosophical as well as psychological.[20] A clearly relevant facet of this work involves distinctions between jealousy and envy. Jealousy is the emotion attached to holding onto something or someone, involving fear of loss and anger or grief at its prospect; it might even serve, in social terms, as the emotion of the upper classes, who have more to lose. Envy is different: it involves coveting something or some attribute that someone else has, with more lust attached and less fear; and it might be the emotion of the lower orders, who have more to gain. Distinctions of this sort make a great deal of sense, and this study is not directed toward disproving them in any systematic way. It will be obvious, however, that the book uses a somewhat more encompassing sense of jealousy, overlapping with envy in what, from the definitional standpoint, might seem sloppy ways. In defense of this procedure, I would argue that the usage corresponds to common twentieth-century American parlance, in which envy is rarely voiced as a term and in which the emotion is in fact usually called jealousy, and that one real point about jealousy's evolution, by the twentieth century, is that it came to embrace a good bit of envy, to such an extent that the distinction, though still theoretically possible, lost much of its meaning. This claim, laid out in chapter 6, includes an attempt to explain why this change has occurred. Here again, historical analysis is meant to contribute some theoretical weight of its own, toward advancing our understanding of current and past emotional styles alike.

Jealousy Traditions in the West

Although most comments on romantic jealousy in the United States are narrowly focused, aside from highly personal statements as in Nancy Friday's rambling book on the subject, there has been some sense of the emotion's complex place in American life. Willard Waller, one of the most perceptive students of romantic relationships between the wars, noted the odd situation of jealousy in the culture.[21] He illustrated through cases such as a man's marrying a former prostitute, apparently accepting her past with equanimity, but later killing someone who insulted her at a dance. The general point, though, was twofold: first, that American jealousy was open to considerable reconditioning but from a basis in which the emotion, as a response to sexual or romantic threat, ran quite strong; and second, that a variety of complex tensions surrounded the emotion. While Waller did not explore the general issues more fully, his sense was accurate, and a larger historical view will in some ways substantially embellish it.

The history must begin with patterns of jealousy in preindustrial Western society. Although no thorough research is offered here—and the topic might well reward an enterprising early modern historian— some sense of jealousy's place before 1800 is important for two reasons. First, traditional concepts about the emotion—indeed, traditional disagreements about it—provide an ongoing thread in the emotionology of the nineteenth and twentieth centuries, even amid great change. Second, while there is little explicit evidence, some suggestions about a partial recasting of jealousy's valuation do emerge from the eighteenth century. As a baseline for understanding continuities, and for assessing major changes in context, and finally as a means of launching the subject of change itself, a sketch of the Western approach to jealousy can quickly be offered.

Western culture early constructed some of the ambiguities about jealousy that bedevil Americans still. As in most areas of emotions history, change involves embellishments and shadings, of real significance, rather than stark before-and-after contrasts.

Christianity, as modern commentators have noted, set a basis for attacks on jealousy, for God's love was available to all in Christ's central message. Narrow, selfish love might thus be condemned, as Paul did in his comments on marriage. Yet the God of the Old Testament was an explicitly jealous divinity, insisting on exclusive worship; here, as later monarchist theorists observed, could be a model for legitimate jealousy of power and conceivably an exemplar for a more possessive kind of personal love as well. Christianity, as in so many aspects of emotionology, could go both ways.[22]

Later Western commentators on jealousy abundantly reflected the same kind of ambivalence. Condemnations continued to rain down. Seventeenth-century Jesuits blasted jealousy as a "monstrous" passion, the antithesis of real, spiritual love; a jealous husband, through his ravings, actually incited a wife to sin in retaliation, while the role of jealousy in crime was even more obvious. La Rochefoucauld applied aphorism: "If love is judged by its effects, it resembles hate more than friendship." Shakespeare described the "venom" and "misery" of jealousy tragically illustrated in *Othello*, while Alexander Pope termed it simply "hateful."[23] Jealousy was attacked because it produced cruelty, adulterated real love with baser passion, and led jealous individuals to tragic loss of control.

Yet jealousy was also accepted, even approved. A French courtly-love writer of the twelfth century put the point simply: "He who is not jealous cannot love. . . . Real jealousy always increases the feelings of love. . . . Jealousy, and therefore love, are increased when one suspects his beloved."[24] More cautiously, seventeenth-century commentators granted that jealousy was an inevitable part of love, though they worried that its excesses could stifle this same affection. Jealous men were often heroes in literature and drama, as they defended their honor and that of their faithful women. British plays of the seventeenth and eighteenth centuries underwrote the enjoyment of flirtation as the basis for making a lover jealous, so long as it was kept within bounds so that a threatened love did not turn to dislike; the same drama held women to stricter standards, wanting no qualifications, even playful, to their fidelity.[25] There were those, finally, who argued, reasonably enough, that jealousy, if not carried to obsessive or naggingly suspicious lengths, served as vital defense of family. "There is a just and an unjust jealousy. Just, is with married partners who mutually love each other; there is with them a just and prudent zeal lest their conjugal love be violated and therefore just grief if it is violated. . . . That zeal is a just protection against adultery is plain. Hence it is as a fire flaming against violation, and defending against it."[26]

Several key traditional elements are clear, beyond the important ambiguities, and they formed something of a Western cultural arsenal from which later American as well as European views of jealousy evolved. First, the idea that love naturally included jealousy, or a potential for jealousy, was deeply rooted. Advice might caution, and tragic examples of jealousy run amuck were available, but the basic linkage was accepted. Some might find in this not only inevitability but merit, as jealousy could deepen love or simply make it more lively, ensure fidelity, or even (within bounds) provide some enjoyable emotional spice.

Second, in many treatments the jealousy associated with love was closely related to that assigned to power.[27] Jealousy here was the emotional basis and legitimacy for ensuring good authority and order, and while it might become excessive it was in principle open to rational control. Many authors invoked the linkage between jealousy and zeal in this connection, urging the appropriateness of an emotional spur to defense of suitable constancy and property. Jealousy-zeal, of course, provided the basis for mobilizing in defense of honor, either for one's own name and reputation or the fidelity of a wife or daughter. Love and marriage, in this formulation, were closely akin to outright property, and jealousy was assumed to be a particularly masculine emotion in support of proper patriarchal governance.

Somewhat ironically, in a culture where a modern sense of self was largely absent, a supremely selfish emotion won wide approval. Yet precisely because individuals were not taught to define themselves through carefully crafted personalities or achievements, jealousy was essential in protecting the reputation and power that served in their stead to give a man a feeling of importance and pride. Absence of a

careful sense of individual personality may have heightened the need
to express a jealous ego, where power permitted, defining self through
honor and property. Here, clearly, is a facet that warrants further
exploration, lest "absence of sense of self" be rendered too simply for
the early modern West. When a newer kind of self took shape, jealousy
would become more widely questioned. Much of the modern history
of jealousy involves efforts to support individuality sufficiently to
render jealous possessiveness unnecessary. More directly still, traditional views of love diverged from more modern standards, though as
with definition of self some customary impulses long persisted, visible
even in the later twentieth century. Love, in the traditional formulation, had less to do with romantic delight or devotion and more to do
with family hierarchy than would later be the case; hence the widespread confidence in jealousy and its clear gender base.

Actual jealousy, of course, did not necessarily stick to the traditional
rules. Women thus may frequently have been jealous, despite considerable absence of cultural sanction. An aristocratic Englishwoman of
the eighteenth century, Elizabeth Stafford, protested loudly and pub-
licly when her husband took up with another woman, and while she
did not refer to jealousy directly the emotion may well have spurred
her frenzy. In claiming that love had informed their marriage at first
she was obviously observing the traditional affection-jealousy link in
her outbursts, but the fact remains that they were unusual for her sex,
according to prevailing judgments in emotionology.[28]

With the important exception of our ignorance of women's feelings
in an age of male dominance, however, there seems to have been some
real correspondence between articulated cultural assumptions about
jealousy and actual emotional experience. Jealousy was recognized as a
legitimate emotion in courtship and family life, at least for men, and it
could be and was invoked in cases of honor where family sanctity had
been violated. Dueling, violent vengeance, and frequent insult could
express a jealous concern for family and honor, providing a powerful
spur to action whose legitimacy was hard to deny. How many people
tormented themselves with jealousy-clouded love, in courtship or extramarital liaisons in the best chivalric fashion, cannot be determined,
for the widely accepted idea that love involved jealous pangs may have
been distant from reality; in the upper classes, though, some jealous
swoonings may have been taken as standard fare. Husbands' suits

against adulterous wives, with punitive damages assessed on lovers, in upper-class England into the late eighteenth century provided institutional expression for a vivid emotion.

The acceptance of ideas about legitimate jealousy, however, was severely qualified, particularly for the masses of peasants and artisans, and particularly in the American colonies, absent an aristocratic honor code, by strong community controls over behavior. Literary invocations of jealousy did not contradict beliefs, though they may also have provided some outlet for feelings that could not quite be articulated in real life. There was nevertheless a gap between values and occasions for expression, caused by the realities of marriage and group sanctions. Adult supervision of often rather unromantic courtship, and the frequency of arranged marriage, served to limit the need for active jealousy in heterosexual relationships among adolescents and young adults. Relatively little outright premarital intercourse occurred, until a couple was firmly pledged; courtship periods often saw young men and women deliberately focusing on a number of possible partners rather than zeroing in, with intensity, on a single individual until the last minute.[29] This might have occasioned some moderate jealous rivalries, but not extreme possessiveness. One opportunity for jealousy—and it would persist as a theme through the nineteenth century—involved siblings' sentiments when one of their number married. In seventeenth-century England, special rites were established (wearing and dancing on green stockings) to express but relieve this discomfort, allowing siblings to join in approval of the marriage.[30] So while courtship was not jealousy-free, there was little normal need to indulge in the emotion extensively, as a few rituals supplemented normal behavioral controls. The same pattern applied to marriage. Relatively little sexual infidelity was possible, given community supervision of behavior in most villages, and jealous outburts or utilization of laws that could have channeled jealous vengeance were rare simply because they were not needed. An apparently common aversion to sexual activity outdoors curtailed one obvious chance of escaping the neighbors: most people clearly found community control either inescapable or positively desirable. The fact was that traditional Western society looked down on love itself, at least until after marriage, as dangerous, and to the extent it kept this emotional complex in check it automatically controlled jealousy; there was no need to distinguish love and jealousy as impulses.[31]

The point need not be pressed too far. Jealousy was not seen as bound up with romance alone, and it may have spurred the many disputes about property and dignity that dot the records of early modern Europe and colonial America.[32] Aristocrats and Southern planters had more opportunities for romantic dalliance, and therefore jealousies, than did the ordinary run of folks. So the legitimacy accorded to jealousy was by no means entirely idle.

The combination of community behavioral controls and the emotionological support for jealousy had one further result in early modern society: there was no felt need to teach children about the emotion or its management. The idea that love and jealousy might mix and, even more, that jealousy had legitimate patriarchal uses seems to have been widely accepted in the signals given to children. The problematic results of jealousy were, after all, to be handled through restrictions on behavior, not through emotional control. And jealousy otherwise was seen as a suitable motivation for children in their attempts to establish their place in the world. The existence of childish jealousy thus passed unremarked, whether parental emphasis otherwise was on strict discipline or a more tolerant enjoyment of childish foibles.[33] The topic and the very word cropped up neither in religious advice about children nor in parental diaries. The way premodern village children banded together for play, across age groups, suggests that childish jealousy itself may often have moderated in favor of cooperation against the adult world, despite the hierarchy and rivalry implied by systems of unequal inheritance. This we cannot know, at least as yet. It is clear, however, that in parents' eyes the emotion was a nonissue, another sign of a regime in which emotional precision was reduced through the reliance on community monitoring of behavior.

One final element must be added to the traditional brew: wider changes in emotionology in the later seventeenth and eighteenth centuries raised some new questions about jealousy in Western culture. Growing hostility to emotional spontaneity could add a new ingredient to emotionological attacks on jealousy; thus in England and New England, emphasis on steadiness and self-control argued against facile indulgence in an emotion that could so easily run wild. In the same period the literary treatment of jealousy in France moved toward firmer recommendations of control.[34] There is some evidence that the promiscuity of upper-class men declined in eighteenth-century En-

gland, as marital fidelity won new adherence. Changes in male friendships, as commercial relationships added a competitive edge and reduced emotional intensity, may have cut into another source of jealousy,
though a less familiar one, from an additional direction.[35] There are
signs, in other words, that both in experience and in emotionology,
jealousy was winning some new and disapproving scrutiny in the
eighteenth century, though more clearly in aristocratic Europe than in
the United States.

These changes, however, did not necessarily shift popular emotional
habits. There are no signs of altered efforts at socialization or increased
frequency of expressed concern. The transition is significant nevertheless, for it would feed some more widely popular changes in the
approach to jealousy in the nineteenth century. Prior to that point,
however, new jealousy standards were only sketchily evoked, and they
had far less impact than concomitant alterations in the emotionology
of anger or even of love. The probable reasons were twofold, though
in absence of explicit evidence we must inevitably speculate. First,
popular habits about jealousy may have been unusually difficult to
dislodge. Thus as love received new emphasis as a basis for courtship
and marriage in the eighteenth century, which was the case in many
groups both in Western Europe and the American colonies, the result
—because of the popular definition of love—may have enhanced approval of jealousy, running thus against some new theoretical concerns. Second, since control of jealousy depended primarily on community supervision of family norms rather than on internalized emotional
rules, new anxiety about jealousy in principle would not necessarily
spur widespread adjustment in fact. To be sure, the family institution
did suffer by the later eighteenth century, with growing rates of
illegitimacy and youthful defiance of parental authority, but for the
most articulate, property-owning groups family values still largely
prevailed. Institutions, in other words, kept the need for active jealousy in defense of romantic goals in check in the middle and upper
classes: courtship led usually to marriage, and most women were
faithful once married. There was no widespread reason to reassess the
approach to jealousy, and no sign that such reassessment took place.
The idea that jealousy linked to love, but that ideally the behaviors of
those in love would be sufficiently controlled to prevent active expressions of the emotion, continued to prevail. Jealousy itself went undis-

cussed, even amid popular reevaluations of other emotions; it served at most, and again only in Europe, as a literary embellishment, as in the superficial love-rivalry plays of Marivaux. In real life, jealousy continued to be at most a rare factor in sexual and marital activities, more visible in spurring zealous defense of property and honor. And it continued to be ignored, left unlabeled and unremarked, in the training of children.

Much of this traditional structure would change in the decades after 1800, beginning with shifts in community and context plus a further heightening in the value of romance and the moral qualities associated with true love. Change built on earlier patterns, however, and strong vestiges of traditional attitudes, including a pervasive unwillingness to look too closely at children's jealous emotions, would long persist. As a benchmark for change but also an ingredient in the changes that did develop, the complex traditional outlook toward jealousy left a mark in American life.

Conclusion

A history of jealousy embraces the impact of new factors on a sensible traditional formulation of jealousy standards and emotional management. It incorporates what we know about the emotion in contemporary life, including relevant components of theory, and what we know about the history of other emotions and about how to interpret this history. The treatment does not provide explicit knowledge of "what to do" about jealousy. This is not a how-to book; our culture too often looks for fixes instead of understanding. Yet in discussing a wider range of alternatives in approaching jealousy than many contemporary Americans realize, in dealing with the reasons we react to jealousy as we do, and in assessing the results of the dominant approach, we can hope to provide insights that may go beyond the strictly academic realm. Jealousy has changed a great deal in American society, particularly during the past seventy years. The shifts have brought stress, and some acknowledged confusion. A historical approach, focused on this change and its costs, defines one of the emotional battlefields of contemporary life.

CHAPTER 2

Jealousy in
Nineteenth-Century Life

Changes in American society and culture in the late eighteenth and early nineteenth centuries opened a period of unusual complexity in the evaluation and, to some extent at least, the experience of jealousy. Complexity requires attention to a number of different strands, and while these will be rewoven at the chapter's end they can be tagged at the outset. The dynamic to be assessed lasted from the century's early decades until the 1890s, when a new series of shifts began to force revisions in the most characteristic approaches to jealousy.

The new context for jealousy involved two principal ingredients. The first was cultural: the redefinition and heightened valuation of heterosexual love and of familial affection in general, which was launched in the seventeenth century but which reached interim fruition in the love-drenched family manuals of the 1830s onward, urged a more consistently hostile stance toward jealousy than had been normal in Western culture. Jealousy and real love did not mix. At the same time, declining community cohesion made traditional enforcement of sexual fidelity less reliable. Courtship and other male-female contacts became freer, particularly in the urban lower classes but to a degree for the middle classes as well. New opportunities for sexual jealousy opened up, particularly given the importance attached to romantic relationships. Because Western popular culture had never focused explicitly on the suppression of jealousy, save through institutional arrangements that had limited the occasions for the emotion, it is hardly surprising that actual experience and widely held emotional standards butted against the new cultural aversion to jealousy.

One result of this newly complex context was a great deal of diversity in jealousy reactions, a theme that would persist into the later twentieth century. The Victorian decades produced freewheeling indulgence of jealousy and at the other extreme, experiments in alternatives to marriage that entailed, at least in theory, full personal freedom from the emotion. Diversity had regional dimensions, with Southerners, delighting in codes of honor, far more open than middle- and upper-class society in other parts of the nation. But tensions and ambivalence surfaced everywhere, even within individuals.

One outcome of the new tensions about jealousy was silence: more than in prior centuries, more than in the century to come, Victorian society proved reluctant to talk about jealousy. The emotion surfaced surprisingly infrequently in popular literature or in accounts of love relationships. This reticence makes it difficult—despite the deliberately grandiose title with which this chapter opens—to pinpoint how jealousy was actually handled and perceived, even in the reasonably articulate middle classes that serve as our primary focus.

On the whole, however, though certainly not in all individual cases, jealousy issues do seem to have been resolved in nineteenth-century life, in ways that reflected but did not entirely embrace the new cultural standards. The resolution helps account for the pervasive silence: despite the new context, jealousy management was not broken, so it did not have to be loudly fixed. One sign of the unproblematic appreciation of jealousy was the absence of any attempts specifically to introduce explicit attention to jealousy as a part of childhood—particularly early childhood—socialization.

The several components of the nineteenth century jealousy experience thus include a new context; some new manifestations of active engagement in jealousy, with considerable popular sanction; an important new emotionology, or set of cultural rules, that attempted to dissociate love and jealousy, yielding some interesting if abortive experiments in a jealousy-free adult life; a de facto resolution of conflicting strands, based on family cohesion and some fundamental changes in gender attributes; and finally, a desire to bathe jealousy in considerable silence, reflected most clearly in a belief that the emotion did not qualify as an item on the do's and don't's list for shaping children's character.

A First Impression

In some respects, traditional approaches to jealousy persisted in the nineteenth century: it was still widely assumed that love legitimately brought the possibility of jealousy but that well-arranged love would limit its sway. That jealousy still went largely undiscussed by family-and-romance experts and ordinary people alike is one infuriating result, so that conclusions about jealousy's actual role and value have to be worked out somewhat indirectly or by speculation from the basis of a small if interesting body of explicit evidence. There were, however, important changes both in family context and in emotional standards that subtly moved away from traditional norms. Frontal assault on jealousy assumptions provide only one facet of a considerable reevaluation.

One of the most revealing nineteenth-century American treatments of jealousy, intended for a popular audience, was inserted almost randomly in a housewife's manual, written in 1858. The wife described how jealousy came as a "cloud" to shade her happy life with her husband. Her jealousy had nothing to do with another woman, "for my husband not only professed to love me, but treated me with remarked attention in the society of others; and often when I saw married men display their gallantry to any *but* their wives, I felt proud of those *preferring* attentions, which Edward directly, but without display, tendered me."

The jealousy focused on the husband's work, his growing commitment to his law practice, and his habit of studying during the evenings. He neglected his wife, frequently forgetting to take walks with her, or at least delaying them. The wife was ashamed of her feelings, and so told him nothing; but she grew thin and sad, and this he did notice. She also threw one of the law books across the room in the presence of a neighbor boy, who finally spilled the beans. The husband apologized and began including her in his work (though in appropriately simple terms). She began to share his ambition, and all was well.[1]

Jealousy, as this story suggests, began to win growing disapproval by the mid-nineteenth century; it increasingly focused on women, at least in public comments; it reflected a new family setting in which work and home were separated. But it also, though complicated by disapproval and embarrassment, could be worked out, not simply through institutions that would inhibit it but through mutual emotional interaction of a loving couple.

The New Context

Despite widespread linkage of love and jealousy in popular belief, colonial Americans do not seem to have been much bothered by problems of romantic jealousy in practice. Each of three main reasons for this, however, began to be reshaped by the early nineteenth century.

A commitment to love as the basis for marriage, and as a key emotional bond between parents and children, gained ground steadily. Despite the important Puritan discussion of love as an ingredient of a good marriage, colonial Americans had not encouraged ardent passion as the primary foundation of marriage. They cooled potential jealousy by stressing love as a *product* of the marital relationship, not as a preliminary. While economic and other factors hardly disappeared from marriage arrangements in the nineteenth century, the search for true love and sexual fulfillment undoubtedly increased, and with it the possibility at least of jealous efforts to protect one's love or to protest its loss.[2]

More important still was the erosion of institutional arrangements that had inhibited jealousy in the colonial era, whether or not love was involved in a relationship.[3] Sexual infidelity or even a significant threat of infidelity had been limited by close community supervision, by laws and church rules, backed by a willingness to enforce, against adultery and other sexual excursions. Few crimes of jealousy surfaced in colonial society, not because jealousy itself was under control but because the behaviors that might trigger it were so carefully restrained. This pattern, too, began gradually to crumble during the early nineteenth century. Growing urbanization and heightened population mobility reduced the ability of neighbors effectively to supervise the behavior of individuals. Privacy increased, as did the value placed upon it.[4] Freedom in courtship became more extensive, giving young people even in the middle class considerable opportunity to develop romantic attachments. Belief in choice and commitment by young lovers themselves gained ground. More generally, middle-class men encountered a growing number of unsupervised lower-class women, in factory employment and household service. Prostitution increased. Young middle-class women, though circumscribed, had some social freedom at dances, concerts, and other public occasions. Opportunities not only for romance but also for rivalries, changes of mind, and disappointments grew. Significantly, and also symbolically, institutional enforcement of sexual fidelity declined, as laws against adultery were modified or less regularly enforced.

To be sure, Victorian society attempted to construct alternatives to earlier community enforcement. A new gender ideology that stressed the importance of female virtue and, in some articulations, passionlessness accompanied vigorous efforts to keep "proper" women confined to domestic functions. These arrangements, widely if imperfectly accepted in the middle class, continued to limit opportunities for provocation of jealousy, at least among men. They did not, however, entirely replace earlier community sanctions. Coupled with the new emphasis on romantic intensity, opportunities for provoking jealousy undoubtedly climbed.

Finally, while actual occasion for romantic jealousy in colonial life had been limited both by a tendency to downplay intense love—particularly before marriage—as opposed to other, often economic criteria, and by the pervasive and intrusive community supervision of behavior, colonial society had also seen jealousy as an emotion that went beyond sex and romance. As we have seen, jealousy could undergird appropriate concern about one's own or one's family's honor; it could be equated with zeal, not only in affairs of the heart but in more general conduct. Outside the South, the nineteenth century saw increased conversion to commercial codes of behavior in which concern for honor seemed anachronistic, even dangerous. Vigorous motivation remained important, but it should spring from a strong will and a rational calculation of commercial advantage. Relationships between people outside romance should stress controlled, contractual interaction, not impulsive attention to honor. Opportunities to express jealousy legitimately outside a romantic context thus declined—witness, obviously, the disappearance of sanctioned dueling outside the South —which tended to focus attention more narrowly, but also more intensely, on affairs of the heart.

Given the most obvious changes in context—the heightened valuation of love and decline in community controls over sexual and romantic behavior—plus the more subtle movement away from honor-based motivation, it was small wonder that nineteenth-century discussion of jealousy redefined the emotion as attaching almost exclusively to threats to sexual and romantic goals. A traditional prop for jealousy was thus removed—almost no popular voice referred to a link between this emotion and commendable zeal after 1800—even as traditional inhibitions on the experience of jealousy in courtship and marriage declined somewhat. Here, already, was a newly complex equation that could prompt a variety of responses.

Southern Jealousy

One logical reaction to the new context was, simply, to express jealousy more openly than had been common in colonial society. If love and family cohesion were important but newly vulnerable, jealousy could be used as a prop, to spur attacks on rivals and to justify measures to protect sexual possession. Jealousy had always been seen as an appropriate attribute of love in popular culture, whatever the interesting debates at a more intellectualized level. Now that there were more occasions to experience jealousy as part of courtship or marriage, it was hardly surprising that some groups responded by exhibiting the emotion with new vigor.

This response was an ingredient of several larger strategies, including attempts to ensure marital fidelity by insisting on the Victorian sexual code of female passionlessness and male restraint; we will turn to these patterns in later sections. Strong pockets of a more traditional approach to jealousy persisted in other respects, through the nineteenth century and beyond. Novels frequently portrayed the use of jealousy in romance as a normal stratagem; thus Charlotte Brontë's Mr. Rochester tries to get Jane Eyre to fall in love with him by making her jealous. Here and elsewhere the idea of jealousy as a natural stimulant to love merits no special comment.

A jealous response was particularly open, however, in the one American region that did not move away from an attachment to honor. Southern white men used jealousy actively, without apparent compunction, precisely because they combined a full array of justifications for the emotion—its role in zealous honor as well as love—with the decline in traditional restraints on the occasions that might bring jealousy to the fore.

Jealousy played a vigorous, though rarely acknowledged, role in the South, both in family relationships and in wider dealings among men. The sense of rivalry ran high in a society acutely aware of issues of honor and bent on intensifying the emotional basis for marriage. It was interesting that jealousy was almost never identified by name— here the South may have shared the growing disapproval of the emotion current in the North—but there is every reason to see the emotion as a prominent ingredient of Southern social relationships. A major source of violence, including dueling, thus involved defense of family sanctity. Men sought to redress wives' infidelity through private, emotionally charged action, though divorce could be a recourse as well, as Southern law (again not legitimating jealousy by name) castigated any "degrading" behavior on women's part. As in earlier patriarchal societies, women were expected to keep any jealousy of their own strictly under wraps, and their reactions to sexual adventures on their husbands' parts were rarely recorded. Intense concern about slave relations, however, may well have vented women's jealous anxieties at an acceptable remove. Among men, jealousy flared nearer the surface, not only in marriage but also in courtship rivalries among suitors (which not infrequently led to violence) and in defense against insults to honor.[5] Jealousy's role in a distinctive Southern emotional culture was vital, but it is also important to note that many Southern families were also open to injunctions against the emotion that were spreading more generally in the United States.

Crimes of Passion

Outside the South, open espousal of jealousy-based actions was far less common. More characteristic was the timidity of the housewife jealous of her husband's books, who was too embarrassed to express her emotion openly even when, as things turned out, greater openness could lead to resolution of the problem. In discussing significant cases where jealousy was overt and also approved, in adult life, we are dealing with a logical but infrequent response to the new context for romantic relationships.

One other channel, however, did pick up, in a fairy uncomplicated way, on the impulse to meet new threat with newly intense jealousy. The period from the 1850s to about 1900 saw a number of celebrated murder trials in which a jealous husband—and in one case a fiancé, in one other a father avenging his daughter's honor—was acquitted for murdering a rival on grounds of legitimate if blinding outrage.

The number of cases in which homicide was excused was not great; twenty or thirty cases dot the decades between the first full invocation of the "unwritten law" in 1859 and the end of the century. All the cases involved upper-class characters, for defense attorneys capable of mounting this defense cost money, and community standing helped with juries as well. Lower-class crimes of passion were unjustified. Further, the "unwritten law" did not rely on jealousy alone; it related to larger issues of Victorian behavior and judged women's combined purity and frailty in desperate need of defense.[6]

With due caution, however, one can suggest that some of the trials, and the surrounding doctrine that passion might justify otherwise criminal acts, allowed a number of Americans to indulge a sense of jealous outrage that they either did not need or could not freely express in their own lives. The unwritten law defense was novel, though its partisans often claimed traditional sanction. Because of community supervision and peculiarities in English common-law precedent, un-written-law defenses were neither necessary nor possible in colonial society. As community protection against adultery declined, however, imaginative lawyers managed to argue on a number of occasions that jealous outrage so legitimately and intensely consumed an offended husband that he was rendered temporarily insane and so not responsible for his acts. Furthermore, these cases and approving popular response cropped up in all sections of the United States, not just the South. They reflected elements of a jealousy-linked code of honor—male-based honor, since with rare exceptions women could not make the same arguments, whatever their jealousy in fact—not confined to a particular regional culture. Finally, many of the celebrated acquittals won widespread popular attention and excited approval. Acquitted husbands could be mobbed by happy crowds of men and women alike, as packed courtrooms exploded in wild applause. Banquets and campaigns for contributions reflected still wider interest. To some extent, then, the idea that jealousy could legitimately contribute to acts of violence in defense of personal honor and family purity (defined as women's sexual fidelity) served as a symbolic outlet for large numbers of people who thought jealous possessiveness and married love went hand in hand.

"For jealousy is the rage of a man; therefore he will not spare in the day of vengeance. . . . Those who dishonor husbands are here warned of their doom. . . . Jealousy, which defies and bears down all restraint, whether it be what we technically call insanity or not, is akin to it. It enslaves the injured husband, and vents itself in one result, which seems to be inevitable and unavoidable." So argued that successful attorney for Daniel McFarland in 1870, an acquitted defendant who received public adulation from hundreds of well-wishers. While the invocation of jealousy was somewhat double-edged, for a defense lawyer had to show that it produced a momentary insanity and its boundlessness might trouble tender souls, it was clear that jealousy motivated an appropriate, God-ordained—if violent—behavior.[7]

Amplifying these sentiments was the first unwritten-law defense, of Daniel E. Sickles in 1859, when he killed his wife's lover of a year: "he would have been false to the instincts of humanity if that rage of jealousy had not taken possession of him."

"Jealousy is the rage of a man;" it takes possession of his whole nature; no occupation or pursuit in life, no literary culture or enjoyment, no sweet society of friends in the brilliancy of sunlight, no whispers of hope or promise of the future, can for one moment keep out of his mind, his heart or his soul, the deep, ineffaceable consuming fire of jealousy. When once it has entered within

his breast, he has yielded to an instinct which the Almighty has implanted in
every animal or creature that crawls the earth. I cannot speak of the amours or
jealousies of the worm; but when I enter the higher walk of nature, when I
examine the characteristics of the birds that move about in the air, I find the
jealousy of the bird incites him to inflict death upon the stranger that invades
his nest, and seeks to take from him the love which the Creator has implanted
in him, and formed him to enjoy. . . .

"Jealousy is the rage of a man," and although all the arguments that my
learned opponents can bring, or that can be suggested, that a man must be
cool and collected when he finds before him in full view, the adulterer of his
wife, to the contrary notwithstanding, yet jealousy will be the rage of that
man, he will not spare in the day of vengeance.[8]

The juries that accepted these arguments, the newspapers and crowds
that trumpeted approval, showed the simple power of beliefs in jealous
response and may even have had cathartic effect in a time in which
actual emotional life, for most people, was more complicated. Interestingly, as we shall see, the power of these arguments about justifiable
(if insane) jealousy began to diminish after 1900 just as jealousy standards underwent further reappraisal.

Yet the direct indulgence of jealousy, even far short of homicide,
was not the common American response to the new context for love
and courtship in the nineteenth century, among men as well as women.
Jealous honor in the South, plus the popularity of the new legal
invocation of jealous vengeance expressed powerful impulses, and in
many senses unsurprising ones given the application of the earlier
appreciation of jealous defense of love to the new, less structured
settings of American personal life. Other strands gained ground still
more rapidly, reflecting a new culture that, in direct contrast to the
code of unwritten law, held that jealousy and love were enemies, not
allies. Clearly, jealousy was part of a complicated nineteenth-century
puzzle, where the pieces did not neatly fit.

Emotionology: Toward a New Culture of Jealousy

Growing disapproval of any linkage between jealousy and love, was
the most striking change in this aspect of American emotionology in
the nineteenth century. This built, of course, on older Western cautions about the emotion, but it began, at least at the emotionological

level, to eat away at the traditional ambiguity in favor of undiluted hostility. We move here from the frenzy of a few show trials to the more pedestrian but probably more revealing world of popular family reading. The growing roster of advice manuals to families and to "young men and young women" did not necessarily mention jealousy —again, there was substantial silence about the emotion even amid growing interest in love and romance that must be accounted for—but they did touch on the subject with some frequency, as an emotional issue worthy of some attention though not usually pressing or unmanageable. When they commented, moreover, they made it clear that the basic standards were unwavering.

Thus, while admitting that some men might be jealous of a girl who had been previously engaged while others would be unfazed (the standard recognition of individual variability), a popular commentator around 1900 insisted that affection was incompatible with jealousy: "There is no real love where there is no abandon and complete confidence." Jealousy, as against an earlier Western tradition which the author mentioned and condemned, was not an adjunct of love but a defect of character. It was also unwise, for it actually raised the prospect of infidelity.

The exclusion of jealousy from a newly idealized love became indeed a standard refrain. Love, whose "truest, purest, highest form is that of strong, unselfish affection blended with desire," "ennobles" the individual; it is "the beautifier, the glorifier, the redeemer."[9] Small wonder that jealousy had no part to play in this emotion or that couples should be urged to put aside any resentment over each other's involvements prior to the advent of true love.[10] The point, once more, was strategic as well as principled, for jealousy might lead a spouse to precisely the errancy that was feared. "I have repeatedly known ill-grounded suspicions and jealousies to lead one or both parties into profligacy and ruin." Hence the emotion should be avoided, as well as flirtatious behavior that might arouse it.[11] Psychologists like G. Stanley Hall added some pithy comments on jealousy's frequent role in crime, but at the level of popular emotionology the main point was the new rift between jealousy and the ideal of love as a joyous, generous experience.[12]

Why did the love ideal become jealousy-free? Victorian beliefs about sexuality contributed: respectable behavior involved such strict sexual restraint that, in the view of some, the occasions for serious jealousy would be limited before as well as during marriage.[13] Larger Victorian standards of self-restraint came into play as well, as they worked against any emotion that might threaten loss of control or public outburst.[14] Stereotypic Victorianism, however, should not be over-done in this area, for the actual strictures against jealousy in popular manuals were not immune to ideas of desire and, in their enthusiasm for love itself, hardly bent on emphasizing emotional restraint above all.

The antijealousy thrust stemmed primarily, at this level of theoreti-cal emotional standards, from an Enlightenment-fed belief that human motives should be pure, untainted by selfish impulses, and that per-sonal relationships built on love should be similarly free from possess-iveness, a voluntary result of positive emotional attraction. Thus Rous-seau had written against the commonplace idea that jealousy might usefully spur achievement, claiming in *Emile* that he would "prefer a hundredfold" that a child not learn at all than that he learn out of jealousy or vanity. All the more clearly, as the valuation of romantic love increased, did purists seek their emotional utopia unclouded by base—because self-centered and proprietary—sentiments. Jealousy and the love ideal now clashed head on, because the ideal had changed, separated from selfishness because of the moral transforming power now attributed to love. Scientific commentators, interestingly enough, might still see some value in jealousy, through its role in turning courtship into union or in defending marriage and fidelity, but the popular marriage experts would have virtually none of this logical argument.[15] Thus Darwinian contentions about jealousy's evolution-ary functions, though written into some late nineteenth-century psy-chology, were ignored in popular advice literature—in contrast to lively interest in other emotional implications of Darwinism. Only occasionally, and inconsistently, did a sneaking admission that a bit of jealousy might add "piquancy" to courtship qualify the general con-demnation at the popularized level. At no time, at this same level, did even the most ardent advocates of conventional marriage, as against free love doctrines, seize the obvious ploy of urging that some jealousy enter the protection of fidelity. To them the love ideal would produce faithful union rather than promiscuous experiment, but this same one true love would be free from any petty emotional trammels.

Emphasis on the theoretical redefinition of love as the cause of the new emotionology of jealousy gives primacy, obviously, to cultural causation. Both the Enlightenment and, in the United States, evangelical religious strains pushed toward an upgrading of optimal human nature, which Romantic novelists mentioned even as they gushed about love; and this trend suffices in explaining the new stance on jealousy. A more psychological explanation (not necessarily incompatible with cultural factors) might urge exploration of a new or heightened set of jealousy impulses, given new courtship habits and urban temptations, which the purified standards were designed to inhibit or deny. More emotionally intense parenting, for example, and particularly the growing emphasis on maternal affection might thus have roused in nineteenth-century children a growing proclivity toward jealousy in love, first as an attempt to monopolize cherished parental fondness and then by extension in courtship and marriage. New strictures on jealousy would thus follow from a growing problem, not simply from a new culture of love. Some signs of this more subtle causation are visible, as we shall see in exploring other shifts in the emotionology of jealousy, but its fuller manifestations would await the twentieth century. In terms of cultural standards, in an age bent on using the loving family as a leading symbol of harmony and sanity in a complex industrial society, a primary explanation in terms of theoretical principles seems adequate. Only in later articulations, and in actual emotional experience, did a more nuanced, partially unconscious dynamic come into play.

Somewhere between psychology and culture rests a final restatement of the basic nineteenth-century shift. In the preindustrial West, love itself had often been seen as a virtual illness, because of the pain and irrational behavior it could produce. The nineteenth-century middle class completed a reversal of this equation, in arguing that love, far from causing pain, could cure. But jealousy, traditionally seen as part of love's discomfort remained pain—and so it had to be cast out, removed from healing love.

The Experimental Impulse

The effort to remove jealousy from ideal love went beyond popular marriage manuals into the various experiments with alternatives to marriage itself during the nineteenth century. Proponents of free love warred implicitly or explicitly with jealousy. Their efforts are interesting in themselves and in foreshadowing similar experimentation in the twentieth century. They also serve as a comment on more mainstream middle-class values. Although free lovers were a decided minority in the United States during their mid-century heyday and were often bitterly attacked, they illustrated many broader values as well, as recent scholarship has demonstrated.[16] Their approach to jealousy is a definite case in point.

Free lovers, in their writings and in the communities they established, agreed wholeheartedly with the idealization of love itself. They wanted affection that was spontaneous and voluntary. They argued, however, that marriage, because of the exclusiveness and possessiveness it entailed, ran counter to the essence of love. Fundamentally, they held that the new emotionology of jealousy was valid and vitally important but that it required the further step of abolishing legal ties, which were rooted in real or potential jealousy.

Thus Angela Heywood, coeditor of *The Word,* found the key to free love in the integrity of each individual. She admitted that people often confused passion with love, implying that in the baser forms of attraction jealousy might well be a problem.[17] Thus Marx Lazarus, attacking jealousy more directly, blasted its origins in "the false conception of a chattelism or exclusive property in the person beloved."[18] Thus Robert Owen, rejecting both marriage and polygamy for their assumptions that women were mere property, argued that both arrangements tended "to make men and women weak, jealous, irrational beings."[19] Many free lovers, of course, themselves enjoyed extremely stable unions, in which jealousy was no problem. Others, including many who initially entered the utopian communities, assumed that new arrangements would downplay sexuality, thus avoiding any conflict between jealousy and ideal relationships. Like most nineteenth-century Americans, at least in the middle classes, free lovers were reluctant to discuss jealousy too elaborately, hoping that their hostility to the emotion could be expressed through the positive force of pure love and, of course, some important institutional reforms. They differed from the mainstream, in this emotional area, only in their heightened sensitivity to individual free will and their desire to avoid any imposition, through jealousy and proprietary arrangements, of one person on others.

The most striking explicit attack on jealousy stemmed from John Humphrey Noyes, founder of the Oneida community. Some have contended that Noyes's hostility to monogamy derived from earlier rejection by a woman he courted; he thus sought alternative arrangements as catharsis, to spare himself the need of admitting his own guilt and jealousy directly.[20] Noyes himself revealingly argued that man's love was inherently noble and free, in contrast to woman's debasingly selfish love, and he sought a community in which the purer male standards might prevail. He urged that young women pledge to "put aside all envy, childishness and selfseeking," and for men and women alike he sought an end to "private feelings" that held back group harmony and individual development.[21]

Reality was less pleasant. Communities like Oneida that went furthest in direct experiments with alternatives to marriage, instead of emphasizing discussion or more purely economic communalism, suffered from frequent jealousies and resultant bickering. Oneida itself broke up in part as a younger generation returned to acceptance of traditional marriage arrangements; as Pierrepont Noyes put it, while not denying directly economic clashes over community controls, "possessiveness in sex and family . . . [made] economic communism unattainable."[22] Pressing the campaign against jealousy too far had backfired, a point to which we must return in assessing the impact of nineteenth-century emotionology and which foreshadowed dilemmas in the still more general war against jealousy in the twentieth century.

Yet failure to root out jealousy is not the only point to draw from the free-love experiments. A few couples, at least, managed to override the emotion, and felt better for it. One of the most dramatic scenes in all of nineteenth-century free love involved Moses Hull and his revelation to his wife that he had begun sleeping with other women. Mrs. Hull was outraged, and even the garrulous Moses refused to unveil her jealousy in full. "I told my wife all; the scene which immediately followed I will not relate, as it was only the process of bringing the more remote, beneficial and lasting results."[23] Mrs. Hull eventually came around to her husband's point of view, defending him as having become a better man because of free love; her suffering vanished when she got over the mistaken notion that she owned Moses.[24] This was an unusual incident, in that free lovers, in the best nineteenth-century fashion, usually went out of their way to avoid direct confrontations with jealousy. While the result may be idiosyncratic, and certainly was atypical, it may also suggest that standards that urged individuals to rise above jealousy were being implanted even in some nonbelievers, like Mrs. Hull: it was fine to triumph over the base emotion, even though most Americans planned to stay within marriage to achieve this.

The theoretical disagreement over free love involved dispute over true love's exclusive nature, not over the admissibility of jealousy. Mainstream opponents of free love argued that true love led naturally to a single union, which free lovers dismissed as arrant possessiveness. Neither side, however, condoned jealousy, and neither side was eager to discuss the emotion as a problem.[25] Free love in this sense sprang from the new emotionology of the nineteenth century, with its insistence on jealousy-free relationships and the importance of love and purity itself. It confirmed, in its maverick fashion, one of the century's key shifts in emotional definition.

The Gender Factor

The attack on jealousy—vigorous if largely implicit because of the belief that true union or some experimental arrangement would bypass the emotion in favor of right love—was not the only emotionological innovation of mid-nineteenth-century decades. One other revealing change occurred, which at once confirms the disapproval of jealousy in the dominant feeling rules and gets somewhat closer to the actual emotional experience of the nonexperimental majority of middle-class Americans.

Women, as J. H. Noyes had argued, were now held to be the principal bearers of jealousy, an emotion that in centuries past had been a largely male prerogative in theory and—from the standpoint of overt, approved behavior—in fact as well. Male proclivity for jealousy—and it may be relevant to recall that among lower animals males alone demonstrate intense jealous-like behavior in sexuality—showed obviously in defense of honor and female fidelity but also, even when jealousy was twined with love, in the assumption that this emotional pairing primarily involved females' ability to spark anxiety in men. Special—indeed, naturally or divinely ordained—jealousy rights for men persisted in the gender-skewed reactions to the killing of paramours, where husbands had leeway firmly denied to wives.

In explicit, popular discussions of jealousy, however, the gender tables were turned. "As in matters of the heart in general females are more susceptible to the passion than men."[26] This judgment reflected the widespread belief in greater emotionality on women's part, and their particular concentration on issues of love and family. It also reflected a realistic appraisal, on the part of advice writers, that men were more likely to be unfaithful than women, particularly after marriage, which left women—given the general disapproval of jealousy—in greater need of counsel and restraint. "Jealousy is, on several counts, more inexcusable in a woman than in a man." It made her vulnerable and also, horror of Victorian horrors, left her open to retaliatory indiscretions. Female jealousy might indeed break up the family, by driving men away. Hence wives should close their ears to gossip about their husbands, and if by chance they learned of an indiscretion they should respect their spouses for trying to shield them from pain. On no account should they display jealousy or even admit knowledge of extramarital activity, because husbands would usually come back unless they had been humiliated through jealousy-inspired attacks. "The best way is to pass over." "Never search after what it will give you no pleasure to find."[27] Situational differences, in other words, along with the female need for love caused the new linkage of woman and jealousy, which became an unexamined assumption by 1900 not only in popularized advice but in social-science research extending through the first half of the twentieth century. The result was yet another area where women were subjected, at least in theory, to special emotional controls, urged to restrain some basic impulses in the interest of the higher goal of family preservation. While jealousy concerns did not produce huge tomes of advice to women—the problem was less acute than several other emotional and sexual issues, it did generate discussion in many pamphlets directed at marital and courtship behavior. It also helps account for the extensive fascination—though not, ultimately, full sympathy—the nineteenth-century public displayed for female crimes of passion, the dark side of the gender shift in jealousy focus.[28]

The need for women to wrestle with jealousy in a male-dominated society was by no means new, nor was some backhanded societal recognition of the emotion in females, but the focus on this issue was novel. It reflected the more general increase in the disapproval with which jealousy was regarded in the ascending emotionology. It could serve as a convenient dodge by which men might periodically stray from sexual rectitude without jeopardizing family comforts or legitimating female retaliation—in which sense it obviously fit Victorian beliefs about greater male sexual appetites.[29] It also, however, in shifting away from concern with male jealousy, suggested some more subtle changes in the ways jealousy was defined and valued, which can be linked to the actual impact of new standards in emotional experience.

The gender reordering of jealousy suggests, finally, some unexpected complexities in nineteenth-century love ideals—for again, failure to consider jealousy has been a serious limitation in our understanding of a wider emotional canvas. Women were most naturally loving, but could also most readily defile love with jealousy. This dilemma could be resolved by careful emotional restraint, and there was a spark of hope that true love could emerge jealousy-free in either gender. Nevertheless, though the dilemma was never probed very deeply by nineteenth-century commentators, it remained interesting. The female love-jealousy tension reflected some reality: women needed family more than men did, in the middle-class economic context, and so may well have become more openly possessive. The tension reflected something of the good-bad woman polarization visible in other facets of male-dominated nineteenth-century ideals: good women could love purely, but jealous women were worse than men. The tension, lastly, may have reflected some heretofore unnoted male ambivalence about women's love, even in its idealized version. On the one hand, men revered women's loving potential as the basis for family life and

emotional solace. On the other hand, they feared its ensnaring qualities, and the disproportionate attacks on women's jealousy (plus the
new impulse to claim that men were freer from the emotion) expressed
this fear. Here was a tendency that would expand further in the
twentieth century. Attacking jealousy became a safe way of articulating otherwise forbidden doubts about love itself.

The Emotionological Shifts: A Summary

While nineteenth-century emotionology did not produce a neat, explicit redefinition of jealousy overall, furnished with some commentary
on change, it is possible to combine the novel ingredients into a
somewhat coherent whole. More pronounced disapproval of jealousy,
producing among other things some experiments designed to demonstrate unusual freedom from the emotion, plus the shift in gender
definition add up to a substantial movement away from conventional
patriarchal emotionology. Not, one hastens to add, away from a male-
dominated statement, as the potential uses of attacks on female jealousy make clear; but away from strict patriarchalism.

Beneath the surface—and it must be emphasized that almost no
commentator seemed explicitly aware of the shift in context—jealousy
was being moved away from its traditional service as an emotion that,
for good or ill, would protect honor and property as extensions of self.
At least at the emotionological level it could no longer be invoked to
defend power or appropriate order. The emotion was now clearly a
sign of weakness—hence its special attachment to the feebler sex, and
the growing sense that it stemmed in either gender (though particularly
in men) from inadequacies of character. Even in the exceptional case
where some husbands were exculpated for paramouricide, jealousy
was defined as a consuming and momentary insanity, not an ongoing
emotional resource. Relatedly, the emotion was now narrowed to
issues of love pure and simple. The idea of a wider application of
jealousy, including love but also other issues of power and honor,
faded from view. This negative claim is supported by the absence of
discussions of jealousy, either pro or con, in nineteenth-century work-
ethic stories, or advice manuals for young men in the business world
where its appearance might have been expected had the emotion's

range been updated beyond the romantic sphere. Pamphlets that showed how anger could be channeled into proper motivation ignored similar possibilities for jealousy, now held to be a perversion of love and no more. Competition was praised, of course, but it was meant to be internally and positively generated, not inspired by anything so base as jealousy. Thus when psychologists took up discussions of jealousy late in the nineteenth century, as in the work of G. Stanley Hall, they focused primarily on sexual and romantic jealousy, reflecting as well as promoting the more limited definition of the emotion advanced in popular discussions earlier on. Similarly, the more abundant work personality literature of the first half of the twentieth century did not address jealousy as an explicit topic, even as emphasis on the importance of cooperation increased. A link between work concerns and jealousy did develop around this point, as we will see in the next chapter, but it applied to socialization, not to explicit discussion of jealousy in the workplace.[30] Jealousy reflected emotional need alone, in an age that increasingly believed in the importance of love as the basis for key relationships.

Finally, love ideals themselves, of course, moved away from possessiveness and hence from any legitimate jealousy; an individual should love, but love freely. Women, quintessentially loving but dependent creatures, must especially be taught not to ensnare with jealousy, but the lesson was by traditional standards even more novel for men, who could no longer see jealousy as an appropriate response to threat or a valid motivation for defense of their sphere of control. Jealousy's scope narrowed to emotional relationships alone, and its acceptability vanished as these relationships were redefined as spontaneous flowerings of unselfish love.

The new emotionology of jealousy did not capture all expert opinion, though as the gender assumptions suggest it affected psychologists along with ordinary folk. Scholarly work on jealousy through the first quarter of the twentieth century would recurrently recall the link between jealousy and zeal—which suggested that jealousy might be channeled into useful achievement; it could note jealousy's utility in defending family bonds or converting casual courtship into deeper links; and it could occasionally discuss jealousy in settings other than romance. Most popular writers, however, hewed to the new emotionology more strictly, finding no use for jealousy above all because it contradicted healthy—and all-important—love. Jealousy became a petty emotion, and a potential problem, rather than serving as love's inevitable companion and a vigorous, if admittedly complicated inspirer.

Standards and Experience: The Problem of Interaction

Whenever emotionology changes, questions must be asked about resulting impact. The jealousy standards of the nineteenth century were not entirely new, in that they heightened concerns about the emotion, its selfishness and compulsive qualities, that had existed in traditional literature. Nevertheless, the unqualified disapproval, the exclusive focus on matters of love, the new link between jealousy and women did call for adjustments in the ways people actually evaluated jealousy and, ideally, the ways they experienced it in fact.

Assimilation of change is always gradual. It is easier to alter advice than to adjust deeply felt emotional values. The experiments with jealousy-free environments showed an impact of the new standards, but the results also demonstrated severe limitations. Some people, clearly, wanted to feel less jealousy than they did feel. A few, including a handful of husbands of promiscuous women, even took pride in full tolerance. Nevertheless, the ongoing signs of more traditional beliefs, as in the sympathy for husbands who committed crimes from jealousy even apart from the honor-pledged male culture of the South, suggested tensions with the rising advice literature. More generally, pleas for less jealousy were complicated by the new context in which sexual and romantic behavior was less regulated by community supervision: simply put, the nineteenth century formed a difficult environment for the full and ready integration of new aversions. In essence, the dominant emotional culture posed a challenge, asking people not only to alter older ideas but also to react counterintuitively to innovations occuring in family context.

The new standards for jealousy had some impact on actual emotional experience and to a degree picked up on changes in this experience. Not surprisingly, given the changes in family context, the novelty of the standards, and the fact the standards remained secondary amid the complex emotional lessons preached during the nineteenth century, emotion-fed behavior did not convert completely to the reigning emotionology. As always, it is far more difficult to describe emotional experience than to detail recommended values, but it is possible to speculate, on the basis of scattered but revealing evidence, about the relationship of the two facets in a century of change.

Despite disapproval, the experience of jealousy continued. Advice writers themselves referred to anxieties about former loves that could complicate courtship or marriage. Attachments to past loves, even after a broken romance, left men as well as women vulnerable. One young man described how he "felt as if a sharp knife had pierced his heart" when he learned that a girl he had simply fantasized as a bride was engaged to be married.[31] Pious advice to the contrary, many young women clearly provoked jealousy as part of their courtship procedures, either to fan the flames of romance into commitment or simply to watch a covey of suitors squirm. In a century that touted love, encouraged attention to courtship, and allowed considerable latitude therein, jealousy undoubtedly played a role as ingredient or by-product, even aside from straightforward cases of continuity from past standards such as that of the American South.

It is also possible that women's jealousy increased or at least became more articulate, in a pattern that paralleled some shifts in emotionology but complicated the imposition of new emotional restraints. The division between home and public life, and men's growing latitude in this latter sphere, could easily provoke jealous resentments, not only of possible other women but simply of the freedom to engage in varied pursuits while women became increasingly domestically defined. The stories that focused on wives' jealousy of their husbands' work picked up on this theme, and suggested its reality. To the extent they internalized not only their real dependence on family life, but also their special entrancement with love and matters of the heart, women might have become more aware of jealousy, or their right to express jealousy, than had been the case in more traditional periods. A more egalitarian atmosphere, combined with the real and growing inequality between men and women in ability to escape family confinement, produced a climate ripe for increased articulation of jealousy, perhaps even experience of jealousy, on women's part, especially in a context in which romantic expectations were encouraged. Experience and emotionology, as far as women's jealousy was concerned, may have been mutually supportive to some degree, though with results different from those the standard setters urged.

Certainly women commented more freely on their jealousy than men did, in the nineteenth century. Young women thus talked of their jealous feelings for sisters, while resentment of suitors who came to take a favored sister away was a common theme in popular novels. Jealousy also spilled over into the intense friendships women formed with each other. Carroll Smith-Rosenberg thus describes apparent (if somewhat rhetorical) rivalries with men for friends' affection, as women wrote of wishing they could replace a husband in bed.[32]

Men undoubtedly maintained earlier jealousy themes and may also have become more vulnerable as their own interest in romantic courtship increased. Their lesser emotional and material dependence on family, however, and their ability to form extramarital liaisons while remaining reasonably confident of their wives' fidelity, limited their openness to jealousy, even as prevailing advice urged them to avoid the emotion or keep its expression under wraps. Emotionology and the context of the Victorian family thus reduced the explicit admission of jealousy by men.

While the generation of a powerful, if largely implicit masculine culture bent on downplaying jealousy was a key result of the antijealousy standards, women unquestionably grappled with the emotion as well. While diary references to jealousy do not seem to have been common, they could take on a certain fervency, as up-to-date women tried to build jealousy control into their arsenal of domestic virtues, much as they had begun to comment on their need to master anger a century before. Thus Lucilla McCorkle, a Southern minister's wife, urged the following duties on herself, in her private journal: "Self-denial—in food & clothing & keeping the *tongue*. early rising—industry—economy system—cheerfulness & sobriety—keeping down & quelling the spirit of malevolence, fault finding—covetisness or rather jealousy," adding that she feared she suffered from "that *disease*." Here, clearly, was a woman who had imbibed the new emotionology and viewed it as a major personal challenge; and there were doubtless many more like her.[33]

Overall, however, the most striking feature of the actual record of
romantic jealousy in the nineteenth century was the absence of frequent comment. This suggests that while the new emotionology made
jealousy problematic, it was not fully internalized, yielding more complex reactions that might best be veiled. While the pervasive silence
applies most obviously to men, it also describes women who wrote of
marriage and courtship. A period that touted love, that on the whole
encouraged more romantically charged interactions between men and
women than ever before, outside upper-class circles, and that might
therefore have seen an increase in the incidence of jealous anguish, did
not produce open evidence of widespread emotional issues in this area.
Students of courtship practices in the period and relevant records such
as diaries and letters rarely comment directly on jealousy in romantic
relationships. This is why advice manuals, though clear in their negative rating of the emotion, normally dealt with it only in passing:
jealousy was not a major problem. Nor, as we will see, were there
careful efforts to identify and reprove jealousy in children, a result that
might logically have followed from the clear-cut disapproval of the
emotion. Children's jealousy was seldom identified or labeled and was
never described as a systematic concern. The resultant silence about
jealousy as a real experience is frustrating to the historian of emotion,
forced more than usual to read between the lines; but it does permit of
interpretation.[34]

Silence as Strategy

The absence of probing discussions of jealousy during most of the
nineteenth century, despite potential confrontation between old standards and sincerely (if quietly) preached new ones, despite dramatic
focal points such as the unwritten-law defenses, suggests an implicit
strategy. Jealousy in real life had become too complicated for fully
coherent assessment, and silence might ease a family's management of
the emotion as something other than a pressing problem. That the
Victorian middle class used a certain amount of hypocrisy construc-
tively, defending family cohesion while in fact recognizing some complicating impulses, has been suggested for kindred facets of behavior
such as sexuality.[35] The argument here is that the failure explicitly to

recognize how complex jealousy had become not only reflected a lack of crisis but promoted calm. Silence allowed contradictory values to coexist without undue stress, particularly for men but to an extent for women as well.

Certainly the silence about jealousy's potential storms, as against prevailing cultural standards, extended interestingly to nineteenth-century popular literature, particularly from mid-century onward. The contrast between earlier literary use of the emotion, extending into early nineteenth-century fiction, and also to the fascination that resurfaced in twentieth-century fiction and film, was again striking.

Given the tensions surrounding romantic jealousy and the increasingly frequent discussions of romantic love, one might have expected a strong literary usage of jealousy themes, even if these were surrounded by greater reticence in daily life. Stories might have provided guidelines, or surrogate outlets, or both. In fact, popular literature joined diaries and letters in keeping the emotion under wraps and assuming that its role in love and family was unproblematic.

No generalization about nineteenth-century jealousy is flawless; the emotion was complex, if not prominently visible. While the dominant tone of popular literature involved silence tempered by occasional pious disapproval, some stories cut closer to the bone. George Eliot's *Mill on the Floss*—to be sure, neither American nor produced in the most popularized format—built on several emotional tensions, including jealousy. The protagonist clearly envies her best friend's good looks, though the emotion is not explicitly explored. Later she falls in love with the friend's suitor. Yet the friend rises above the petty jealousy; the protagonist loyally refuses to marry the man; and the epic ends with spiritual redemption and death by drowning. Jealousy does not win out, and it may contribute to the semitragic end in the best Victorian tradition. Here, certainly, were potential lessons in full keeping with dominant emotionology, including the concentration on female emotional temptation. While one should not minimize cases of this sort, however, when fiction might substitute for the more explicit advice books, the point is that they were unusual. Most widely read fiction, perhaps particularly in the United States, where the idealization of family and love was so intense, was more evasive.

There were occasional stories or poems about jealousy in the most popular nineteenth-century magazines. *Godey's Lady's Book* ran a verse on "The Jealous Lover" in 1841, terming the emotion "worst inmate of the breast; a fell tormentor thou, a double pest, wounding thy bosom by the self-same blow thy vengeance wreaks on the imputed foe." After echoing the new emotionology in ringing terms, the poem further drove its message home by describing a situation where the suitor's passion is completely baseless; his lady is blameless, because she has pledged her "solemn promises of love." Jealousy thus becomes shameful, in its contradiction of what one should know of love, as well as agonizing.[36]

Still more interesting was the treatment of jealousy in an 1876 story, "Amiability vs. Jealousy." Despite the title, the bulk of the story involves a convoluted account of the gradual emergence of love. Jealousy intrudes only briefly at the end, when a cousin of the woman in love, who loves the same man, learns of the announcement of marriage. Briefly assailed by the "old demon in her breast" (which in fact the story had not discussed), the cousin is comforted by her father and drives "the ill-adviser" from her bosom. She bravely decides to attend the wedding and discovers that she enjoys it, for she gained "pleasure from this victory over self, to which her former selfishness had made her a stranger." As the story ends, the cousin rejoices to God "for awakening her to a nobler life and higher aims than that of mere self-gratification."[37]

Clearly, some popular literature existed to disseminate the new emotionology that sought to equate jealousy with selfish possessiveness, to label it the antithesis of true love. The jealousy message was vague—the emotion was not probed save to be condemned as devilish. Remedies for its emergence were vague as well, a theme that would carry into the twentieth century. Self-control, some good advice, and otherwise the jealous person was on his or her own, so obviously in the wrong that more detailed support was unwarranted.

More important than the characteristic approach to jealousy in Victorian fiction, however, was its rarity. It was simply not an interesting emotional focus for nineteenth-century popular writers, as the normal vagueness in exploring it in the few relevant stories already suggests. Jealousy did not achieve equal status with some of the nastier passions —sexual seduction, for example—that Victorians might, even with some indirection, evoke.

Thus, over a four-decade span, a periodical such as *Godey's* (surveyed from the 1840s through the 1870s) featured only four items that referred to jealousy beyond the most fleeting aside, including the two already described as emotionologically characteristic. In contrast, as we will see, women's magazines in the twentieth century readily included jealousy as one of their endlessly recycled topics, yielding in the case of any given periodical at least one explicit article every two to three years. Nineteenth-century short stories shunned even casual inclusion of jealousy, and there were no nonfiction items to compensate. Discussions of love were noteworthy for their neglect of the subject, even for castigating a darker emotional side.

Aside from the implication that jealousy was simply not a compelling problem, the frequent discussions of romance and marriage provided additional reasons for the restricted focus. Their subject matter was too vital, in its positive ideals, to be sullied by potential emotional distractions. Married love, particularly, involved such complete and fulfilling merger of two individuals that jealousy could not conceivably enter in: "Though I have obtained the mastery of her soul to an extent quite unusual, I see with pleasure that she intimidates me, and so long as I love her as I now do I feel sure that no wrong thing will have dominion over me."[38] Marriage itself "is complete union of amity and love, of life and fortune, of interests and sympathies, of comfort and support, of desires and inclinations, of usefulness and happiness, of joys and sorrows."[39]

Obviously, these idealized definitions were fully compatible with official disapproval of jealousy as a selfish intrusion on true love. Atypically, one marriage column urged avoidance of the "demon-monster" as part of a larger recommendation of "implicit and unwavering confidence in each other," which included not only banishment of jealousy but also exclusion of mutual criticism. The point is that, normally, the extension to comments on jealousy was not judged essential, either because the emotion would slumber more surely if not evoked, or because it was genuinely believed that love would not normally be troubled by it.[40]

The tendency to leave jealousy unexplored, to avoid it as a subject so long as disapproving standards were occasionally reasserted, recalls other targets of Victorian morality. Sexual ethics were discussed more often than jealousy was, though particularly in nonfiction settings; but

Victorian literature readily yields a sense that sexuality should not be explored too deeply beyond an assertion of appropriate behavior. Anger was another contradiction of loving family life, in the more purely emotional realm.[41] Again, stories about familial anger were considerably more common that those involving jealousy, but there was a similar inclination to insist on ideal, conflict-free love rather than to deal with potential problems in any depth.

Obviously, then, the Victorian neglect of jealousy related to a more general insistence on idealizing family relationships and their base in unselfish and reasonably unsexual love. The accent was resolutely on the positive, with the transparent hope that good emotions would readily conquer the bad. Gender distinctions were added in each case to catalyze the correct emotional formula. The sexual purity that was part of true love was maintained in part by women's fortuitous freedom from undue sexual desire. Good women were also by nature unaggressive, which helped them avoid anger and allowed them to help men calm it as well. The gender equation for jealousy was a bit different: women here, in the newest formulas, had the more substantial problems because of their greater sexual fidelity and their particular responsibility for fostering love. Women's good behavior and men's superior control of jealousy could combine to avert emotional collapse. The net result in popular reading was the same: an undesirable emotion could be simplified—call it a demon and let it go at that—and largely ignored in favor of unequivocal attention to the ideal. That the results often intertwined, that discussions about avoiding a first married quarrel abutted the brief reminders about jealousy, and that they seem comparably naive to twentieth-century eyes, simply reminds us of their common root in the deep Victorian need to insist on emotional optimism. Tawdry emotions might exist, but they should not be paraded even in aid of the cherished standards, and if the results in real life involved more than a bit of hypocrisy, at least the stated goals could be maintained in full purity.

Though the approach toward jealousy linked to the resolute insistence on idealization in other areas, however, this emotion was far more thoroughly neglected than were sexuality and anger. Stories about disastrous first marital fights, for example, were something of a staple, suggesting an awareness of an issue—anger—even if a concomitant insistence on surprisingly unrealistic standards and remedies. The silence on jealousy, however reflective of idealized love, remains somewhat distinctive. It reminds us that when common emotional labels are not in use, some important emotional experience may pass unperceived—which in nineteenth-century eyes could be functional where jealousy was concerned.[42] Further, the silence was echoed by an almost unanimous aversion to attending to jealousy as part of childhood socialization during the nineteenth century—again in contrast to other passions on the reproved list. Victorian parents, though prone to idealize childish innocence, were notoriously capable of active insistence on appropriate sexual standards, as in monitoring potential masturbation. And they definitely talked about problems of angry personalities among children, and how these might be countered. Jealousy produced no such comment. Parental nonchalance in this area reflects rooted idealism, to be sure—a particular need to believe that the family was indeed one big happy unit distinguished by exceptional cooperativeness among the offspring. Again, however, additional factors were involved, which explains the differentiation, in parental comment and childrearing advice literature alike, between jealousy and other, more readily perceived issues. It is time to add this final piece to the puzzle before sketching the nineteenth-century middle-class synthesis.

Siblings Without Rivalries?

Compared to the parental anxiety with which many Americans became familiar in the twentieth century, compared even with the relatively infrequent attacks on romantic jealousy in the nineteenth century itself, Victorian comments on the subject of childish jealousy are striking in their absence. Parents and parental advisers might discuss various failings of children, from precocious sexuality to sloth to carelessness with property, but jealousy simply did not make the list. The phenomenon was known, of course, and children themselves learned a relevant vocabulary. Letters by sisters in the middle-class Hills family abound with references, as siblings carp at each other's purchases, receipt of letters from their mother ("I thought it very strange you should have written Emily first. . . ."), and so on. "I suppose Papa told you of how jealous I was when I heard you are going to allow Emily to go to the Phi Psi musical for it did not seem at all like you to let a *child* like her go to any such things." "I am very jealous of Emily for I think she has more than her share of gaiety when I am away." But an idea that such emotions merited any particular notice, much less parental attention or criticism, is oddly missing. Missing also is denotion of jealous reactions by very young children, as on the birth of a new baby.

Indeed, letters like those of the Hills sisters suggest precisely that middle-class parents had not worked to banish jealousy. To twentieth-century eyes, the poutings of the Hills sisters seem like the scribblings of four-year-olds (were they magically or tragically literate), expressing sibling rivalry in the starkest form short of violence. Yet these laments to mother about feeling jealous because sister got a letter first were being penned by a twenty-year-old, who clearly had not been taught, as Americans were to be taught in the following century, that jealousy even if experienced should be veiled more cleverly lest one be labeled childish. They compare oddly, for example, with the deliberate efforts to "outgrow" jealousy reported as standard from roughly age eleven onward, in the mid–twentieth century, by Gesell and his colleagues.[43] They also contrast with abundant nineteenth-century interest in dealing with anger among children, in the family context and as part of character formation. Unlike anger, jealousy seems not to have been an issue.

The same negative finding about nineteenth-century concern over childish jealousy applies to virtually all the popular childrearing manuals before the very end of the century. John Abbott, to be sure, mentioned the possibility that a girl might refuse to share a bed with her sister (in which case obedience must be insisted upon), but the word *jealousy* was not used, and the context, focusing on proper parent-child relations, had little to do with judgments of sibling emotions. Marion Harland described situations in which a girl might well have been jealous of her brother's privileges, and the favors granted him by a sexist father, but again overt jealousy was neither described nor invoked. Jacob Abbott talked of childish boasting and its immaturity, urging that parents avoid punishment for this offense but guide the child toward more mature behavior—an approach suggestive of twentieth-century tactics on jealousy—and he wrote widely on how to handle disputes among children, with use of dolls and calm mediation. He may thus have been writing about situations resulting from jealousy, but he was not writing explicitly about jealousy itself, and when he turned to emotions that needed attention, such as childish fears, jealousy was simply not listed.[44] Christian manuals urged that children be taught to work together (by their sixth year, argued one such in 1919, they would be "habitually cooperative"),[45] and general invocations of Christian goodness, obedience to adults, respect for the property of others, and generosity may have addressed the problem of jealousy. Again, however, it is striking that the emotion was not mentioned, even as an illustration of original sin or, in milder treatments, an example of the barriers posed to desired virtues.

Family manuals in fact manifested consistently high expectations about the importance and normalcy of brotherly or sisterly feelings. The pervasive family idealism surely entered into this picture, but it was noteworthy that no inherent or common impediments to the ideal were cited. In contrast to adult romance, there were no demons to belabor even occasionally, much less to exorcize. Adult advice manuals maintained the theme by including sections on utilizing good relations with brothers or sisters, and the image of a large group of siblings engaged in a common activity, such as music, was common. Among younger children ungoverned temper might briefly cause flare-ups, even violence, but jealousy did not enter the picture, and there was no durable tension under any other label. A girl strikes her younger brother in T. S. Arthur's 1856 manual, but she is immediately sorry: "She had no animosity against her little playmate; on the contrary, she loved him dearly." L. H. Sigourney, noting that parents can help soothe competition and compose differences, urged that this approach could build on a fraternal love "planted deep in the heart," which "seldom fails to reveal itself." Many authors noted how frequently siblings grouped together (respectfully) to plead the cause of one of their number against parental discipline. The image of an older sibling's aiding younger kin cropped up frequently, with rare admission that a younger child might be "jealous" of this kind of authority.

Catharine Sedgwick's popular manual conveyed the common view. Children in a large family grouped together. A new baby boy was "an object of general fondness." Jealousy was nonexistent. Its possibility came up only in young adulthood, when two brothers loved the same girl. Even here, however, the earlier "home cultivation of affections" had produced a "glare of fraternal love," which allowed the brothers to master "the most selfish and exorbitant of the passions." This view of a loving, envy-free childhood obviously set implicit standards against jealousy, but it conveys no sense of a common emotional problem in early childhood that must be combated, in contrast to other emotional issues, such as temper (or indeed jealousy in siblings as young adults), where high standards were also asserted but against recognized if unfortunate impulses.[46]

To be sure, Bronson Alcott in 1837 (but in a context wider than explicit childrearing advice) briefly mentioned the possibility of a "moment of jealousy" in which a child, frustrated at her older sister's receiving a picture, said she hated her father, who responded by getting a picture for her too but also by pressing her to understand that it was better to give than to receive. The jealousy—and this is an unusual use of the term in talking about children in the nineteenth century—was "understandable" because "she is a very little girl"; no huge crisis was involved. Alcott quickly moved on to other illustrations of mastering appetites. Lydia Child, in her popular manual wrote nothing at all about jealousy and very little about siblings. She did talk about children's propensity to quarrel and urged that brothers and sisters be kind. "Any slight rudeness, a want of consideration for each other's feelings, or of attention to each other's comfort, should be treated with quite as much importance as similar offenses against strangers." Again, quite apart from the implicit quality of any reference to jealousy, the tone was matter-of-fact, with no indication of a major problem under consideration, and the author quickly went on to note how sisters often helped each other.[47] Indeed, predominant literary treatments of siblings in nineteenth-century America, such as *Little Women* or the widely popular Rollo series (featuring Rollo aiding his sister), joined the family manuals in stressing easy sibling harmony.[48] As late as 1904, in another popular manual, an incident that a quarter century later would be invoked with howls of anguish was virtually brushed aside. Mrs. Theodore Birney describes a child's biting her baby sister, without apology; the advice to parents is to strike the girl "lovingly" in the same place, to show her it hurts and to bring home the suffering of the baby "of whom, in her baby way, she was very fond." End of lesson, with no portents of dark passions that must be leashed.[49]

Jealousy, then, continued to be played down, in some cases well into the twentieth century. If mentioned at all, it was usually treated in passing and certainly never given an entire section, as became commonplace in manuals by the later 1920s. The few examples cited referred to sisters, doubtless a reflection of an expectation that girls should behave better than boys but possibly a result also of girls' greater domestic dependence and confinement and their proneness to sibling tension in early childhood. Here was a link with the new female emphasis in questions of romantic jealousy. Nevertheless, one could sum up the evidence on actual family life, as reported by participants, or suggested in family advice or portrayals in the nineteenth century, without mentioning sibling jealously as a perceived issue.

Inattention to jealousy among younger children is partly explained by a belief that the emotion cropped up seriously only as a component of puberty and early romance. At this point, control became part of the responsibilities for character building so seriously laid on teenagers and young adults by a society that saw personal discipline and moral development as lifelong tasks. Childhood, in other words, loomed less large in overall socialization than would later be the case, and distinctive attitudes toward sibling jealousy reflect this fact. Many late-nine-teenth-century experts, certainly, linked jealousy tightly to sexual maturation, influenced by Darwinian efforts to identify the evolutionary utility of major emotions. This was the case with G. Stanley Hall, who largely condemned jealousy—placing his comments in a section on juvenile criminality—but referred its source to puberty, not, in twentieth-century fashion, to earlier childhood experience.[50] Popular fiction cushioned even this kind of concern by discussing tensions that arise among older siblings confronted by an outsider able to take one of their number away through courtship or, perhaps, by the love two siblings might bear for the same individual, instead of focusing on direct rivalries among contesting suitors. Here, sibling cooperativeness supplemented personal maturity and self-sacrifice in damping down potential friction, and the "lessons" bore more on the idyllic happiness of brothers and sisters than on issues of emotional control. Still, the possibility of some jealousy in early adulthood contrasted with the absence of explicit warning flags earlier on; by the same token, when jealousy issues arose they did not signal failures in earlier personality development. Parents had no reason to seek special strategies or even precise labeling: as with true love, childhood and jealousy did not mix. Appropriate adult control might be prepared by more general character building, including the experience of joyous cooperation with siblings, though this link was not specifically drawn. One result of the sense that childish jealousy was at most an incidental issue, not a significant focus, was naïveté, and parents felt no little shock when such a problem was newly identified in the early decades of the twentieth century. Nineteenth-century thinking was especially unprepared for the idea of jealousy's flowing from child to a sibling baby, for what few jealousy references there were normally involved a younger child's resentment of the attainments of an elder, as in Bronson Alcott's lesson.

Several other factors explain the nonchalance about childhood jealousy, shared by parents and advice writers alike. Neglect of childish jealousy built on tradition: there is no sign of explicit antijealousy concerns among American parents before the nineteenth century, and Victorians to an extent simply maintained this stance. Lack of innovation was enhanced by the special, ubiquitous family idealization characteristic of the nineteenth-century middle class. Here, precious values were new, or newly intense, but they did not conduce to careful inquiry into children's jealousy. To note frequent clashes among children, of the sort rooted in some endemic emotion, would challenge belief in the family as a loving, cohesive unit, and not only childrearing experts but ordinary parents seem to have preferred imprecision to sobering reality. To this extent, of course, the approach to childhood jealousy mirrored the impulse to assume that love readily preempted jealousy in adult life.

Yet Victorians did grant a need to lay down basic, condemnatory standards for adult jealousy: the problem emotion was not viewed as compelling, but it might exist. And while idealization of childish innocence doubtless inhibited comment on jealousy, it did not have quite such a thorough deterrent effect with regard to sexuality or anger. Childhood rivalries did not command even this degree of attention. Again, more general invocations of obedience or attacks on quarrelsomeness did part of the job, encompassing jealousy-inspired behaviors without evoking the emotion directly. Parents could note fights or obedience issues that by the twentieth century would be seen as instances of sibling rivalry. That nineteenth-century views of children sometimes used a broader brush does not mean that specific emotional issues went entirely unperceived. And in insisting on docility, generosity, politeness, or simply emotional restraint and self-mastery, parents may well have been combating the effects of jealousy. Parental tolerance must not be too sharply drawn.

Nevertheless, lack of reference to jealousy involved two other ingredients, besides traditional inertia, idealization, and more general behavioral controls. One derived from features of nineteenth-century childhood itself; the other related to additional complexities in parental expectations.

In the first place, there was not as much childhood jealousy as most American adults, and many children themselves, would come to expect as normal by the mid-twentieth century. Silence on the subject reflected in part a different reality. This is, to be sure, a quantitative claim without quantitative evidence, but the probability is strong, not only because adult silence serves as an indicator. Victorian families were relatively large on average, and there is considerable contemporary evidence that large sibling groups produce less rivalry for parental affection than do smaller broods.[51] Older children tend to take responsibilities for their younger brothers and sisters, thus diluting the intensity of links to parents, and numerous siblings often band together against their parents instead of trying to conquer parental affection by dividing from their fellow siblings, as is more tempting when these fellows number only one or two. To this general point about large sibling cohorts, which helps explain the absence of concern about young children's rivalries in earlier centuries as well, might be added the possibility of some special impulses toward sibling cooperation in the nineteenth century itself. Here, it must be stressed, we can only speculate, given the lamentable lack of historical research on sibling relationships. Victorian parents highlighted cooperation more explicitly than earlier families had done. More to the point, other new tactics in childrearing, such as the emphasis on guilt rather than shame, might have encouraged children to unite, thus downplaying mutual rivalries. Guilt strategies, to be sure, were meant to isolate an offending child— go to your room!—but they might elicit a quiet sympathy that earlier shaming techniques, specifically designed to evoke peer reaction, had not done.[52] In any case, whether or not the Victorian decades differed from times past in the amount of young sibling tension, they certainly stand out from what was to come: jealousy in early childhood was less pronounced than it would be later on, and this helps account for its failure to provoke elaborate adult concern.

Many emotions researchers would hope here to see more detailed invocation of current child-development beliefs. Some authorities now downplay the inevitability of sibling rivalries, seeing them as probable only when the oldest child is a boy, while stressing abundant possibilities for cooperative relationships. This trend helps situate an argument that nineteenth-century sibling tensions were less acute than might be expected, but it does not directly support specific historical claims about changes in average experience over time. Current theory would argue that lower levels of childhood jealousy helped prepare less jealous adults, yet here again jealousy may be more malleable over time than present developmental beliefs allow for. Thus before the nineteenth century great jealous intensity might develop among older siblings, as they vied for parental property or honor, without extensive reports of hostility in earlier childhood, and while sibling cooperativeness may have contributed to the tone of Victorian adulthood it hardly ensured a jealousy-free romance. Sibling history is not precise enough definitively to qualify existing theories about personality development, but it probably involved sufficient change to impose some caution in applying the developmental patterns of one time period to the characteristics of another—especially when recent findings themselves have been in flux, from Freudian certainties to a recognition of greater childhood diversity.

Contemporary data combined with Victorian reactions suggest that the emotional life of nineteenth-century children involved greater limitations on the spontaneous generation of jealousy than would later develop. This probability, in turn, helps explain larger childhood experience and adult perceptions alike. The argument is not, however, that sibling jealousy was absent, only that it was somewhat less acute and common than would be the case a century later. One final factor, beyond idealization or more generalized labeling, explains why the childish jealousy that did exist went unlamented.

Many parents, even amid middle-class families striving to be up-to-date, found jealous sniping among their children not only natural—as unwritten tradition may have implied—but even useful. Some may indeed have welcomed a certain amount of jealousy (particularly when it was sporadic rather than consistent or intense), on grounds that—as John Locke had stipulated—it might spur achievement.[53] There was little articulation of this parental belief in the nineteenth century itself. Later authorities, however, would frequently lament a persistent, and hardly novel, parental tendency to play children off against each other in order to motivate good behavior. Parents who normally valued cooperation might be tempted to call John's good behavior to Ben's annoyed attention when provoked—and there were no explicit guidelines to inform them that they erred. Jealousy as disciplinary tool would not necessarily threaten the loving emotional ideal of the family, and particularly parent-child bonds, because it recalled more the older tradition of rivalry for honor than the newer (and far more clearly condemned) tendency to befoul true love with the same emotion. Interestingly, what little perception there was of early-childhood jealousy in the nineteenth century judged it more as rivalry for power than as competition for affection; hence the focus on jealousy of younger against older. If this sense of contest were not stretched too far, and if it were occasionally used to prompt a younger child better to emulate an older brother or sister, parents might be willing to put up with a certain amount of attendant grief without spinning out an overall strategy or grand theory.

Traditionalism, idealization, utility, and possibly some unusual sibling cooperativeness combined, without full consistency, to explain the absence of great parental concern about jealousy and the lag—compared to other emotional areas—in developing explicit strategies for control. Where parents eagerly discussed ways to channel anger, for example, by the 1870s, they continued to pass over jealousy among children; even the gender distinctions, developed quite clearly for adults, were not applied in describing young children—in contrast to anger or sexuality.

All this added up, in turn, to a setting in which children gained little sense of an onus attached to jealousy. They might acquire this sense as adults, when the special demands of unselfish love were brought home to them, but they faced these emotional issues with no elaborate prior baggage. The dominant parental nonchalance, and some probable vacillations in fact, help explain why even adult jealousy was not viewed as a major problem, despite the pervasive condemnations—for no sense of childhood failures fed into it. The same lack of concern also reflects jealousy's special status as a reproved emotion that nevertheless required no major campaign of either prevention or control. And this returns us to the larger issue of how the various nineteenth-century ingredients fit together in accommodating new standards and old, new hostility alongside a reduction in customary behavioral controls over jealousy provocations among adults—without becoming, save in the eyes of utopian experimenters, a major issue.

Handling Jealousy and Love

For jealousy to remain a low-priority emotional issue in the nineteenth century, as was at least superficially the case, two kinds of tensions—or rather, a set of tensions that can be described in two ways—had to be managed. Traditional beliefs in jealousy as a concomitant and defender of love had somehow to reconcile with the new emotionology, and in a changing setting in which community supervision had markedly declined. In the second place, children who had not been given an explicit set of jealousy guidelines had to adjust to courtship and marriage situations in which new tensions might easily arise—a prospect not only plausible in theory but suggested by the recurrent if brief comment on the subject in advice literature and some popular fiction. How did individuals like the Hills sisters, so open about minor sibling squabbles, adapt their jealousy stance when involved in romance? Could they easily internalize the suggested restraint?

A number of different ingredients, some of them directly contradictory, competed for a place in defining adult behaviors and evaluations concerning jealousy. One result was, unsurprisingly, considerable diversity. Nineteenth-century culture, even apart from more private sentiments, remained capable of varied formulations:

A proper amount of this passion (jealousy) is most desirable in both romantic and conjugal love.[54]

We may even blight and blacken our happiness by jealousy, which is really an admission of our own inferiority, of our own cowardice and conceit.[55]

Diversity is certainly no stranger to an assessment of jealousy; it remains a standard feature in the later twentieth century. Yet the opportunity for diversity may well have widened during the nineteenth century, depending on individual openness to the new emotionology or reliance on more traditional standards. To diversity must be added internal inconsistencies. A given individual—particularly a middle-class male—might preach freedom from possessive jealousy while cheering on a beleaguered murderer in a romantic-triangle trial. Parents urged cooperation while sporadically promoting jealous emulation. Again, inconsistency is hardly unusual, and it would certainly persist into our own day, but opportunities for it opened considerably during the Victorian decades. Here were ways, however messy, in which conflicting currents might continue to coexist.

The silence on romantic jealousy in real life, as in popular fiction, reflects a combination of partial internalization of the new emotionology and considerable continuity from the past, extending the possibility of inconsistency amid deeply felt standards. Americans did not, as the advice givers urged, really believe that jealousy was inappropriate in love. Men as well as women still had strong possessive feelings, as the failure of some free-love experiments suggested. While institutional arrangements, such as women's domesticity, helped cushion jealous feelings (at least for husbands), there remained considerable potential for romantic anxieties. And young adults, not taught explicitly as children that jealousy was dreadful, might be ready to express the emotion when and if encountered—though here women were prepared to be a bit more open than men. Indeed, the new attention to female jealousy, though accompanied by promptings to restraint, might have encouraged some women to feel that at least limited jealousy could be expressed, in defense of higher values of family formation and integrity. Again, novel standards could produce diverse reactions as well as varying degrees of acceptance.

The new disapproval of jealousy, however, had an impact in several respects, quite apart from its literal citation in some private diaries. First, the disapproval unquestionably made suitors and spouses less willing than in the past to admit that they were jealous, lest they seem vulnerable, anachronistically possessive, or ungenerous. Emotionology, while not yet used in elaborate socialization programs for children, bore some fruit in keeping young adults silent, whatever their real feelings. Self-censorship, then, was one reason for the absence of a jealousy record, and particularly for the reluctance to use the word itself, in nineteenth-century romance. Many couples discussed their fears of deception in love, particularly early in the nineteenth century, while urging the importance of candor; surely this suggested some concern about provoking jealousy, while equally surely reflecting an aversion to admitting the problem outright. Self-delusion, as well as concealment, was another probable result of demanding standards amid the uncertainties of middle-class courtship.

One interesting manifestation of self-censorship involved the termination of the intense friendships many middle-class young men formed with a peer of the same sex, when one of the pair moved toward matrimony. Deep feeling produced complaints of inattention, when a courtship began to break into earlier emotional intimacy, and warnings about the married state, but it did not yield a direct admission of jealousy (in contrast to some comparable situations among close women friends). Most men rather dropped significant contact with their once-boon companion, in preference to accommodating jealousy to new complexity—or, possibly, to admitting their feelings even to themselves.[56]

Silence and self-censorship were only one way to adjust new standards to ineradicable impulse. Another mechanism, more familiar in Victorian family history, involved concealment not of emotion but of jealousy-producing behavior (or of open awareness that would require a confrontation with one's own jealousy). The classic scenario here involved double-standard sexuality, in which male infidelities were handled discreetly, away from wifely gaze, while women themselves deliberately failed to acknowledge what they half knew.

Here, for all the idealism normally attached to definitions of love, nineteenth-century advice givers could be surprisingly frank. They praised men who took the trouble to conceal affairs, for showing due concern for their wives' feelings, and as we have seen they urged wives to let sleeping dogs lie. The shift in gender attributions, where jealousy was concerned, neatly supported a family system in which men had substantially more freedom to pursue other sexual interests, or even to entertain themselves simply by pondering options, than women did. The basic Victorian role separation between the genders had a host of causes aside from its function in limiting the need for male jealousy, but this function was very real. Many societies with a high jealousy potential—such as Islam—manage to construct systems that, through constraining women, reduce the need to deal with jealousy as a normal emotional issue. Victorian society, though less thoroughgoing in its confinements, had some of the same qualities; for example, it withdrew middle-class women from participation in their husbands' stores and factories, after a first generation of fruitful collaboration—ostensibly lest women be distracted from their high domestic calling, but in practice also to limit public contacts and attendant temptations. In essence, the fuller domestication of women at a time when the male sphere moved outside the household allowed the family to compensate, as a regulator of sexual behavior within the middle class, for the decline of community supervision, not in all cases but in the main. Here was a key reason that the new context of urbanization, declining church and government control over morals, and increasing anonymity among strangers did not produce the anxieties, and so the need to deal with jealousy in detail, that might in theory have been expected.

As noted, some of these effects were doubtless fortuitous, the product of the separation of work from home and the pragmatic need to redefine the family division of labor as a result. Yet the unstated role of jealousy, and particularly the desire to avoid the pain the emotion could cause, should not be entirely ignored. Even when it admitted a jealousy impulse linked to love, as in courtroom dramas, nineteenth-century society was prone to emphasize, more fully than did traditional characterizations, the agony and obsession jealousy could bring. References to an enhancing piquancy, a supplement to love's games, did not disappear, but they moved to the wings in favor of jealousy's more distressing qualities. Avoiding such distress was no small boon, even aside from living up to new emotionological promptings about the pleasure to be gained from rising above jealous selfishness. Arrangements that allowed men to win this avoidance of distress, while offering some protection to wives, however hypocritical, may have reflected some real emotional needs. Jealousy's silence, in sum, should not be equated with inactivity. The emotion helped prompt familial arrangements that then kept it at bay.

Finally, lest Victorian systems be oversimplified yet again, the management of jealousy also depended on considerable mutuality within marriage. Here was the most interesting and revealing adjustment of all. It functioned particularly, of course, where man and wife were both faithful, though it was not absolutely incompatible with highly discreet indulgence in a double-standard sexuality. Mutual concern to avoid provocations of jealousy figured prominently in marital advice, in interesting contrast to the twentieth-century approach that rested more purely on self-control. Thus husbands were urged not, in their wives' presence, to "enthusiastically praise the sterling quantities of other women," while wives should not "invidiously eulogize the seemingly incomparable character of other men."[57] Mutuality of this sort followed from the goal of placing family integrity above potential jealous onslaughts. It may have been prepared by childhood socialization that, though not directed explicitly against jealousy, urged a cooperative sensitivity to jealous reactions of one's siblings.

Certainly most married couples, at least in the middle class, did accept the incompatibility of ongoing jealousy and true love, though not in the sense of requiring total individual control over the emotion regardless of stimulus. They bought into this feature of the new emotionology, in agreeing love was better when jealousy-free, while not expecting love to be as automatically pure as the popular theorists proclaimed.

While the Victorian silence on jealousy reflected personal repression, then, it also reflected the willingness of many couples to avoid extended provocations of jealousy and to deal supportively with the emotion when it did crop up. Jealousy was not elaborately discussed, because of its negative connotations, but repression did not totally impede communication. Thus the housewife who envied her husbands' books found it difficult to admit her pettiness, but jealousy did come out—and when it did the husband recognized his responsibility to deal with it.

The standard mutual approach emerged even more clearly in a mid-century manual on letter writing for lovers. The male suitor writes of his great and exclusive devotion to the only woman he can ever love. But there is a problem, for his love has provoked jealousy. "Do not think I assume the right to control your actions; but I love you too fondly to share our smiles with another." No accusations here—the cautions about expressing jealousy, particularly of the traditional, patriarchal kind, are largely observed, and the emotion is not designated explicitly. But the message is clear enough, and what is more important it is understood and dealt with. The woman responds that she will never flirt again, never give reason for jealousy. The manual's author goes on to offer the usual lecture about jealousy's normal baselessness, particularly where men are concerned, but the interchange itself bore a slightly different message. Jealousy might well exist, particularly amid prevailing courtship practices, but it was painful and should be handled, as part of true love, by careful reassurance.[58]

Real emotional experience, then, produced more intense jealousy than the prevailing emotionology acknowledged; it also produced an undocumentable amount of silence on the part of people unwilling to admit their own encounters with an emotion that was now allowed no easy outlet. It also encouraged new familial controls over women's activities. Many people developed a creative mixture of the new emotionology with an ongoing willingness to recognize that jealousy was a fairly normal part of love—but a part that should be conscientiously addressed and reduced. Love really did mean considerable candor and devotion, or great deal of discretion, and jealousy should not be part of its regime. Old assumptions were not entirely jettisoned, but the disapproval central to the new emotionology, and the concurrent decline (outside the South) of some of the most obvious traditional outlets for expressing jealousy through dramatic challenges to rivals, did gain ground. Jealousy was not a common romantic problem, because people were learning increased reticence about admitting the emotion, but also because couples were sensitive to mutual obligations to keep it at bay. Individual control over jealousy ran less deep than the new emotionology urged, yet the results of some mutual restraint and communication, along with the other adjustment mechanisms, worked to something like the desired end: jealousy was not seen, either by advice writers or by most middle-class couples, as frequently fouling love's nest.

This nineteenth-century paradigm, in which new values blended with some older ideas, was in many senses transitional, reflecting the first impact of new jealousy standards and a widespread reliance on family formation and stability. It did not last, in part because some assumptions of the new emotionology were more fully realized, in part because the willingness of couples to sacrifice independence for reassurance began to decline. Jealousy would become a problem, all the more when measured against the success of many nineteenth-century suitors and spouses in keeping it under control.

The varied strategies designed to minimize jealous tensions in nineteenth-century life won considerable success and played no small role in shaping family ideology and many personal relationships, yet the significance of the emotion itself, or its avoidance, remains elusive. Certainly at the level of public comment, and insofar as can be determined in most personal evaluations as well, jealousy was not a focal emotion in nineteenth-century life. Only the variety of resources mobilized to keep it under wraps, plus the innovations in emotional standards however briefly and infrequently stated, suggest a larger if partly unconscious role.

Jealousy control helps explain, and certainly illustrates, the Victorian reliance on family cohesiveness, now understood to include sibling cooperation as a key ingredient and embellished with the idealization of childish innocence as well as marital love. It provides an additional angle for assessing shifting gender differentiations. Jealousy was now seen as an annoying aspect of female dependency and emotionality, a problem to address. At the same time, jealousy more subtly fed the web of contradictions surrounding middle-class men by 1900:[59] with men held to be guarantors of female fidelity yet somehow magically jealousy-free, it was small wonder that symbolic outlets such as the loud exonerations of a few prominent paramour-murderers gained significant role. Still, while the theme of jealousy illuminates several new corners of Victorian life, it hardly recasts what is already known, precisely because middle-class families compensated so well for potential problems without reaching for heroic emotional control.

To a great extent, as a result, nineteenth-century jealousy must be understood as a backdrop for later change. To be sure, it offers an interesting theoretical illustration of lags between radical innovation in standards and sluggish behavioral and socialization response; the abortive results of most collective experiments in conquering the emotion constitute a graphic illustration. Because we know that the Victorian adjustment did not endure, it may be too tempting to stress the fragility that resulted from this same gap between standards and practice. The nineteenth-century ability to ignore jealousy depended on a good bit of turning a blind eye toward sexual infidelity, on a good deal of oversimplification or idealized glossing, on some unresolved tensions between jealous revenge and rigorous control. Fragility was enhanced by the very real changes occurring in emotionology, in the new gulf defined between jealousy and love. As Victorian adjustments began to break down by the 1890s, in part because of fuller internalization of the new antijealousy standards, jealousy and its management were poised to become more active, certainly more recalcitrant ingredients of American emotional history.

———

CHAPTER 3

Jealousy Moves Front and Center: 1890–1920

There's nothing *new* about adultery. What's new is the carelessness.
JULIA O'FAOLAIN, *No Country for Young Men*

The first symptoms of new uneasiness about jealousy cropped up at the end of the nineteenth century. They resulted not from major new ideas about jealousy, for the emotionology pioneered in the nineteenth century persisted, but from the application of these very values to new behaviors in sex and love. Jealousy began to become a new concern at the experiential level, in dealing with siblings and lovers alike; standard-setting experts picked up the theme after 1920, and at that point began to incorporate the perceived problem of jealousy into an intensified emotionology.

This chapter focuses on the decades of transition, when jealousy began to emerge from nineteenth-century patterns of accommodation to become a serious, much-discussed emotional problem. The full statement of the problem awaited the 1920s, when the transition was completed. Only at this point, furthermore, did it begin to become clear what the response would be. Between 1890 and 1920, we pick up only straws in the wind, along with many complacent assumptions that older adjustments still held sway.

Focus on transition, however, allows particular attention to problems of causation. One advantage of a historical treatment of emotion is that aspects of emotional style are seen as both mutable and explainable. Mutability plays against some impulses in psychological research to seek unchanging response alone, while the effort at explanation departs from tendencies in anthropological study of emotion to focus on cultural variation amid a sense of timelessness that exempts the researcher from attention to causation. With jealousy, the factors that would prompt a radical new concern unquestionably coalesced at the turn of the century, even if their full result had yet to emerge, depending as it did on a serious reconsideration of entrenched reactions and still further intensification of the new factors.

The causation was predictably complex. The ingredients needed to move an emotion into new prominence as a significant issue are rarely simple. To an extent, contradictions visible in retrospect during the nineteenth century, amid new standards and altered family context, but successfully downplayed for some time, came home to roost by the century's end. But new ingredients forced the issue. Many of these are familiar enough, in areas of courtship, child care, demography, though attention to jealousy allows understanding of interactions among them that have previously gone unnoticed.

Without oversimplifying, it is well to note in advance that a primary ingredient in the causal brew was cultural—the moral stance toward jealousy refined during the previous century. Only the dominant emotionology, steadily gaining ground as part of middle-class outlook, explains why new developments in gender relations or child care were interpreted as they were, as adding up to a new need for firmer strategies against the emotional green-eyed monster. The idea of cultural causation's prompting not only a shift in standards, which is obvious enough, but ultimately at least partial changes in emotional experience may jar somewhat, and indeed we will fudge a bit by noting a linkage to concomitant shifts in occupational structure and business organization in determining direction of change as well activating new levels of attention. Yet ideas about emotion do have a shaping role, as scholars have demonstrated for earlier periods in discussing the impact of emerging Protestant emotionology and, more recently, in explaining the rise of new maternal emotional standards in the nineteenth century, though in these instances too a link with structural change—

growing commercialism in the Protestant case, the work-home separation with maternalism—existed as well.[1] Nevertheless, the power of
culture in itself should not be downplayed, particularly, in the modern
American case, where family ideologies are involved. Cultural causation was not fundamentally responsible for the new intensity of concern about jealousy, but it unquestionably guided its direction, its
anxious hostility.

The factors that did come together around 1900 shaped a substantial
transformation in emotional management in American life, setting a
framework within which many Americans still evaluate their experience and train their children. The unexpected crescendo of concern
about jealousy was a significant ingredient in this transformation,
which also entailed other new strategies toward anger, grief, and other
emotions whose integration seemed newly complicated in relation to
social and personal goals.

The idea of an early-twentieth-century watershed risks seeming
either obvious or startling. Most historians dealing with emotion have
focused on a prior modern shift, taking shape in the seventeenth and
eighteenth centuries, traces of which helped redefine jealousy's relationship to love. Their chronological emphasis suggested a premodern-
to-modern transition in which directions set by the later eighteenth
century defined trajectories from then on. One family historian directly contended, in fact, that the redefinition of love sketched by 1800
reached fruition only in the twentieth century—a straight-line connection that in his judgment did not require demonstration.[2] Against this
view—while not at all contesting the significance of the first modern
transformation—evidence about jealousy, linked to findings about several other emotions, describes a second, more recent shift, perhaps not
quite so fundamental in that ingredients of the earlier redefinitions still
applied but certainly substantial in reshaping perceptions of what
constitutes an appropriate emotional life. On the other hand, emotions
researchers, less concerned with history for its own sake, eagerly seize
on the idea of twentieth-century differentiations from an often amorphous past in which Victorian traditions blur with earlier antecedents.
This view can risk exaggerating twentieth-century change—as in a
misguided effort to define emotional modernization as a purely contemporary phenomenon best seen as an attempt to liberate the individ-

ual for maximum possible freedom of emotional expression.[3] It risks, also, a readiness to see fundamental change at every subsequent turn, so that popularized decadal or generational fads are ranked with more basic recasting, as if emotional styles could shift significantly with every breeze.

The transition in jealousy that opened in the 1890s was not casual. It had important roots in the eighteenth-century redefinitions, from which modern emotional culture and a tendency to look to childhood socialization as a key management tool both sprang. But it was not a minor blip on an existing screen. At the same time, the transition did not set in motion a series of subsequent oscillations. It must be seen, and explained, as a relatively unusual kind of reassessment, within which interesting but much less durable or fundamental fluctuations —such as the 1960s youth culture as it related to jealousy—could emerge.

Signs of Change

During the 1890s, a new and explicit concern about jealousy among young siblings began to sprout, though very tentatively amid predominant complacency or silence. The change may first have been noted among parents themselves, faced or believing themselves faced with unexpected unpleasantness among younger children, particularly on the arrival of a new baby. When experts nationwide picked up the idea, in the 1920s, they indicated that parental anxieties, reported in counseling sessions, had helped pinpoint their own concern. It was from childhoods in the later nineteenth century also that autobiographers would report jealous tensions with younger siblings—like Helen Keller in the United States, who wrote about losing her "only darling" status when a baby sister was born, or, in Vienna, Sigmund Freud, who wrote his own jealousies as first child into a general theory. This is impressionistic, to be sure: full descriptive evidence of parental redefinition emerges only in the 1920s. Nevertheless, even if this later point is taken as the definitive break, it is important to search a bit earlier for the causes that would prompt parents to see a problem— indeed, a massive problem—where none had existed before.[4]

Suggestively, the first popular manual to take up a new-style sibling-jealousy theme was Felix Adler's *Moral Instruction of Children* (1893), the most widely read pamphlet in the field to appear in this decade. Adler talked about inequalities among brothers and sisters that resulted in "ugly feelings in the hearts of the less fortunate," unless parents were carefully evenhanded. He moved beyond invocations of generosity specifically to urge children to "be more eager to secure the rights of your brother than your own. Do not triumph in your brother's disgrace but rather seek to build up his self-respect." Parents who did not get to the root of children's quarrels might promote an "incipient hatred" of brothers, despite the fact that love should form the basic center of family life. Here was the kernel of what would become, three decades later, a veritable flood of concern about sibling relationships. Adler's approach remained transitional, as he continued to emphasize childish innocence and scattered his remarks about brotherhood rather than concentrating them in a powerful single section, with elaborate tactical advice bolstering the central message.[5] In his concern, Adler long stood alone among American experts, but he had sketched a redefinition of the child's jealous nature, its dangerous long-run potential, and resultant parental responsibilities whose appearance was not accidental. Something new was in the wind in parent-child relations.

At about the same time, scattered symptoms of a new concern about romantic jealousy began to emerge among American adults. Timing cannot be pinned down too precisely, and though impressions begin to clarify after 1900—a decade or so after the emergence of new sibling-rivalry themes—the main point is the essential coincidence of the two strands, which reinforced each other despite the absence of explicit links. As with sibling tensions, the innovations in romantic jealousy occurred first in actual experience, in what some courting and married couples newly perceived as problems. Only later did these new perceptions feed a formal literature. Marriage writers picked up the theme after 1920 and at that point began to incorporate the new sense of jealousy as an adult issue into an intensified emotionology. But again, the new context predated the full explosion, which aids in identifying the first forces of change.

The concrete evidence suggesting a new impatience with romantic jealousy early in the twentieth century is twofold. A substantial number of young women (though by no means all of those who faced the issue) began more openly to report jealousy at the knowledge of their fiancés' use of prostitutes. Most continued to accept the idea of more chaotic male sex drives, which in combination with the continued need for "good" middle-class girls to avoid intercourse before marriage created some undeniable tensions. And some women were able to acknowledge casual male sex without a sense of threat, or at most a fear of venereal disease. But the tone of jealousy was fierce on the part of many interviewees, and of course it corresponded to mounting turn-of-the-century feminist rhetoric against double-standard sexuality. Young women's jealousy reflected heightened willingness to admit emotional discomfort during the courtship period, and it may also have followed from more blatant—either more frequent, or less covert—pursuit of sexual pleasure on the part of young middle-class men. New behaviors and a new sensitivity to jealousy that could not be resolved by simple mention of the problem to one's partner added up to a new sense of tension about the emotion itself. Some women were beginning to challenge the bases of nineteenth-century adjustments that had kept jealousy under more careful wraps.[6]

The second sign of altered context came from the male side, in growing complaints by husbands about their wives' jealous nagging. This was to become a common male grievance (matched by an almost equally frequent female charge about undue attention to other women). Here, even more than with the issue of brothel visits during courtship, was a sign that the nineteenth-century paradigm was breaking down, as a comment by a wife that behavior-roused jealousy was increasingly taken not as a signal to apologize and conciliate but as an unacceptable intrusion, a nagging effort to control. Possibly husbands did have more roving eyes by the early twentieth century, or at least grew less concerned about subterfuge—again, a combination of new behaviors and, in this case, mutually heightened sensitivities prompted disputes about the appropriateness of jealousy.[7]

The two symptoms of growing recognition of jealousy and disagreement about it developed only gradually. Both were more firmly stated by the 1920s and 1930s than before, so the assignment of their initial stages to earlier decades must be somewhat tentative. Furthermore, reporting on both symptoms (young women's reports and husbands' reports) resulted from new social-science inquiries on courtship, marriage, and emotional issues therein; these inquiries are not available for the nineteenth century, yet had some equivalents been produced they might well have unearthed at least hints of tensions that available documentation does not reveal. It is important to recall that jealousy problems did exist in the nineteenth century, as the attention to gender differentials suggested. The argument here is simply that they began to play a more central role, began indeed to be less commonly resolved by mutual recognition of the responsibility to reduce jealousy anxieties as part of true love, than they had been previously.

The basic nineteenth-century pattern was starting to transform, though gradually and with many individual variations: concern for individual autonomy and pursuit of pleasure was rising, and resentment of jealousy rather than willingness to reassure began increasingly, in actual emotional interactions as well as prevailing emotionology, to shift the burden to the person experiencing jealousy rather than to the behavior that occasioned it. This change corresponded to the emerging concern about jealousy among young children, where heightened attention was vital precisely because internal, individual controls had to be built in, as a matter of personality development, in order to produce appropriately jealousy-free responses in the child and later the adult. The sensitivity to others that earlier emphasis on sibling cooperation had implied gave way, in the jealousy area, to attention to individual emotional restraint regardless—within reason—of external circumstances.

While rising concerns about childish and adult romantic jealousies were ultimately part of a common process, reinforcing each other in various ways, explanation of the transition from nineteenth century nonchalance is best divided. When we know why parents began to worry more about jealous children, we can turn to the question of why adults began to worry more about themselves and their partners.

Causation: Why Young-Sibling Rivalry Was Invented

The causes for unprecedented parental anxiety about jealousy among young children, as this began to emerge around 1900, centered on three concurrent changes. Childish jealousy, particularly of the sort that would respond to the advent of a new baby, began to increase.

Parental personality goals for their children began to alter, making jealousy less palatable than before in light of a new eagerness to inculcate smooth collaborative work habits. Finally, adults began to push off on their children their doubts about their own romantic and sexual impulses and about the jealousy attached. Any one of these factors guaranteed some reconsideration of childish emotions. In combination, they were to produce, after 1920, a veritable frenzy.

Before treating the basic casual trinity, however, we must sketch an alternate channel that fed into the ultimate response to sibling jealousy but did not in fact set the new tide in motion.

The most obvious explanatory path, relevant but deceptive in its simplicity, would see parental attention to sibling jealousy as an anxiety created by experts, a specific instance of the larger pattern of professional child-guidance types muscling in on parental, and childish, autonomy. A considerable industry has grown up around the theme of intrusive social control: self-proclaimed authorities undermine family confidence through their incessant invention of new problems. The revision of emotional standards could be a significant case in point.[8]

We have seen already that an early sign of new concern about siblings was Felix Adler's guidance pamphlet in 1893. This work foreshadowed a larger flood of expert writing three decades later, fueled now by theoretical underpinnings. Spurred by the dissemination of Freudian theory, child psychologists unquestionably became more attuned to childish jealousy on the basis of theoretical preconceptions and to childhood generally as the source of adult personality. These predictions were in turn confirmed by a raft of studies from the mid-1920s through the 1930s that investigated actual incidence of jealous symptoms among various groups of children in both institutional and family settings. The studies differed in some particulars, arguing over whether jealousy varied with children's age and the family's social background. Particularly important was dispute as to whether extended family settings heightened or diminished the chance of jealousy and whether strict discipline favored or discouraged the emotion in young children. But the studies almost uniformly claimed a high rate of jealousy, usually in over half the sibling groups studied, and normally claimed as well that the emotion was most commonly experienced among girls. The results of these studies routinely found their way into general treatises on child psychology, which were in turn utilized (and sometimes even given credit) by the popularizing authors of childrearing manuals and periodicals.[9]

So the experts found or invented a problem, often using research methods that would today be questioned but finding what they expected to find. Their message battered at parents through the child-rearing literature—not surprisingly, reaching suburban middle-class parents most readily—until parents, too, came to see a problem where none had existed before. One could add to this picture the increasing conversion of American families to an emotion-based view of children[10] and to emotional rather than strictly economic functions more generally, a conversion that helped parents see what had previously been judged normal quarrelsomeness in more dire terms.

Expert opinion surely helps explain the acceleration of awareness of childish jealousy and the precise vocabulary it acquired, including the standard use of the term *sibling rivalry*. It also helped form compensatory tactics, which will be explored in the following chapter. But persuasive experts do not primarily account for the popularity of the sibling-jealousy issue or its widespread acceptance among parents. Thus many experts also pushed the idea of basic oedipal conflicts, and resultant jealousy between child and parent, which did not win nearly so much parental attention. To be sure, parents may have artificially turned away from this aspect of jealousy because it struck too close to home and involved a frank recognition of childish sexuality for which many were still unprepared. Or, as one French observer claimed (imaginatively, but with no effort at proof), oedipal conflicts may have been muted in American families because of the sexlessness of parents themselves (in contrast, of course, to *la belle France*).[11] The main point is that expert findings on childish jealousy were not uniformly embraced by American parents. It was sibling jealousy that hit home, because it was sibling jealousy that merged expert recommendations with what American parents themselves were experiencing. Indeed, it is probable that experts turned to sibling jealousy in part because parent-clients were telling them, in counseling sessions, that it was a problem.

With the important exception of the Adler pamphlet, the expert outpouring awaited the 1920s, when the bases for actual parental concern about sibling rivalry were well established. Dominant authorities continued to reecho the nineteenth-century approach well into the twentieth century. Thus a major American collection of 1919 modified the nonchalance of the previous century only slightly, noting that boys might not be "naturally" chivalrous toward their sisters. But the explanation focused on natural masculine rough-and-tumble, plus a tendency to tease when allowed to be too idle. There was no fundamental problem, certainly nothing in the emotional sphere. Parents should keep children busy, while understanding that a certain amount of quarreling was normal and might even usefully spur competition. At most children should be given specific competitive outlets, such as boxing or spelling competitions, while allowed some toys earmarked as individual possessions. The encyclopedia referred to parental expectations that might be excessive, like a father who believed that "it should be instinctive in a manly boy . . . not to hurt his sister," and to this extent nineteenth-century confidence about sibling cooperativeness might be qualified. But the manual suggested no issue that required major new strategies, no sense that parents needed outside guidance to handle an emotional tension that presented unrealized dangers.[12]

Precisely this new worried tone would become dominant just a few years later, and the change owed something to the slightly belated spread of new ideas such as Freud's. But the change was undergirded by other factors, outside the expert realm or at most affecting this realm and middle-class parents simultaneously. The invention of sibling rivalry as an explicit new problem constitutes an instance where expert renderings responded to amorphous parental concern and where parental enthusiasm for the new advice literature that began to issue from the mid-1920s was provoked not by authorities' persuasiveness (for again they never managed to inculcate a full Freudian agenda) but by changes in actual family life and its social context. And here we return to strands that actually wove major innovation in parent-child relations, in advance of expert response.

The fact was that jealousy among young children almost certainly increased in the later nineteenth and early twentieth centuries, for the simple reason that family conditions became increasingly favorable to it. Obviously, jealousy among young children had existed before, and changes in incidence cannot be precisely measured. We have seen, however, that the absence of much explicit comment on jealous reception of new babies before the turn of the century resulted not only from distinctive adult vocabulary and expectations, including the ideal of a conflict-free family, but also from a distinctive actual experience. By the later nineteenth century the framework that had conduced to low-level jealousy among young children was beginning to change.

Jealousy most frequently arises when mothers are intensely affectionate. According to most findings, it is most common when discipline is not severe (for harsh discipline helps unite siblings against parents). By 1900 maternal intensity was definitely on the rise, prepared of course by a prior centering of emphasis on mother love, but now facilitated by more exclusive mother-child ties. Furthermore, discipline was probably moderating. Advice literature was in fact reaching a pre-1940s pinnacle of emphasis on love and tolerant flexibility. Jealousy among young children may also have been heightened by the increasing practice of using hospitals for delivery of infants, which could exacerbate the tension, the apparent threat to maternal affection, experienced by an older child when a new baby was born. Above all, sibling jealousy is most common in small families, where children do not see themselves as part of a larger group with mutual responsibilities for their own maintenance.[13] And smaller families were becoming increasingly common, particularly in those middle-class circles that most readily reported jealousy as a problem.[14] While the American birthrate had been declining for some time, only toward the end of the nineteenth century did families of two to three children become at all standard. It was the expanding middle class that pioneered in this new demography, which helps explain the social basis for the advent of a new concern over sibling jealousy. The various criteria commonly used to distinguish among family types, in terms of susceptibility to jealousy by young children, thus also operated over time. American families by the 1920s normally involved small sibling sets, enmeshed in abundant maternal affection whose disruption could be therefore more easily perceived, with children seeing themselves as rivals (sometimes, given encouragements to competition, prodded to do so)[15] instead of primarily as companions. Widespread parental reluctance to prepare a child for the arrival of a new baby, lest embarrassing sexual questions be raised, in favor of claiming that storks or doctors suddenly produced the new intruder, added to the mix.[16]

A number of other changes, again coming to a head by the early twentieth century, added to the impact of declining birthrates and growing maternal intensity. The use of live-in servants declined in the middle class from the 1890s onward, and soon thereafter coresidence with an older relative—a grandparent or maiden aunt—also began to drop. Here were key factors in the greater exclusivity of mother-child bonds. The nuclear family drew tighter, more isolated. Obviously, young children in this setting encountered fewer caregiving adults in the home, which encouraged greater emotional attachment to their mother and subsequent rivalry.[17] School demands, beginning to affect a growing number of adolescents, also reduced the likelihood that older siblings would play such an active role in childrearing. A number of factors thus combined to reorient mother-child contacts and interactions among younger siblings, augmenting the jealousy potential. In an interesting but somewhat vague sketch of the rise of intense nuclear-family interactions by the end of the nineteenth century, Richard Sennett posited a significant shift in personality formation and a reduction of emotional flexibility; the increased battle for maternal affection, and the consequent reduction of sympathy among siblings, is one area where this kind of change prevailed.[18]

The combination of changes in the treatment and context of children must be emphasized particularly in light of current child-development theories that sensibly downplay the universality of sibling tensions. Unquestionably, the explosion of anxiety that emerged for several decades after 1920 had more to do with parental shifts, in assessing the impact of children's squabbles, than with childish emotionality itself. While development experts long supported the campaign against jealousy in young children, playing to parents' fears, many authorities more recently have emphasized that only certain contexts are likely to generate serious resentments; primary among these is the presence of an older brother, particularly when this brother is the oldest sibling, who can focus resentments of superiority based on age and often on gender.[19] Obviously, lots of families at the turn of the century had a female oldest sibling. Reports of jealousy in these families may have been particularly exaggerated, as a result of skewed adult perceptions heightened by prevailing belief that jealousy and femaleness easily combined. Yet the possibility of somewhat more generalized jealousies at that time should not be discounted entirely. Peculiar maternal intensity (which has lessened since 1950) and the withdrawal of other adult agents could foster systematic jealousies that have since declined. These might be disproportionately directed not against a superior older brother but against a baby seen as superior in getting love. Maternal concern about infant welfare, at its height early in the century, would simply exacerbate a dynamic that has since abated. Current developmental wisdom, in sum, may not accurately fit the situation of a few generations back, which was then ballooned into mythic proportions for other reasons.

Although one cannot pretend precisely to measure change in children's emotions, the simple fact was that early twentieth-century families were different from those of the mid–nineteenth century and somewhat different from families today, and heightened jealousy was a key product of this distinctiveness. It is no accident that several features prominent in nineteenth-century discussions of sibling affection figured among the changes. Thus the happy large sibling bands idealized by many stories and manuals gave way to dyads and triads as the birthrate dropped. The growing concern about sibling jealousy, and particularly its identification among young children rather than, nineteenth-century fashion, among older children preparing to dispute a suitor or a patrimony or dowry, responded to fact as well, as competition for maternal affection rose. Indeed, expert attention itself almost surely resulted in part from the novel childhood experiences of the experts themselves—including Freud, a jealous first child par excellence—whose own emotional context reflected the shifting conditions of family life. Though impossible to demonstrate without some circularity, then, one of the two greatest factors in the heightened concern about sibling jealousy was heightened sibling jealousy. Expert advice was to a great extent directed, as in urging that children be given some responsibility for babies, at modifying some of the changes that had produced more jealousy, though few authorities more than dimly perceived this historical perspective.

A new reality was only part of the story, however. The kind of adult concern that found expression by the mid-1920s greatly exceeded any conceivable increase in actual sibling tensions. These were not new, and they surely varied even amid new pressures more than adults were to realize for several decades. Along with new troubles among younger children, then, the invention of sibling rivalry reflected shifts in adult standards that would have made even earlier levels of quarrelsomeness unacceptable.

Thus declining infant mortality rates, another turn-of-the-century phenomenon, produced growing concern about infant health in general, as expectations shifted. This in turn could trigger new guilts and anxieties about babies that could spill over into declining tolerance for even modest potential roughhousing from older brothers and sisters.

While parents responded to new facts, as well as to subsequent expert pressure, they also reflected other ingredients that colored their perceptions, beyond what the facts warranted. From the early part of the century middle-class parents began to redefine the kinds of personalities they wished to raise, in response to alterations in business climate that stressed bureaucratic and service talents over entrepreneurship. They heightened their emphasis on social skills and became increasingly ambivalent about emotions that supported competitiveness. This tendency ultimately showed in a reevaluation of anger, and it also, still earlier, generated greater sensitivity to jealousy. Here too, expert guidance picked up cues from the audience, in stressing that childish jealousy might unfit an adult personality not only for familial love but for work habits as well. Not surprisingly, when evidence became available, by the 1930s, about the social basis for particular concern about sibling tensions, middle-class parents, and especially the newer kinds of service professionals and corporate managers in the suburbs, displayed disproportionate anxiety.[20] The link between a changing occupational structure, in a mature industrial economy, and the desire to foster harmonious personalities cut into lingering traditional tolerance for jealousy among young children and into the desire to use such normal sentiments as a spur toward achievement. The tie between economic change and familial goals showed in the frequent references to the damage unchecked jealousy could do not just to a new baby or the family, but to the ultimate personality of the jealous sibling, among other things hampering the poorly socialized adult in proper work relationships. Here also was the clearest tie between the perception of a new jealousy problem and larger changes in the context for American emotional standards and emotional repression.

A final factor in the new perception of the sibling-jealousy issue was more specific to the emotion itself and, along with actual sibling changes, particularly revealing of why jealousy won new reprobation in advance of anger and other emotions unsettling to bureaucratic smoothness. In their zeal to ferret out childish jealousy—and particularly in their professed shock at the signs of such jealousy, as if no sibling squabbles had clouded their own early years—parents in the first decades of the twentieth century were projecting onto children a novel tension they themselves experienced in dealing with jealous emotions in a culture that attacked their validity. In other words, the more thoroughly nineteenth-century standards penetrated, convincing adults that romantic jealousy was wrong, the more tempting it was to turn on children the disquiet felt in oneself. This was all the truer, by 1900, in that provocations for romantic jealousy were also on the rise.

The declining gender rigidities, the wider socializing, and the looser sexual tone that described middle-class life from the early twentieth century onward stimulated new pangs of jealousy that culture refused to countenance, as discussed in greater detail below. One recourse was to attack childish symptoms with unprecedented zeal, buoyed by the belief that children would grow up freer from emotional strain as a result. Here was an important intersection between the startling new emphasis on childish jealousy and the wider experience of the emotion in twentieth-century American life.

The war on childish jealousy responded to a variety of interlocking factors, from expert prodding to a significant shift in the emotional experience of many children. The war reflected a growing need to answer change with change, to restrain jealousy even as it threatened to burst into more vigorous bloom.

The specific pattern of causation for the shocked awareness of child-ish jealousy ran as follows: middle-class Americans were conscious by the 1890s of an emotionology that strongly urged a contrast between jealousy and real love, and even if they had not actively integrated this contrast into their emotional perceptions they were certainly attuned to an equation of family and love. Then, through an interlacing series of shifts including new demography, they increasingly confronted a family situation where sibling jealousy was likely. Some resultant manifestations, such as threatened violence to babies, might have been inherently disturbing, but the pattern was particularly distressing in light of existing expectations about family life. Signs of new tensions over childish jealousy began to surface in the 1890s and troubled many parents before they gained widespread public articulation. Experts then aided this articulation, developing a more elaborate set of emotional standards regarding jealousy. Parental interest in developing more cooperative personalities for a corporate world and parental anxieties about combating their own jealousies encouraged an exaggeration of the actual problems of sibling jealousy, and the sheer novelty of the issue worked to the same effect. Nevertheless, in contrast to most known cases, where emotionologial change normally precedes shifts in actual emotional experience—as with anger or love in modern Western history—the rise of the sibling-jealousy issue moved more from actual emotional changes on the part of children and parents in combination with a heightened specification of standards.

Uncertain Romances

The development of new opportunities for jealousy in courtship and marriage, signaled by signs of tension over double-standard sexuality and women's "nagging," rose in close correspondence to the discovery of jealousy in young children as a key problem. Here too, the 1920s would see excited discussion of issues that had clearly been incubating for some time. Chronological congruity helps explain how parents might seek to express doubts about their jealous reactions through their shock at their children's possessiveness and by seeking to improve their offspring's adaptability as adults through earnest control of jealousy in early life.

Certainly, without major alteration in nineteenth-century beliefs about adult jealousy and love, several trends could induce new concern. The context for romance was changing rapidly around the turn of the century, and although the leading developments cannot all be directly linked to new emotional tensions, they are consistent with

growing concern about responses to jealousy, and some tied to romantic anxieties directly.

Rising divorce rates and, in the middle classes, the increasing use of
mental-cruelty provisions in divorce could link to jealousy in several
ways. As marriage was judged in terms of emotional harmony, which
"irrational" nagging or blatant infidelity might intrude upon, jealousy
problems could be seen as an issue that need not be met by compromise and conciliation. At the same time, divorce itself could occasion
substantial outpourings of jealousy, as partners tried to adjust to their
loss and to affiliations of former spouses with others.[21]

New public roles for women provided yet another context for uncertainties about jealousy. Middle-class men now—after 1900—commonly worked with female subordinates, often young ones, with one
result that advice to wives now frequently included injunctions not to
be jealous of secretaries. Rule number one: "Avoid Being Jealous."
Rule two, just in case the point wasn't clear: "Refrain from Envy."[22]
For a younger group, coeducation during adolescence became a normal
experience, with the rapid gains of the high schools plus expansion of
the female contingent at the college level.

Shifts in the wider culture contributed confusion. Films made sex
objects visually accessible to the masses, and, equally important (in
contrast, say, to clandestine pornography), the accessibility was obvious to lover or spouse. Jealousy could thus focus on a real or imagined preference for an early Hollywood idol.[23]

The removal of courtship from the front porch, and from some adult
supervision, began to create the practice of dating during the decade
before 1920; dating, in turn, particularly in its earliest manifestations,
frequently meant playing the field. The whole practice was infused
not only with adolescent sexual anxieties but with contests for popularity and status among peers—a ready setting for frustration and jealousy as a heightened part of the teenage experience.[24]

Changes in courtship and marriage, and the significant if still limited
shifts in women's roles in work and public life, were particularly likely
to provoke jealousy among people who retained traditional views of
gender or of romance. This correlation is hardly surprising—indeed,
it still prevails—but it served as a particularly dynamic factor in
decades during which innovations in behavior could so easily outstrip

flexibility in outlook. Even for some who eagerly embraced change, jealousy could express concerns about appropriate values or a desire for more radical action than could yet be risked. Some of the new jealousies in marriage, for example, might reflect appetites for infidelity and not just distrust of spouse, at a time when conventional standards were becoming less secure but still held considerable power. It was easier than during the Victorian decades to project jealousy on a spouse or a lover that in fact expressed one's own guilty desire to experiment.[25] Adolescents could experience understandable confusion in a dating atmosphere that combined romantic aura with practiced lack of commitment.

These developments took place, furthermore, in a culture in which sexuality and sexual satisfaction were becoming more overtly important. New and more revealing costumes for women, reports of growing eagerness on the part of middle-class wives to learn about the experience of orgasm, the increasingly charged atmosphere among college youth as the boundaries of "petting" expanded—all these expressed and might provoke this new interest.[26] Actual intercourse behavior may not yet have greatly changed, but appetites were less concealed, and this could make the more definite behavior changes productive of heightened jealousy.

What was happening, overall, was a tendency to move away from Victorian conventions that had downplayed jealousy potential by separating the genders outside the family context and keeping sexual interests under partial wraps. Just as the Victorian accommodations had helped explain why jealousy did not emerge as a major issue, so their decline triggered vigorous new concern.

Changes in childhood experience, particularly before being countered with firm parental tactics, might feed into this fire as well. Many experts, certainly, soon came to believe that teenage or adult jealousy problems had little to do with actual romantic situations, deriving instead from unresolved issues earlier in life—the "carry-over of traits established long before."[27] Jealous children, it was argued, were less likely to see the emotion as monstrous, regarding it instead as a natural, even desirable part of love. This hypothesis need not be pressed too far, for the new factors in the context of courtship and marriage contributed directly and abundantly to jealousy, serving as ingredients of change in their own right. But increased childhood jealousy added to the overall evolution.

Increasingly, jealous siblings were confronted by parents often newly uncomfortable with their feelings about jealousy, which could add to the confusion. A final reason for tensions surrounding romantic jealousy, then, was the strong likelihood that many lovers brought a somewhat different emotional baggage to their adult experience, deriving from incompletely resolved childhood jealousies, than had been the case in the nineteenth century and before. Children raised with substantial adult attention, who had been less subject to the compromises of growing up in large households, might also feel, as adults, that their interests in autonomy and pleasure deserved particular respect, and so be less patient with the jealousy of others.

There are a number of signs, certainly, that the balance between individual and family was beginning to shift early in the twentieth century, though more clearly on the part of men than on that of women. As middle-class Americans became somewhat more comfortable with the basic conditions of urban, industrial life, the need for emotional idealization of the family—including denial of jealousy or its careful handling—diminished.[28] The lessened willingness to dilute individual whim, so widely noted after World War II, in fact took root earlier, and both jealous response and attack on jealous response were key symptoms.[29] The growing sense that jealousy was a problem followed from a number of fairly familiar changes in American family culture, but they suggest how deeply these changes could cut into emotional experience and self-evaluation, producing additional adjustments of no small importance.

Conclusion

The simultaneous emergence of factors prompting concern about sibling emotion and those urging new attention to jealousy control in romance was obviously not accidental. Children whose early rivalries with brothers or sisters were more deeply rooted and were nourished at this point particularly by confused parental reactions might find greater uncertainties in courtship than had been true during the Victorian decades, always granting that shifts in childhood experience were by no means complete. Even clearer was the linkage that ran the other way, from adult uncertainties to perceptions of children's emotional deficiencies.

The temptation to displace one's own conflicts about jealousy and fidelity onto children, the leading cause of the gap between perception and reality in defining sibling problems in the first place, helped produce an approach that depended on appropriate socialization as the only logical escape from untenable emotional traits. As concern about adult jealousy mounted, if only because of the new uncertainties of romance, the question of what to do with unwanted jealousy obviously intensified. Nineteenth-century emotionology had offered no clear answer in theory: the emotion was not supposed to exist, and should be overwhelmed by true love. In practice, of course, many nineteenth-century couples dealt with the issue by reporting the problem, however hesitantly, trusting that the partner would reassure. This strategy by no means vanished after 1920, but it did become more difficult given the growing insistence that jealousy was an unwarranted intrusion, to be handled by the jealous individual rather than foisted on a partner. So what could be done? Experts turned to childhood as the only logical escape. If children were emotionally trained to control their jealousy, with a focus on issues that arose very early in sibling life, they would not present problems as adults, and so the need to handle jealousy in romance disappeared. Jealous adults were people who had not been properly raised. This theme, reechoed from the 1920s onward, still begged the question of what to do with these unfortunates, but it did focus attention squarely on explicit emotional management during childhood, and the first years of childhood at that. This was the logic of the situation, given adult anxieties as they followed from implementation of the antijealousy emotionology of the previous century applied to a changing context of gender relations.

The twentieth century has seen doubts about childish emotions built into childrearing advice on many fronts, with promptings of appropriate restraint and a sense that raw childish impulse was dangerously immature unless guided by adults until greater reason could take command.[30] Concern about childhood jealousy fits this picture nicely. But one should not sanitize childhood jealousy by lumping it too thoroughly with other emotions: it became a special problem area, achieving this status quite early in time compared to other emotional management areas, and it helps explain why twentieth-century experts and many parents came to focus so resolutely on early childhood rather than childhood in general. For the intensity of concern about managing jealous emotions by age eighteen months to two years calls attention to the unusual features of childrearing beliefs in the twentieth-century United States as they contrasted with most cultures and with the American approach itself during the nineteenth century. Many Americans came to believe that problems started early and must be handled early; there was no conventional waiting period in which infants might be regarded as helpless animals or blessed innocents, prior to the possibility of imposing clearer standards. American anxiety about early childhood was encouraged by expert theories, Freud's chief among them, but it had other and earlier bases in what parents came to perceive in the interactions between a toddler and a baby brother or sister. Gradually, the idea of launching emotional management among young children spread to other areas, as in growing concern about infant tantrums, but the first breakthrough came with jealousy. This is turn was due to the new priorities adults came to feel about consistency in handling jealousy, whereby appropriate adult restraint had to begin with what were now seen as the initial, tragically early manifestations of the emotion in human life.

The factors that jointly built anxieties about sibling rivalry and romantic jealousy from the 1890s onward had by no means completed their work by 1920. Causation would continue and intensify. The impact of changes in economic structure—the rise of bureaucracy and the service sector—on personality goals would gain ground steadily. New factors would add in. Thus during the baby-boom years after 1943, close child spacing added to the older factors inducing an upswing in sibling jealousy—at least according to most theories, which argued that children were most susceptible to these emotions before about age three and the development of some interests outside the home. This rise in turn prompted the final upsurge of expert and parental concern, which lasted through the 1950s and then eased somewhat with the end of the baby boom by 1963. Romantic jealousy, challenged already by new gender patterns in the 1920s, received additional pressure from the work and educational roles for women that developed during and after World War II and from dramatic new middle-class sexual habits from 1960 onward. A key result was a new outpouring of advice about adult jealousy itself, after 1945, that soon surpassed attention to siblings. These subsequent developments, including the surges of expert advice, largely built into a framework already established, in basic direction, by the 1920s. Americans were primed at this point for a new campaign against jealousy, with first focus on early childhood but a warning system set for adults as well. The only serious explanatory issue thereafter—and even this would not apply until the 1960s—was whether some countervailing factors had emerged. For several decades, and in most respects through the 1980s, the anxious context for jealousy set in motion during the early part of the century remained in force; Americans simply became more accustomed to working within it. The next step—following on the somewhat disparate changes in childhood, parenting and parental perception, and romance during the turn-of-the-century years—was an explosion of near-hysteria about jealousy during the 1920s, when the changes coalesced and burst into public view.

CHAPTER 4

The Campaign Against Sibling Jealousy

Long a nonissue, at least in terms of any explicit identification, sibling rivalry—complete with the new label—became a staple of childrearing advice and parental discussion from the mid-1920s onward. Not surprisingly, given the urgent factors underlying the concern, jealousy ranked with anxiety as the most frequently mentioned childish emotions in popular manuals from the 1920s through the 1980s.[1] From this point until the 1960s, childrearing manuals uniformly contained comment, usually anguished comment, on the importance of dealing with this aspect of emotional interaction. Particularly as attitudes toward childhood sexuality began to loosen somewhat, as with the declining tension over masturbation, sibling jealousy focused more efforts on reproval and control than any other emotional issue, at least through the 1950s. The contrast with the nineteenth century was simple but fundamental: childhood, and indeed early childhood, became for the first time the key battleground in the campaign against jealousy, and the negative evaluation of jealousy became more unambiguous than ever before.

The Outpouring of Advice

Appropriately enough in terms of standard setting, one of the first salvos in a new war on children's jealousy came in a widely cited government publication on childrearing, by D. A. Thom, published in 1925. "Few emotions are experienced by man which from a social point of view are more important than jealousy," Thom warned, and jealousy takes root in early childhood, preventing happiness and possibly causing violence. "The jealous person becomes an object of dislike. Often he develops the idea that he is unjustly treated or persecuted, and all too frequently this idea causes uncontrolled resentment and disastrous results." So parents should attend carefully to jealousy in their children, doing all they can—and Thom had a few suggestions along lines of impartiality—to prevent it. A more complete set of tactics emerged from the Children's Bureau in 1930, again under the heading "Nobody likes a jealous person. A jealous person is never happy." Fortunately, appropriate tactics on the arrival of a new baby could stem the tide: "Tony was happy again. Now he loves his baby brother. He is not jealous anymore."[2]

Standard privately authored manuals for parents eagerly picked up the theme. The Child Study Association of America, in 1926, while briefly acknowledging jealousy's potentially useful role in spurring competition—and so "speeding up the wheels in the business world" —came down clearly on the side of repression. Jealousy was normal, but if left uncontrolled "so intense that little but harm can come from rousing it in its more primitive forms, and that even in the higher form of rivalry and emulation greatest caution must be used." If a child's jealousy works to hold back his siblings, "There is no limit to the depths to which he may sink." "Children who quarrel because of jealousy . . . are in a serious state. This type of quarreling should be treated at once by getting at and doing away with the cause of it."[3] So much for the unspecific approach of the past century or more: jealousy must now be isolated from other childish attributes and given focused attention. Both the novelty and the gravity of the problem are striking; experts pulled out all the stops in urging high anxiety. Dorothy Canfield Fisher, a prolific writer for parents during the interval years, turned to the problem of jealousy by 1932. The emotion was infantile but not easy to outgrow, yet it could easily distort adult relationships. Parents had a serious responsibility in helping children through the emotion, for the family context was where jealousy began. Failure to staunch jealousy was "a severe indictment of the family." Yet too many parents deliberately encouraged competition among siblings. "In inciting their children to rivalry . . . parents may be wrecking their chance of present and future happiness."[4]

There were, to be sure, some alternative voices on the subject of childish jealousy, particularly during the 1920s and 1930s. A minority of advice manuals simply avoided the subject, as in the older tradition. Watsonian behaviorists mentioned jealousy but tended to downplay it, predictably arguing against any idea that it was instinctive and claiming, correspondingly, that a few simple tactics would prevent its emergence. Avoidance of too much mother love was the key, for parents caused whatever jealousy there might be.[5] More interesting still, and more durable, was the undercurrent of belief that jealousy might in fact be useful, at least in appropriate doses, by spurring achievement. This quite logical line of argument, similar to beliefs about channeling boys' anger to purposes that would serve in adulthood, occurred in a few manuals that attempted to reduce the dominant tone of anxiety about sibling jealousy and also, occasionally, as an inconsistent note in treatments largely set against the emotion. Thus jealousy might encourage young children to learn from their older brothers and sisters —though it should never be used deliberately to motivate. Or, more positively, "To outdo each other, each [child] puts forth more energy, to gain adult recognition." After all, the competitive spirit was fundamental in American society, and it was too much to ask children to love one another. Jealousy, in sum, might have "character-building and creative uses."[6]

This approach was not common, however. Unlike the idea of channeling anger, which received widespread support until the 1940s, jealousy was seen by most commentators as too dangerous to try to use. In fact, in the dominant emotionology of the period from the late 1920s until at least 1960, jealousy required more concerted repression than any other childish emotion. The standard manuals (including Spock) devoted five to ten explicit pages to the subject, more than on

any specific topic other than physical care. Revealingly, individua
manual writers who had not identified the theme of jealousy in early
work, prior to 1930, such as Dorothy Canfield Fisher and Gladys
Groves, converted to vigorous concern in their later writings, recognizing the importance of this emotional issue but also, implicitly, its
novelty as well.

Hostility to jealousy was not itself new, for the redefinition of love
to exclude jealousy had occurred, at least on the adult emotionological
level, considerably earlier. What was novel in the twentieth century
was the intensity of the attack and its focus on early childhood. These
innovations had several ingredients in turn. Guidance experts and
many parents themselves reported a growing anxiety about the direct
results of sibling rivalry in the family. Jealousy was dangerous. It
might, some argued normally would, lead to attacks, even murderous
attacks, on a new baby. Jealousy, unchecked on a new sibling's arrival,
would spoil a brotherly or sisterly relationship well beyond babyhood,
to the disadvantage of the children involved and the disruption of the
larger family. "Unless the parents recognize that jealousy will normally
appear, and are prepared for it, strong feelings of hostility often develop which continue to make life miserable for both children over
many years." Jealousy, quite simply, contradicted the emotional goals
long since advocated for family life, and many authorities cited the
shock parents experienced on witnessing the hatred with which a new
baby might be greeted. Yet, authorities were now arguing, jealousy
among siblings was inevitable. Indeed, insidiously, it was more likely
to be present when concealed than when manifested in overt acts of
violence. This was a subtle emotional monster, whose existence must
now be assumed. "The child whose jealousy is not as easy to recognize
suffers more and has greater need for help."[7]

The new approach to children's jealousy shifted nineteenth-century
emotionology in several ways while building on the disapproval already established. In addition to the intensification and the unprecedented application to the very young and to early personality formation, the new concern adapted earlier beliefs about jealousy as a
consuming force, likely to generate monstrous acts. Now seen as a
distressingly normal drive, jealousy as an impulse to blind violence
moved from exceptionally impassioned adults—the stuff of plays or

courtroom dramas—to otherwise conventional siblings who might readily vent their resentments on helpless babies. The same grip of passion applied, but now refocused from romantic tragedians to the suburban nursery.

Jealousy was a problem not simply during childhood years, however; it could become a permanent liability to personality, unless attacked during those years. "If he [the child] does not have the right kind of help, his personality may be damaged. Unfriendly, disagreeable, self-conscious adults show these traits because of unsolved jealousy problems in their childhoods." Sibling rivalry "indelibly stamps personality and distorts character."[8] It became, indeed, conventional wisdom that jealous adults were defective and that their defects stemmed from childhood jealousy improperly handled. "A prolonged state of jealousy is a symptom of retardation in emotional development and shows itself along with other evidences of emotional immaturity." Unchecked, jealousy could lead to unhappy people, bad marriages, homosexuality, criminality, the works—"we have only to read the daily paper to see the results of ungoverned jealousy in adult life." Here was a huge responsibility for parents, not only in setting the right tone for their own family but in regulating an omnipresent emotion that could ruin their children as adults. Small wonder that specific handbooks dealing with jealousy in children emerged by the 1940s, that almost all childrearing manuals had long and carefully noted sections on sibling jealousy and its prevention, that the columns of *Parents' Magazine* filled with tales of childish jealousy and practical measures to combat it.[9]

In children and adults alike jealousy was bad because it attacked the very values for which the family existed and because it denoted a selfish possessiveness unsuitable not only for family settings but for life in general. Here the emotionology developed in the previous century found full and urgent voice.

Jealousy flourishes in souls where affection and response are wanting.

Jealousy is more than a subversion of love; it is the dark face of love ingrained with fear. The person into whose character habitual emotional insecurity has bitten deep can be so persistently or intensely jealous as to bring constant turmoil into the most promising family life.

We talk about good anger and good fear, but there is no good jealousy.

Its technique is domination. Its method is to enhance one's status at the expense of another. It is not conducive to growth and development. It is productive of strife, disharmony and wasted energy.

Jealousy, in sum, was held to be incompatible with real love and also, in a newer twentieth-century element, to suggest a kind of person incapable of meeting the standards of cooperativeness and ease with others now seen as essential even in ordinary relationships.[10]

Tactics for the Young and Their Parents

The importance of the jealousy problem dictated a variety of tactical responses, normally listed in childrearing manuals from the 1920s onward. These responses were viewed as feasible and productive but not, at least until the 1950s, automatic. They required effort and some careful planning, even some rethinking, by parents.

Beyond sheer effort—and Dr. Spock specifically urged that the problem of childhood jealousy was so acute and menacing that "a lot of effort" was essential,[11] in contradistinction to the easygoing tone of most of his child-care manual—the treatment of childhood jealousy rested on two basic ingredients. First, parents must recognize that children could not handle jealousy themselves. Left unchecked, the emotion might take on a disguise, but it would only fester and worsen. Second, the logical response to overt acts of jealousy, punishment of some sort, was directly counterproductive. For though jealousy subverted love, it must be answered, at some sacrifice to short-run parental ease, with still more love.

Jealousy was caused, of course, by the child's perception of a threat to his claim to parental, primarily maternal love. "No one, not even the most enlightened adult, can accept without many pangs the idea of sharing a love relation with a rival. We must remember that the child has been in the possession of all his mother's love; now he is called on to share it with another. . . . If we succeeded in getting him to accept the situation happily, we have done much towards making him grow into an adult who looks upon all love as a sharing with others, not as a possession which must be calculated and selfishly held against all comers."[12] Though extremely undesirable, in other words, jealousy was also supremely understandable, because it rested in a loving relationship.

Yet while handling sibling jealousy required massive doses of parental love—so that on the arrival of a new baby, the older child realized that the affection directed at him was in no way reduced—it also required recognition that sibling love could not be insisted upon. Parents must let their children articulate a dislike for new babies. "A child should know that he is entitled to feel any way he wants to about his brother or sister, and he is not to think that he is a bad child because of it." Avoidance of guilt was as crucial to the development of secure, jealous-free personality as was the attack on the emotion itself. Parents should tell the child that he "sometimes won't like the new baby at all. Sometimes you'll be mad at momma too. You'll want to tell her 'stop loving that little red baby. Come and love me.' Of course momma will give you more loving whenever you want it. So, be sure to ask." "I know how you feel, dear. Come on over and I'll give you a hug and we'll see if that doesn't help." "I know how you feel; you wish there were no baby; I love you just as always." Here, obviously, was explicit recognition, as against the more optimistic nineteenth-century renderings, that family and love were not indissolubly linked in the child's eye, though the solution was still more insistence that love could conquer all.[13] Jealousy entered the twentieth-century American pattern of emotional repression in which undesirable feelings were to be circumvented, rendered largely passive, rather than directly attacked.

Specific tactics within this overall framework became increasingly standardized, after some vagueness in the 1920s. They are of interest particularly because, at least in the eyes of experts, they ran counter to common parental impulses in some instances. Children must be carefully told that a baby is coming, as against some modest tendencies to duck the subject lest awkward questions be asked. If a child had to be moved to make room for baby, the move should come well in advance of the newcomer's arrival. Sharing should be downplayed. If at all possible children should be given separate rooms, furnishings, toys, and clothing. Where sharing was economically essential—and Spock and other urged that unexpected expenses were worthwhile in this endeavor, as in possibly hiring a nurse to take care of baby so that maternal attention could flow to the older child—it should be masked by repainting furniture or dyeing clothes. Grandparents and others should learn not to make a great fuss over babies turning instead in preference to the older child. Invidious comparisons should never be made among children, and an atmosphere of careful fairness must prevail from the outset. Babies should be brought home without fanfare—there was some disagreement over whether older children should be present or not—and attention should immediately turn to the older child, even at some expense to the infant. After all, babies sleep a lot and a bit of neglect would not hurt them. Fathers, those vestigial remnants of traditional family life, actually had a role as well, in helping to divert the older child when the mother was inescapably preoccupied with the baby. Feeding the infant, particularly breastfeeding, was seen as a traumatic act, best done when the older child was diverted (and it was better to let a baby squall a bit than to turn away from the older child's needs). Finally, older children should be given responsibility for helping with babies, as well as treated to confidential asides about what a nuisance babies could be. Children should be given evidence, as one *Parents' Magazine* contributor noted, that "the baby was his."[14]

Some authorities went further still in urging sensible spacing of children, now that most parents were aware of birth control. There were some amusing disputes about the ages of greatest vulnerability to jealousy, with opinions including two to three, four to five, and even seven to ten, but ultimately considerable consensus emerged that the greatest danger of jealousy's taking root came in very early years, before children had any outside interests. Sensible spacing thus dictated two- or three-year intervals.[15]

At an extreme, of course, parents had to guard against violence to babies. Some experts treated this problem as dire indeed, urging that a child never be left alone with a baby as though murder were an almost predictable result. Finally, persistent or deep jealousy should be turned over to expert counseling, for the emotional bomb simply had to be defused.

The goal, of course, was to stem serious jealousy before it could start. Some experts were optimistic that their recommendations could produce full family harmony as well as a healthy personality in the older child. Others, while claiming that personality development could indeed be set aright, admitted that recurrent, if relatively minor, outbursts of jealousy would continue, as part of a family life that fell short of ideal.[16]

The burst of concern about attacking jealousy in young children involved a number of expert-urged approaches against more traditional methods of discipline. Parents should respond to jealousy-induced quarrels not with a heavy hand but with fairness, empathy, and assurances of love. They should not push generosity to the point of counterproductively insisting on down-the-line sharing. They should not expect their own joy at having a priceless baby to be shared by their own children. They should guard against their own impulses, for sheer power could not permanently prevail against jealousy and short-term repression simply made matters worse. They should take seriously newer approaches to housing, feeding, and even spacing children. Experts obviously seized on jealousy as an occasion to assert their authority over what they assumed to be widespread parental errors, and they moved generally in the direction of great permissiveness. Yet the real innovations rested not on tactics alone, but in the very issue that occasioned them: jealousy in children was being redefined as at once inescapable and dire.

Audience Response

Parents responded both to the recommended tactics and to the novel identification of the emotional problem. The crescendo of appeals for serious attention to sibling jealousy and for concrete steps of remediation won wide attention, precisely because so many families shared the expert perceptions and wanted to know how best to act. Guidance authorities of various sorts reported widespread parental concern over jealousy in their young children. Letters from parents to family magazines show a similar reaction, as parents readily seized on a new problem and often indicated their personal shock at the manifestations of jealousy in the bosom of the family. In a standard pattern, one woman wrote to *Parents' Magazine*, in 1955, that jealousy was "by far the most troublesome, the gravest issue I've met so far in my career as mother." Many of the interwar experts who included sections on sibling rivalry in their manuals specifically noted that their interest had first been piqued by the sheer numbers of parents who brought the problem to their attention in requests for counseling and guidance.

The chronicle of parental woes could be endless, with innumerable variations on the same theme. In 1954, a parent gives milk money to her eldest child, causing jealous tantrums from the preschool sibling, until the parent allows him to "buy" milk from her each morning. In 1953, a mother has to organize weekly tea parties to distract her six-year-old from jealous biting fits directed against two younger siblings. In 1955, a ten-year-old broke her baby brother's gift toys until parents hit upon the idea of letting the child write thank-you notes on the baby's behalf. In 1957, a two-year-old refuses to climb stairs if a mother carries the baby up. And virtually monthly, through 1959, accounts appeared of needs for special reassurance of an older child, explanations of the infinite capacity of love ("love was big enough for two") in a wearying battle against the green-eyed monster, juvenile division.

With this drumbeat of parental concern, fed by the experts but essentially antedating widespread expert advice, it is hardly surprising that strategic recommendations seem to have found a receptive audience. Recommended tactics were widely adopted, and some experts noted such enthusiastic response that older children were actually lionized or made to feel wronged by the apologetic presence of a new baby.[17]

A poll taken in the mid-1940s drives the point home: middle-class parents agreed that jealousy was a major issue and were ready to shape family strategies accordingly. In a survey of 544 families, 53 percent reported significant problems of jealousy among siblings, rating this the third most important issue in dealing with children and the most serious of all concerns about children's personality and temperament. For suburban parents, sibling problems stood in fact second on the overall list, compared to an eighth-place ranking for urban poor, eleventh for urban wealthy, and fourteenth for urban blacks. The problem was most acute where only two children were present—a clear reminder of the demographic factor underlying the deepest new anxieties about children's jealousy. Boys and girls ranked roughly equally in their parentally judged susceptibility to jealousy, with girls leading by a small margin.[18] Jealousy among children had become a leading emotional concern, indeed emotional annoyance, of family life, as parents joined expert standard setters in their readiness to identify and condemn this common impulse.

The contrast with nineteenth-century unconcern, still granting the extent to which many nineteenth-century parents had attacked the problem through generalized efforts to limit quarrelsomeness, was dramatic.[19] While the surge of expert advice demonstrates the new climate most readily, parental eagerness to agree, to share experiences in the columns of *Parents' Magazine*, to learn the necessary counterstrategies, testifies to a widespread sense of shocked surprise at the depth of an issue parents themselves had not been schooled to expect. The adults who responded so powerfully to the sibling-rivalry concept in the 1930s and 1940s had not themselves been taught, in childhood, that the underlying emotion must be labeled and carefully managed, and this was precisely why their openness to the large sibling sections of every childrearing manual was so great.

Parental response and expert advice alike signaled other changes in American middle-class socialization patterns, beyond the careful identification of jealousy in young children itself. Heightened anxiety about the overall emotional as well as physical context of early childhood was one important concomitant. Many parents were spending far more time than before in trying to shape two-year-olds, by explicitly conditioning their responses through a combination of diversion, reassurance, and subtly reproving labeling, than their own parents had done.

Parents were also altering their expectations about sibling interaction in ways that could have larger effects for the family and for adult life. In contrast to the nineteenth century, siblings were not being told to love each other, to cooperate on the basis of deep and positive emotional bonds. Coexistence without violence and constant bickering was a sufficiently demanding goal. The tactics for handling rivalry placed parents as intermediaries, carefully reassuring and protecting children as individuals when attempts to keep them apart had failed. Here, surely, was vital encouragement to more fully individualistic personalities, buttressed by conscientious efforts to separate rooms, toys, and other paraphernalia of childhood living. More specifically, a sense of separateness could persist in later life, in contrast to the ongoing vitality of sibling relations sought and often found in the nineteenth-century middle class. Some tensions might be avoided in the process. Studies of American teenagers from the 1930s through the 1950s noted, to be sure, some lingering sibling resentments. Older children could resent the interference of younger brothers or sisters—for example, when starting out on a date; younger siblings expressed even more tension about the privileges they saw their elders enjoy. Yet from age eleven onward, these rivalries were consistently downplayed and at most ages were rated as minor, with the children themselves firmly aware of the infantile qualities of remnant jealousies. The focal jealousies of the nineteenth century, around contacts between older siblings and their parents and particularly around tensions introduced by a romance on the part of one beloved brother or sister, now paled in intensity, precisely because, on average, siblings had already been encouraged toward greater separation. Emotional strains avoided, however, also meant a kind of closeness that might also be missing, as siblings launched into adulthood with far less sense of one another as points of emotional reference than had been the case before. Hard to measure, certainly not totally altered or fully uniform, this pattern constituted a significant shift in the emotional dimensions of American family life well beyond early childhood.[20] An emotionally extended family declined in salience.

The new sensitivity to early sibling rivalry also constituted an important new definition, again by experts and parents alike, of the relationship between emotion and motivation. Childrearing authorities and popularizers were clearly urging parents to abandon traditional impulses to use jealousy as a spur to proper discipline and emulation. The identification of jealousy as a major problem virtually required revision, for the emotion had become too dangerous to try to utilize. Actual parents surely could not be so pure, and the impulse to call Susie's accomplishments to Johnny's attention persisted still. Yet parents did assimilate the new recommendations to some extent, as letters to *Parents' Magazine* attested: they tried to wean themselves from invidious comparisons, and some effort to live up to an ideal that jealousy should not drive children's achievement—at least within the family— entered into parental calculations.

This revision, in turn, fed into a larger shift in socialization patterns, which had been prepared by prior alterations in beliefs about children but which reached fruition only in the twentieth century: emotions that cause discomfort, like jealousy, should not be treated as useful, and motivation should build only on the pleasant and the positive.[21] By the later twentieth century, middle-class American children would stand out, in comparative terms, in their ability to recognize pleasant emotions, and would correspondingly display confusion and imprecision, by the standards of numerous other cultures, in reaction to less pleasurable sensations. This distinctive imbalance involved a reorientation, for had a similar comparison been undertaken in 1900 it would not have produced the same American result. As first jealousy, then anger, drew more consistent reproval in adult life, with attention drawn to the importance of stifling effective expression of these emotions in childhood, the arsenal of acceptable spurs to constructive activity narrowed, with interesting implications for adults who emerged from the revised socialization as well as for children themselves. The idea that some difficult emotions might be trainable, directed toward defined and useful ends despite some discomfort, faded, with the new attack on childish jealousy a key ingredient in the change. Parents might still slip into some encouragements to rivalry, but their intentions reflected the newer agreement that jealousy was too hot to handle. Children, correspondingly, should be enticed by pleasant and positive sensations—including the assurances of love that were to wean them from jealous feeling, with the sterner complexities of emotional life relegated to the shadows. The dramatic new approach to childhood jealousy, in sum, participated in a major recasting of the ways that many Americans were trained to become emotionally mature and of the kinds of appeals to which they were supposed to respond.

The Maturation of the Childrearing Campaign: From the 1960s Onward

Before drawing out the full implications of the new attack on childish jealousy, including the relationships to adult emotional behavior, a final chronological phase must be assessed. There is no question that the expert and parental campaign against childish jealousy took on a new tone by the 1960s. In large part the change resulted from the fact that the hardest battles had been won. The emotionology established during the previous half century remained largely intact, but the sense of urgency and the impression of novelty both subsided. There were, in addition, some contextual changes that added to the mix, making it necessary to ask whether yet another new period in the childhood-jealousy relationship had taken form.

Advice manuals, though varied, on average dramatically reduced their treatment of sibling rivalry. A few dropped the standard section altogether.[22] As early as 1956 Stanley and Janice Berenstain derided conventional expert treatment. "There is so much talk about this phase of childrearing that even fond grammas and misty-eyed aunts generally understand that it's not cricket to chirp at baby while Big Brother is around." The Berenstains argued that children normally liked each other and grew jealous only if parents fouled the nest. They then, despite their amusing counterpoint, carefully repeated all the standard tactics but without any sense of crisis.[23]

Clearer measurements of the new tone come from Dr. Spock and *Parents' Magazine*. Spock in later editions pulled back, though slightly, from his earlier warnings. The phrase about jealousy's meriting a "lot of effort" was dropped, and instead of threatening a permanently distorted personality Spock opined that childish jealousy "may sour his outlook on life for quite a while." Successful management, while it would not eliminate jealousy, can help children grow up and foster more "constructive" feelings. Again the recommended tactics were unchanged, but the setting was less apocalyptic.[24] *Parents' Magazine* continued high-frequency coverage on jealousy through the 1950s, though with increasing emphasis on trusting children by 1959. But the early 1960s carried some articles venturing to deny the inevitability of sibling rivalry along with columns citing the delight that children could take in a new baby. One parent wrote about the attention she lavished on her older child, to compensate for a new birth, "even though she didn't seem to need it." And a 1961 poll on problem behavior (admittedly not comparable to Jersild's 1940s poll because it did not focus on common issues between parents and children), saw no reference to jealousy at all, with quarrelsomeness, the nearest candidate, ranking only twenty-sixth. Clearly, parents as well as experts were redefining urgency.[25]

To be sure, there were some treatments reminiscent of the earlier wars. Frank Caplan, who ignored jealousy in one 1977 manual, in another, issued the same year, wrote that "nothing so greedily consumes a child's inner emotional reserves than feelings of jealousy" and even extended the age of peak openness to the monstrous emotion to six.[26] Sibling advice books remained popular, and some stressed the negative, unless balanced by careful parental strategies. "Whenever a child feels down, shaky, envious or threatened, jealousy crops up again." Parents must be extremely careful to be impartial and to offer demonstrative love.[27]

But the impression of imminent disaster eased overall. Earlier experts were derided, including Spock for his anxiety about breastfeeding in front of an older child. Parents who frantically overcompensated for a sibling birth were ridiculed: "they tended to fall over backwards trying to avoid it."[28] The 1930s social science studies were criticized, as experts more than halved the previous figures of likelihood of significant jealousy, from 44–60 percent to 20 percent.[29] Indeed scientific sibling-jealousy studies themselves dropped from fashion, in favor of careful inquiries into the cognitive impact of birth order. Specific tactics were modified in light of the reduction of tension. Duplicating presents and avoiding any fuss over a new baby were countermanded, as unnecessary and indeed detrimental to the older child's adjustment to reality. A bit of jealousy was still to be expected, but it could be corrected. "It is possible for you to change his emotionalized state with a changed situation."[30] "Youngsters with a sturdy sense of trust can handle these momentary feelings and even benefit." A few authorities returned to the invocation of useful spurs to ambition, while others disclaimed any necessary connection between childish jealousy and the adult emotion. "Children are usually resilient. If one approach doesn't work and sibling rivalry gets out of hand, this doesn't mean the children will be permanently damaged."[31]

While treatments of childish jealousy shifted in emphasis, with less space devoted to the subject and more attention directed to other problems such as low self-esteem, most of the earlier recommendations remained in force. There was simply more confidence that the problem could be managed. "Jealousy is rarely preventable but it need not be extreme."[32] Reading designed for fairly young children carried the same message, thus amplifying the range of signals available to siblings themselves while avoiding high anxiety. Beverly Cleary, for example, used the stubborn jealousy between her protagonist, Ramona, and an older sister as a central theme, treating "siblingitis" as a fact of life while making it clear that mother love would ultimately reduce the strain and growing maturity would take it from there: "[Ramona] was working at growing up."[33] Here is an important addition to earlier advice literature, suggesting greater or more varied dissemination of the basic emotional message even as intensity declined somewhat.

Yet the decline in intensity itself demands explanation. An issue on center stage in emotional socialization for four decades now receded in prominence. Did this constitute a real change in parental expectations and childhood experience, or did it at least presage such a change?

It is certainly possible to discern some serious causes for a new approach toward jealousy among young children, some of them recalling the more casual framework of the nineteenth century. Academic authorities on the subject unquestionably changed their minds.[34] The jealousy experiments of the 1920s and 1930s were derided for their artificial settings and lack of adequate controls. As we have noted in other connections, dominant opinion pulled back from any idea that intense sibling jealousy was a standard experience, particularly where the reactions of older children toward a new baby were concerned. Jealousy might be expected when the oldest child was a boy, on the part of younger brothers or sisters, but this was the only common case and even it was not inevitable. Frenzied speculations about whether children were more jealous at age three or five, when a new baby was born, or about great gender differences, were increasingly laughed out of court. Some of this revisionism entered the more popularized child-rearing literature, where it might be supplemented by sheer faddism. One way to sell advice books, after all, is to attack last year's advice, and so a growing willingness to talk about sibling affection and to downplay the need for panic over small conflicts had solid commercial as well as intellectual roots.

New kinds of advice, and particularly reduced parental concern, had other bases as well. Some of the factors spurring sibling jealousy eased by the 1960s. The rise of outside-the-home employment for mothers, including a majority even of those with young children, exposed many toddlers to a greater array of adult figures, including babysitters, agents at child-care centers, and fathers. This change could distribute the emotional load for children, reducing insecurity about any particular deprivation when a new baby was born. Maternal intensity was on the decline, and with it one of the causes that had prompted increased sibling jealousy in the first place. The spread of contacts among peers and the growing attachment to a peer culture, reaching into grade-school years, could also divert some jealousy-producing intensity as well. Children might not band more closely with siblings, but they had growing links with other children of their own age, and this might re-create some sense of cooperativeness and an ability to downplay any jealous possessiveness of parental love.

The decline in the birthrate, beginning in the last baby-boom years and speeding after 1963, reduced sibling problems automatically in many families—by preventing siblings. Even aside from the renewed increase in single-child families, changes in child spacing probably reduced the worst reactions to the advent of a new baby. Again, developmental models are hardly sacrosanct, but jealousy was probably less likely when children began to be spaced three years apart or more than in the frenzied baby-boom pattern of eighteen months or two years. On the other hand, the increased number of children exposed, as a result of divorce and remarriage, to step-siblings and half-siblings might induce serious jealousy from a new source.

Despite new complexities in family context, it is certainly possible that the real sources of childish jealousy declined by the 1960s. Certainly much of the focused attention devoted to jealousy during the 1960s and 1970s turned more directly to adults, as we shall see, given new antijealousy experiments initially generated by the counterculture. While jealous adults were still accused of insecure childhoods, children themselves became slightly less interesting to antijealousy campaigners if only because there were fewer children, and a great many more young adults, to draw attention.

It might be possible, adding up all the shifts in context, to argue for a new emotional generation of middle-class Americans. Not only journalists but also more serious social researchers interested in change often regale American audiences with an intricate series of generational characteristics, as if each decade or fifteen-year span produces dramatic new trends. While the chronology of children's jealousy is clearly not so volatile—the focus on sibling rivalry lasted for forty years—there may be reason to posit some frequency in oscillations.

In fact, what took shape from the 1960s onward involves a more subtle characterization that allows for some change but insists on maintenance of the basic framework that had taken shape before. Conclusions drawn from the growth of sibling rivalry and concerted adult response that prevailed during the first half of the century must thus be modified for this most recent period, but not reversed.

Basic standards did not change. Childish jealousy was still wrong and dangerous; there was no serious impulse to argue for its utility or triviality. Parents still had important obligations. Expert revisions of the century's conventional wisdom about sibling relationships were not picked up by popular manuals or—save insofar as they had always modified the fiercest anxiety through some common sense about children's variety and resiliency—by middle-class parents themselves. This is why prescriptive literature periodically returned in full force to the tone of the 1940s and 1950s, like the 1987 sibling-rivalry guide that warned parents of the "incredibly difficult task" they faced in their duty to deal with childish jealousy.[35] All the old urgency could return, and as we have seen even more relaxed presentations normally repeated the full range of advice about proper tactics. At most, a slightly greater optimism emerged that with careful management, siblings could develop some warmth in their relationships as they matured: the truce that often seemed the most to be hoped for in the 1930s might be replaced by alliance. In other respects basic adult perceptions—of the need to control jealousy early and of the significance of the task—were unchanged.

What did change, accounting for greater variety in the amount of coverage in the prescriptive literature and—more important—for some real shifts in childhood emotional experience, was the familiarity with sibling jealousy according to the now-established standards. Parental shock at childish jealousy inevitably declined as adults could recall their own childhood, when the emotions had been clearly labeled, expected, and managed. Advice givers, similarly, could assume that their middle-class audience was familiar with basic concepts and needed only sporadic reminders. Motivation for proper parental tactics could also be largely assumed, which excused the standard setters from the scare tactics of earlier decades without really suggesting a reduction of effort. To be sure, lower-class families might not yet be up to speed, a point to which we must return, but jealousy was seen as such a personal emotion that the need to mount a campaign across social levels was less urgent than where a dangerous emotion had more obvious social ramifications.

Parental familiarity extended to tactics. Middle-class adults knew them by heart, for they had lived through them and could remind each other through conversations peppered with wry remarks about siblings. Children were abundantly prepared for new babies, and parents were now aided by picture books specifically designed to tell toddlers what to expect—including some resentment. Parents conscientiously avoided overt favoritism. Their friends automatically brought a token gift for a toddler when showering a new baby with the more conventional birth presents. Family policy toward siblings was far more elaborate than was true during the 1930s, when the problems of jealousy were strange and novel and the tactics had to be newly learned.[36] Adult awareness remained acute, but anxiety levels had dropped.

The goals of jealousy control, and the basic means of achieving them, thus were unchanged even at the end of the 1980s, despite and indeed because of a process of routinization. In these areas, where emotionology interlaced with parental perceptions, and with the ways childish emotion was diverted or handled, no new period had taken shape.

In one important respect, however, more substantial change was probable: there may well have been a diminution of actual sibling jealousy, after the hothouse of the baby-boom years. Declining maternal intensity and new child spacing played a role here, but so did the increasing utilization of the expert-recommended tactics, now standard equipment for middle-class parents. As siblings were reassured, individual possessions defended, praise more evenly distributed, some factors that had initially prompted greater jealousy among young children could well be checked. New research findings that stipulated the lower incidence of jealousy among siblings likely reflected not only improved methods and assumptions but also a genuinely altered experience among children. The tendency to downplay jealousy among sisters, for example, showed a new desire among researchers to rectify earlier errors that had been based on gender stereotypes but also, in all probability, the impact of parental tactics that helped sisters live together with less overt rivalry, even in the small families of the late twentieth century. Jealousy-defusing tactics worked, however imperfectly, and as parents became comfortable with their use—even without strident expert guidance—they introduced a genuinely novel factor into the childhood experience. Granting that some of the earlier reports about rivalry had been exaggerated, the sense of a diminished problem that arose, unevenly, from the 1960s onward reflected an altered reality: siblings were less likely to experience active, prolonged jealousy than they had before the new campaign took shape or even during its early decades.

The periodization of the socialization efforts against jealousy was thus somewhat complex. In important respects, the framework that began to emerge in the 1920s was little changed by the late 1980s. Goals were the same; recognition of the problem was not basically recast; the tactics employed were not changed save that they had become more general and more comfortably accepted with the passage of time. These continuities allow assessment of the meaning of the campaign against young-sibling jealousy over an almost seven-decade span, as a fairly stable feature of contemporary American emotional life. At the same time actual childhood experience did shift, in part because of the ongoing parental campaign; this change also demands assessment, as it echoed in adult experience in various ways. Here, the clearest ramifications will emerge in the analysis of romantic jealousy, where again some continuity in basic standards plays against evidence of behavioral change by the 1960s, when the less jealousy-prone siblings began to reach adulthood.

The Impact of Sibling-Jealousy Control

If experts and parents had merely tried to introduce new judgments about childish jealousy into family life, the topic would constitute a significant ingredient in twentieth-century emotional history. That altered expectations and strategies also seemed to have some impact, in providing a counterattack against some of the factors promoting sibling rivalry, makes assessment all the more important.

The United States in the twentieth century witnessed a significant rise in childhood jealousy, matched, within a preexisting context of hostility to the emotion, by adult concern and some partially successful counterstrategies. Children's jealousy remained a greater family issue in the 1980s than it had been a century earlier, even if it no longer seemed to be running amok. The development of a new focus on sibling jealousy, and particularly the attention given to early childhood, did not constitute simply an episode in parent-child relations, even as some of the most acute tensions eased. The three intertwined strands of the twentieth-century pattern—the increase in jealousy itself, the adult concern, and the repression attempted—all had wider repercussions on the larger role of jealousy in personal and public life. Just as the twentieth-century history of children's jealousy reflected changes in the larger society—including expert role, business personality, and basic demography—so it promoted change.

The implications of the rise and the downturn in sibling jealousy itself are the most difficult to draw out, in absence of an appropriate theory of the relationship between childhood and adult emotion. Whatever the significance of some primal jealousy, inherent in the human animal and inevitably arising, it seems clear that the link between children's jealousy and adult personality is complex, and not merely because of the intermediary of socialization—too complex, certainly, to posit an increase in adult jealousy on grounds of heightened sibling tension in early childhood. In past time, relatively harmonious sibling relations could turn bitter in youth, while the promptings of honor could pull a jealously protective adult from a child not marked by obvious rivalries. Some observers, though mainly non-American, given the national urge to downplay jealousy's value, continue to see a link between jealous children and competitively achieving adults, which would have interesting implications for twentieth-century American behavior both before and after the partially successful efforts to damp down new sibling tension.[37]

Certainly, at a simpler level, the rise in children's jealousy came at a difficult time in American emotional history, given the increasing dependence of families on positive emotional experience—defined as excluding serious jealousy—juxtaposed with the increasing opportunities for jealousy in adult life. One result, as we have seen, was a deepening of the disapproval with which jealousy was viewed. While the emotion had earlier been recast as negative, the intensity of the condemnation rose in response to the heightened threat from childhood. While the inevitability of some childish jealousy was reluctantly granted, many adults could not easily accept its normalcy. As one authority recently put it, the emotion is too awful to be normal. It must be moderated, for its persistence becomes a sign of a "rotten moral fiber." And so the beast must be tamed rather than put to any use.[38]

The resultant campaign must be seen as a significant part of twentieth-century American family and children's history, in which obvious changes in sibling relations and their impact on parent-child contacts have been too long neglected.[39] Many Americans took seriously the charge of defusing jealousy and made a number of adjustments to this end. Some even talked about decisions over child spacing and family size—the idea of curtailing jealousy by having more than two children fit into the middle-class baby-boom enthusiasm—in terms of these emotional goals.[40] Without question the anxious monitoring of jealousy, particularly in the decades when strategies were newly developed, complicated the evaluation of children themselves, seen as bearing new seeds of discord that must be controlled even as other impulses were given freer play. More general policies toward children, such as attempts to modify school settings to reduce jealous competition in favor of greater cooperativeness, reflected the new sense that prior practice must be reevaluated in light of new emotional problems and goals. Here, however, as in dealing with anger, the school environment moved more slowly than that of the family, setting up for children a new version of the public-private emotional dichotomy, with somewhat different emotional rules to be learned for each.

The attack on jealousy was not socially consistent: middle-class families worried far more about their sibling broods than lower-class families did, even during the baby boom, when family sizes were unusually homogeneous, and therefore this source of sibling tension was roughly equal across class lines. The same social differentiation also produced interesting adult results: several family studies showed worker families far more involved in romantic jealousies, founded or not, and also resentments of wives who paid attention to new children, than was the case in the middle class.[41] Here is important if unsurprising confirmation of the impact of socialization efforts, but also a qualification to any attempt to paint these efforts onto too broad an American canvas. Because jealousy's impact was seen as more familial and personal than social, there was less impulse to extend an emotionological campaign across social lines than was true in other areas. Even the interest in controlling jealousy toward smooth work relationships bore mainly on middle-class settings; unlike anger, it did not require intense appeals to workers.

Nevertheless, while granting disproportionate middle-class focus, the concern for jealousy among children linked to a number of important themes in twentieth-century culture. The insistence on dividing emotions between pleasant and unpleasant, and trying to divert the latter, had wide implications. It helped, for example, attune many Americans to the joys of consumer acquisition or sexual achievement while leaving them relatively unprepared to deal with attendant jealousies. Thus while experiments with novel family arrangements in the nineteenth century had normally assumed a certain asceticism as well as an attack on jealousy, twentieth-century experiments typically involved direct tensions between sexual hedonism and unexpected jealousy. Family styles clearly produced a different emotional balance from that characteristic of the nineteenth century, with heightened individualism and a new intolerance of jealous demands by others constituting a key ingredient—again, a result that puts emotional flesh on analytical frameworks already sketched.[42]

The campaign against sibling jealousy has more intimate human meaning as well. Adults who battled against childish jealousy were clearly working out important conflicts in their own lives, linked to romantic and sexual impulses. While urging themselves to support their children's emotional needs, parents may well have battled a certain resentment against this source of demandingness. Certainly the new view of children as emotionally difficult, plus the probability that there was more jealous behavior in fact, played a role in the twentieth-century reduction of parental admiration for children, now seen as less lovable and more problematic. Polls that show a marked decline in parental sense of emotional reward, and an increasing insistence on defining family primarily as a marital bond rather than a parent-child bond, cannot be explained through any single factor, but the new emotional balance sheet surely entered in. The gap between children's perceived nature and "real" emotional maturity widened. In addition, then, to new patterns among siblings themselves, jealousy and control efforts contributed to a readier parental exasperation, helping to account for the transformation of the "century of the child" into the century where children were downgraded.[43]

The key issues, however, involve not parental perceptions alone but the impact of new experience on children and their developing personalities. Here, the obvious point is considerable ambiguity. Sources of jealousy in the young increased, but they were countered at least in part by new strategies. The strategies were predicated on a desire to limit jealousy, but they carefully avoided outright prohibition. Adding to ambiguity was the fact that experiences outside the family, particularly in competitive school atmospheres, could send signals different from those of the antijealousy campaign of a child's first years. Here it was interesting that the peer culture that intensified after World War II typically tried to downplay competition in favor of group harmony— sometimes to the despair of adults who hoped for greater individual achievement and a willingness to separate from the group.

The socialization experience attuned many children to a new sensitivity to rivalrous emotions. Expert-urged tactics helped prevent jealous confrontations, but the process went deeper than this. Even in assuring young children of their sympathy and unbounded love, parents gave signals of disapproval; children, eager to pick up signs adults gave of what properly mature behavior was, learned that a resentment they felt was somehow wrong, even if on the surface it was met by parental reassurance. They learned, quite simply, that jealousy was childish. At the same time they were not given a chance for great nuance in sorting out jealousy, though of course they learned to label it; the lack of complex vocabulary, of the sort that would help distinguish different intensities and degrees of discomfort, also encouraged a sense of shame or embarrassment when the emotion emerged at all. The adult campaign against jealousy, in sum, produced results, though only partly for the reasons that adults acknowledged.[44]

Yet even apart from the commonsense conclusion that no such gentle campaign was likely to root out jealousy entirely, plus the

obvious recognition that many middle-class parents doubtless promoted jealousy—if only as a stimulus to good behavior—while also
downgrading it, the antijealousy message was hardly clear-cut. Children were meant to learn that jealousy existed and might to this extent
find the emotion normal. More important still, they learned that jealousy was greeted not with harshness or punishment but with love and
possibly some bribery in the form of compensatory gift giving. Jealousy might in this sense seem rewarded, its repression tentative and
contingent.

These conflicting effects informed adult experience amid the new
context for romance and marriage that had developed by the 1920s.
Diversity was one result, apart from social-class distinctions. Many
adults emerged from conscientious middle-class childhoods without
much sense that jealousy was wrong, while others were eager to show
their freedom from the emotion. More still were caught with more
complex reactions, stemming in part from their new childhood experience. On the one hand, they often expected quick redress when jealousy was encountered—the adult equivalent of mother's reassurance
—which could heighten the disruptive effects of jealousy within an
adult relationship. On the other hand, they had also learned that the
only person who really qualified for reassurance was a young child;
they were unready to answer the jealous claims of others.[45] And they
were eager to defend their own maturity against accusations of jealousy. They sought to construct a complex personality in which clear
identification of self and self-interest, the "me" impulse, was not sharp-
ened by overt jealous possessiveness. Jealousy, as one 1960s observer
put it, "is well on the way to becoming the New Sin of the liberated
generation."[46] And when the emotion arose, it created discomfort and
also prompted concealment. In a comparative study of the late 1970s,
based on polling responses, Americans were rated far more likely to
feel uncomfortable when jealous than any of the other nationalities
surveyed (57 percent; the next closest—West Indian—was 40 percent), and considerably more likely than most to try to hide jealous
feelings.[47] Discomfort and concealment reflected in turn the evolution
that jealousy had undergone in twentieth-century America. The emotion existed; it would not yield to direct discipline; but it was harmful
and unpleasant, a badge of emotional immaturity.[48] So, though it still

might goad action in personal relationships, it should largely be denied, even tested against an increasing array of situations that in other cultures would readily provoke a jealous response. The battle set up in childhood continued within many an American adult. It is time to turn to the adult experience, which paralleled, and was partly shaped by, the childhood campaigns.

CHAPTER 5

Love and Jealousy in the Twentieth Century

Efforts to uproot children's jealousy from the 1920s onward, while producing complex results, help explain one adult fact: increasing provocations to jealousy, given the new conditions of courtship and marriage, were not on the whole matched by corresponding increases in jealous outbursts. Restrictive socializations and the ability to express some tensions by attacking children's emotions by no means prevented overtly jealous adults, but did limit their number.

Growing concern about adult jealousy produced nothing as dramatic as the identification of sibling rivalry, and no comprehensive new strategies emerged save the idea of socializing children properly in the first place. Yet a new tone, combining disapproval and a grasp of the changing context for romantic relationships, emerged in the 1920s, with a wide discussion of marriage reform—not reflective of popular thinking, to be sure, but eye-catching. From this, by the 1930s, flowed more mainstream advice literature on the dangers of jealousy in romance, aimed both at teenagers and adults; and from this trend in turn, by the 1940s, came new tactics and signs of heightened anxieties in married life. By this time, of course, warnings learned in childhood added to the tensions, when romantic rivalries could not be avoided or dismissed.

Emotionology Restated: Jealousy on the Index

One result of the new context for the experience of jealousy in courtship and marriage was a resounding elaboration of the emotionology
somewhat tentatively inaugurated in the nineteenth century. From a
variety of camps after 1920 came ringing assertions that jealousy was a
foul and useless emotion, incompatible with true love and with healthy
relationships of any sort. This more elaborate emotionology followed
from standards already suggested, and it responded to, and doubtless
enhanced, the growing impatience with jealousy in real life. While the
basic hostility toward jealousy was not new in American emotionology, the vigor and detail of the condemnations reflected the emotion's
more problematic status in actual romantic contexts. Yet, as in the
nineteenth century, while the hostile emotionology had real impact in
reducing tolerance for jealousy, it did not carry the day entirely against
older impulses. Hence, while the preachments against jealousy helped
reduce receptivity to the emotion in some individuals, they also enhanced tensions for those aware of the standards but unable fully to
live up to them. Both results require attention, after the antijealousy
explosion is itself described.

"If monogamy is to be the relationship of the future, it will have to
widen its doors, subjugate its jealousies, and accept many modern
devices for spiritualizing physical passion." So wrote Mrs. Havelock
Ellis in 1921, opening a transatlantic salvo against marital exclusiveness
and its emotional components that drew considerable attention into the
middle of the decade.[1] Judge Ben Lindsay picked up the ball with a
number of widely circulated writings on the American side, his authority bolstered by his experience in dealing with marital disputes in
court. Lindsay's hostility to proprietary jealousy was explicit: "Jealousy is natural, as an instinct that we may observe even in our domestic animals. We become civilized and humane by conquering it, and
those who are unable to do so are unfitted to deal with modern
marriage."[2] Proper love required freedom for other friendships, not
total absorption in the spouse—an absorption wrong in itself and also
productive of unacceptable tensions and even crimes. In Lindsay's
view, 90 percent of all divorces were caused by the strains of jealousy,

which was therefore tactically counterproductive as well as improper: "Any custom that gives two free persons the ownership of each other is a device of the devil."[3] "Anger, hatred, malice, jealousy and the like are far more destructive of human happiness than any amount of sexual irregularity."[4]

The attack on jealous marital possessiveness thus contained important new elements, particularly the claim that the context for modern marriage had shifted and that outside interests were almost inevitable. But the root attack on jealousy picked up on the earlier, nineteenth-century redefinition of love. As Lindsay further argued, jealousy countered "that free and spontaneous intensity so necessary to love. It is a wish and determination to possess another." Sexually up to date, then, the marriage reformers (at least in the United States) also maintained the more traditional nineteenth-century belief in true love, defined as an unselfish contrast to animal like instincts.[5]

Attacks on jealousy were picked up not only by marriage reformers but also by some feminists, who harked back to the use of the emotion to keep women in the fetters of domestic fidelity. More to the point, in terms of converting the new campaign into something more than a 1920s oddity, an emotionological equivalent of nudism, was the extent to which hostility to jealousy began to enter mainstream social science literature. In contrast, for example, to a standard discussion around the turn of the century, in which a psychologist could appraise "a proper amount" of jealousy in love and marriage,[6] social psychology texts in the 1920s began to reverse the editorial twist: "As a rule, jealousy narrows personality, lowers status, and shortens usefulness."[7] The timing of this substantial conversion of social and behavioral science comment to an antijealousy stance was in one sense odd, since Freudianism (as some noted) made it possible to view jealousy as a natural, certainly inevitable human emotion, which therefore might be approached at least neutrally save in excessive outbursts. But the tone of most scholarly literature from the 1920s until the present, if considering jealousy at all, moved toward viewing it as a problem in love and marriage.

Thus Margaret Mead, in the 1930s: jealousy is "undesirable, a festering spot in every personality so affected." Thus Pitrim Sorokin, who contrasted the selfishness of jealousy with love, which "as a psychological experience is 'altruistic' by its very nature." Thus Kingsley Davis, in 1936, in an extensive anthropological review: "Even when affection is not strained jealousy shows on the lover's part a mistrust inimical to the harmony of perfect intimacy." And into the 1940s, Theodor Reik: "You would more willingly disclose that you have hostile, aggressive, mean or perverted feelings; that you are driven by this or that passion, than that you are full of envy," for "the person who confesses his envy admits . . . the complete absence of self-esteem."[8]

The conversion of social science at once demonstrated the pervasiveness of the antijealousy emotionology and extended these same standards. Academic researchers were also central in formalizing what had theretofore been only a tentative suggestion, that jealousy was a symptom of personality inadequacy when normal measurement standards were applied.[9]

The final step in the elaboration of the newly intense theoretical campaign against jealousy emerged from the 1930s onward, as injunctions against jealousy, and demeaning explanations for its existence, moved into standard marriage manuals and advice books for teenagers. Americans began to be barraged by more frequent and detailed condemnations of jealousy than had been true during the nineteenth century, in part because popularizing expertise became more extensive in general, but also because the focus on jealousy grew in intensity and because manual writers correctly discerned new jealousy issues in real-life marriage and dating behaviors.

A 1945 booklet aimed at high-school girls picked up the standard message. "Jealousy is probably the most common of all the unhelpful attitudes"—there was no question of its perverse quality. It had of course an explanation. "Why do we act this way? The reason is that we haven't outgrown the selfishness of early childhood." The solution? "We must grow up," learn to take pleasure in others' success, and in love identify with one's partner's interests—all three achievements possible with maturity and confidence in one's own worth.[10]

Teenage advice literature, particularly but not exclusively that directed toward young women, routinely included a section on jealousy problems during the 1940s and 1950s, uniformly blasting the emotion as "irrational and completely unwarranted."[11] Reiterations of the childishness of jealousy were obviously designed both to accommodate Freud's findings—no one denied that the emotion surfaced at a young age—and to hit adolescents in their aspirations and uncertainties about maturity. "The jealous lover is a child hugging his toy so closely that no one else can see it. Jealousy is almost always a mark of immaturity and insecurity. As we grow confident of love and of our loved one, we are not jealous. . . . we need not cling in desperation." True love, obviously, was "other-centered," prompting a lover to do "anything he can to make his beloved happy." [12] Even friendship demanded full trust, and certainly in love and marriage jealousy could only make both partners wretched. "We may even blight and blacken our happiness by jealousy, which is really an admission of our own inferiority, of our own cowardice and conceit." [13] The popularizers noted that many teenagers did in fact find jealousy a natural concomitant of love, but the existence of a problem to be combated only spurred their efforts: the emotion must be conquered.

Marriage manuals continued the campaign for the next phase of life and love. There was, to be sure, a distinguished exception. Paul Popenoe, a leading marriage expert and a frequent contributor to popular magazines, on this topic swam against the flow, arguing that "Jealousy is one of the greatest civilizing agencies of the human race." He saw the emotion as a vital support for monogamy, though one that must be handled with restraint; it showed that a person cared and could motivate a spouse to be responsive. Even Popenoe, however, urged that jealousy must be "on an adult level" and should not be manipulated flirtatiously because it could so easily pass proper bounds, becoming "a childish and destructive habit." [14]

The vast majority of the manual writers were more straightforward, rejecting Poenoe's implicit attempt to restate the nineteenth-century compromise in which jealousy was meant to promote communication and adjustment. Couples were urged to be faithful but not suspicious: "Therefore surrender all grudges, jealousies and feelings of contempt." [15] Again, the task might be difficult, for some writers noted an American belief, inculcated in childhood, that jealousy was an appropriate emotion in family life. [16] Though natural to a degree, jealousy must be controlled within the individual, for its expression makes marriage a "living hell" for a partner, while demonstrating that "there is something wrong with an interpersonal relationship." The jealous person had a problem that was not dependent on a partner's behavior, and he or she had to heal this problem. Far from being, as some young marrieds still believed, a sign of love, "Jealousy kills love. It is a symptom of weakness and of selfishness. Wanting a suitor, or a wife, or a husband to pay exclusive attention to one has nothing in common with real devotion."[17]

The solutions to jealousy, admittedly, were somewhat vague, as the experts urged maturity and "a full measure of mutual respect." Spouses might help through some understanding and reassurance, but the fundamental responsibility—in contrast to nineteenth-century accommodations that urged discretion, and sensitivity if a partner's jealousy surfaced—lay with the jealous individual, who must devote lifelong "unremitting" effort to the problem.[18] Or—still vaguely, though with all good intent—the jealous person might seek "an enlightened way," and if this way did not emerge there was always counseling. "We don't have to live in the dark about our emotions when available help could let in the light."[19] While there might, to the lay reader, be some question still about remedies, the popularizers left no doubt about emotional evil: "Jealousy is a terrible emotion, one of the extreme forms of psychological cruelty."[20] The twentieth-century version of the antijealousy emotionology even included a revealing new twist on the evil, by arguing that much romantic jealousy in fact reflected not only the individual's immaturity but also a desire for infidelity that was masked through professed suspicions of the partner. This adroit psychological jab (which may well have been correct in some cases, as well as useful in provoking guilt) was interesting in light of the new temptations toward sexual experiment. It was also a good argument for suppressing jealousy in a period of uncertainty about the balance between monogamy and sexual appetites.

After the early 1960s the preoccupation with jealousy in popular writing about love declined somewhat, coinciding with the shifts in childrearing literature though with less intensity because popular women's magazine coverage actually increased. Some marriage handbooks simply did not mention the emotion.[21] Sanctimonious advice manuals for teenagers virtually disappeared as a genre, presumably because their subjects rejected adult preaching or did not read or both.

At the same time, however, there were some new angles of attack. A number of feminists blasted jealousy as a device to keep women in thrall: "A woman becomes the extension of a man's ego like his horse or his car." Germaine Greer thus argued that male jealousy was more selfish and proprietary, less purely tactical, than female, and therefore warranted particular attention.[22] From yet another vantage point a number of mainstream marriage writers, while still attacking jealousy, extended their arguments to include pleas for greater tolerance of outright infidelity. Some jealousy, they urged in the more traditional vein, was simply unwarranted, reflecting a suspiciousness without basis in fact. Even when there were facts, however, the emotion should be kept under wraps. A good marriage could handle outright infidelity, so long as jealousy did not further foul the nest: "We are upset to varying degrees, but usually not so deeply as we think."[23]

Overall, both popularizers and social scientists maintained the anti-jealousy emotionology into the late 1980s, simply reducing their treatment because of an assumption that most right-thinking people were already aware of the proper standards. In the 1980s, indeed, the rate of antijealousy diatribes surged upward once again. Jealousy in love was still abnormal and counterproductive: "Jealousy is its own punishment, though not, frequently, its only one." The emotion resulted from inadequate childhood socialization and resultant possessive insecurity, and the cure was difficult but not impossible. A marriage partner had no reason to put up with jealous accusations, and the best approach was simply to ignore the attacks. True love contradicted jealousy because it seeks unselfish merging of personalities, while jealousy is "a continued compulsion—albeit unconscious—towards separation between two personalities." And the fundamental disgust with jealousy, established earlier in the twentieth-century campaign, could still shine through. Many a careful discussion, after detailing causes and responses to jealousy with something like clinical precision, let the core reaction out. Jealousy was a sign of "rotten moral fiber," no more or less.[24] Again as a sign of expert concern, though at a more therapeutic level, the interest in treating jealousy problems actually increased in the 1970s, as proponents of the prevailing emotionology sought to touch base with popular concerns.[25]

And a magazine article unwittingly but explicitly drove home the point that the nineteenth-century compromise was no longer acceptable: "Jealousy is not a form of communication, any more than contagion is a form of empathy." Another popularized statement showed that the depth of revulsion had hardly changed:

Jealousy . . . exaggerates our own shortcomings and the other's perfections. It makes us our least appealing when we are desperate to appeal. It makes us guilty because of the fantasies of harm we wish upon the object of our jealousy.

Jealousy does not protect love. It does not bind the family of man. . . .

It does not serve as an aid to navigation to heart or eye. It blinds, it warps, it distorts.[26]

In sum, jealousy not only contradicted love, it also ran against proper emotional management and damaged individual self-worth. Though a few magazine articles found tiny windows of merit in jealousy, as against the unadulterated blasts, these were at best silver specks in a very dark cloud.

The point is abundantly clear: for over sixty years almost all the evaluations of jealousy, scholarly[27] and popular, supportive of or hostile to conventional monogamy, had condemned the emotion. A few exceptional comments admitted limited functions for jealousy in calling attention to problems, but most even closed this door, finding green eyes such a bane in their own right that useful service was precluded, particularly in a love relationship. Twentieth-century emotionology was far more discursive on the subject than nineteenth-century advice had been, reflecting a fiercer condemnation and a greater sense that there were real problems to be fought in actual courtships and marriages. The new approach also normally admitted the childhood roots of jealousy, which made attention all the more necessary. But there was continuity as well, in the belief that jealousy was primarily linked to love and, at the same time, that true love and jealousy were incompatible. Even some proposed remedies maintained earlier themes: the injunction to "grow up" or to gain greater self-esteem harked back to nineteenth-century pleas for self-control (and was of equally dubious utility for someone in jealousy's throes), while even a 1930s article might urge a spouse jealous of her husband's success at work to use her energies in activities that would support the spouse toward mutual benefit.[28] Certainly, aside from the omnipresent fallback of therapy, twentieth-century experts confronting adult manifestations had not moved far beyond their predecessors—which pointed up the ongoing problematic that jealousy in love presented. In the twentieth century as before, the emotion should not exist in a loving adult, according to prevailing belief, and when it did, a certain bafflement ensued. One kind of popular-cultural model, to be sure, again with roots in the nineteenth-century idealization, tried to move around the problem by suggesting that only one great love occurred in any person's life, a pervasive American myth as manifested in film. Relationships before the great love (particularly for women) were not really love and so did not require or legitimate jealousy. Many Americans (perhaps somewhat distinctively, in comparative terms) probably were led to wish to believe that both exclusive true love and avoidance of jealousy could prevail.[29] Their hopes were, not surprisingly, unrealistic, but they expressed a powerful set of values, in which love and jealousy were set as opposites, that one way or another has been preached for a full century and a half.

The Impact of Emotionology: Experiments

As with nineteenth-century attacks on jealousy, twentieth-century emotionology had considerable impact on the way many Americans assessed this aspect of their emotional life—indeed, reflecting the durability of antijealousy themes over time, and the heightened intensity of the attacks from the 1920s onward, the negative appraisal of jealousy ran deeper in the twentieth century, affecting both belief and behavior more substantially. Yet, for a variety of reasons, the antijealousy emotionology did not triumph completely, even among middle-class people most exposed to the advice manuals and magazine articles that bore the message. Vagueness of remedy and the tensions between simultaneous promptings toward an exclusive true love and lack of jealousy help explain some of the limits, for the dominant emotionology itself embraced certain ambiguities. It was also true that most Americans tried to combine antijealousy themes with some ongoing belief in the emotion's utility. Their efforts differed from the prevailing compromises of the nineteenth-century, reflecting among other things the greater sway of officially sanctioned values. The fact remains, in turning to actual beliefs and behaviors, that the twentieth-century story involves more than a simple tale of the progressive triumph of the antijealousy view.

One response to the twentieth-century campaign against jealousy involved a new series of romantic-sexual experiments designed (among other things) to demonstrate participants' freedom from the base emotion. The communes and open-marriage arrangements that began to surface in the 1960s recalled earlier free-love advocacies in many respects. Like their nineteenth-century antecedents, they involved considerable variety in actual sexual arrangements and the extent of real, as opposed to rhetorical, defiance of conventional marriage norms. Like their antecedents as well, they responded to a complex causation in which the impact of new or more widely disseminated emotion standards served as only one ingredient. In both cases, however, the experiments were designed to incorporate a surge of antijealousy belief. In keeping with the evolution of emotionology, however, the experiments of the later twentieth-century had wider direct impact than their antecedents (though in both cases there was an important relationship to mainstream beliefs). Reflecting the same evolution, the twentieth-century experiments were much more explicit in their focus on beating down jealousy, addressing the subject directly rather than (in the nineteenth-century fashion) hoping to prevail through silence and implication. Before turning, then, to more widespread and complex results of twentieth-century jealousy standards, it is important to examine people who thought they could meet the standards to the letter.

The advocates of sexual experimentation were clear in their emotional stance. "Jealousy has no place in open marriage. The fact that it is so prevalent in closed marriage does not mean that love and sex must always be accompanied by this dark shadow." Jealousy in this view was a learned emotion, not instinctive, and was a joint manifestation of cultural prescriptions and personal insecurity. It was the antithesis of love; indeed, "it destroys that very love. It is detrimental to it and a denial of a loved one's personal identity.[30] The arguments clearly built on the long-held effort to define jealousy out of real love, on grounds of unselfishness, while adding the more recent challenge to demonstrate resistance to jealousy as a badge of a secure sense of self. Many discussions in fact moved quickly beyond any explicit examination of jealousy, lest they seem to belabor the emotionologically obvious. One open-marriage manual thus gave instructions on what to say to a spouse who called to say he was having a great time and planned to spend the night away—"Fine, I'm glad things are going so well. Enjoy yourself and I look forward to hearing about it tomorrow"—without directly invoking jealousy as a potential problem. And a reviewer, similarly, while praising the basic open-marriage idea, urged attention to possible "insecurities," again without demeaning the brave new world with a retrograde jealousy label.[31]

Many participants in open marriages or communal sex arrangements clearly internalized the antijealousy approach, or at least tried to do so. Some felt no jealousy at all, or were so eager to enjoy the fruits of promiscuity that they genuinely could hold out comparable freedom for their spouse. Others, and particularly those spouses who were brought into the experiments on someone else's initiative, were often intellectually committed to the "new social code," but found their emotions less than fully disciplined. They were typically ashamed of their jealousy: "I think it comes from possessiveness and I'm trying to grow away from that." A common result of this tension between standards and reality was an effort to minimize. Thus the muted remarks, on finding a mate in bed with another: "Somewhat disconcerting"; "It was kind of rough"; "I was sort of put down."[32]

Avowedly "swinging" behavior, as opposed to more clandestine infidelity, attracted only a minority of middle-class Americans even in the heady days of the late 1960s, but it appealed to more widely shared standards, both in its embrace of sexual pleasure and in its attack on jealous possessiveness. Recurrently, since the 1920s, many middle-class Americans had demonstrated their commitment to at least qualified openness, and certainly their freedom from the worst snares of jealousy, by loosening the bonds of monogamy. In the 1920s a new type of "party behavior" spread in many areas, not only big cities but also some smaller communities, to beat back the monotony of strict monogamy. Party behavior involved some regulating etiquette, to be sure: couples could mix through sitting on laps, kissing, sometimes even reclining, but they were not supposed to close a bedroom door.

At the same time, the rules explicitly forbade demonstrations of jealousy.[33] Clearly, the experiments in alternatives to conventional marriage that blossomed around 1970, while they owed something to a particular mood of defiance, built on longer-standing interests. Many Americans had for some time been willing to admit an attraction to sexual pleasure seeking that would move them to new public behaviors, and many Americans had long been positively drawn to arrangements that would allow them to demonstrate an emotional maturity defined in terms of shedding or ignoring jealousy.

While experiments that moved away from exclusiveness in love and sex thus tapped a real strain in emotionology, they also shared a weakness of this same set of standards: it was difficult to know what to do with jealousy that stubbornly refused to disappear. Standard setters urged maturity and the joys of nonpossessive love, but they were painfully vague on the subject of what to do with well-meaning failures. One revealing response was a modest movement during the 1970s, focused on university centers such as Ann Arbor, Ithaca, and Iowa City, to use a workshop approach to sweat out recalcitrant jealousy so that middle-class Americans could live up to their values. Designed for married and unmarried couples alike, the weekend jealousy workshops, run by practitioners such as Larry Constantine and Robert and Margaret Blood, essentially built on earlier party behavior, encouraging spouses to get used to the sight of their mates, being massaged by others. Helpful procedures were also covered (and many actual communes had introduced similar approaches): couples should discuss how much it was comfortable to know about each other's swinging behavior and whether it was useful or disconcerting to have blow-by-blow descriptions of nights out. Whatever the tactical compromises, the goal of the workshops was quite clear. They were designed for "those who are strongly motivated to outgrow jealousy," who recognized its dehumanizing qualities and its barriers to real autonomy. A successful workshop product would appreciate freedom not only for the individual but for the spouse and the whole relationship. "I really appreciate the fact that after you've been with Ann you seem more accepting of me and the children. . . ."[34]

If the experiments with sexual swinging and the resultant battles against possessiveness neatly illustrate one effort fully to realize the dominant emotionology where jealousy was concerned, the limitations on the movement are equally significant. Most Americans—even the majority of young, middle-class Americans—were not drawn into the extremes of the movements. As with nineteenth-century free-love communities, many sexual communes quickly settled into de facto monogamy or some other form of definite commitment, in large part to minimize jealousy. Swinging arrangements also often collapsed on grounds of one partner's irremovable jealousy. Wives, particularly, were often drawn into some kind of spouse swapping reluctantly, in part because of a desire to demonstrate their emotional liberation, only to find that they could not tolerate the result. Having to admit their jealousy, they were forced to try to pull their partner back or, more commonly, abandon marriage altogether: "their relationship seemed more like a strained friendship than a marriage."[35] Frequently, though not invariably, actual emotional experience proved resistant to standards widely accepted in theory. As we turn to more general encounters with jealousy, the resistant strain obviously requires serious attention. The strand of marital experimentation, though an extreme, demonstrates the serious hold that new attitudes toward jealousy could win, inducing efforts to overcome impulse often at considerable cost; but the failure of many experiments, and the decline of the experimental mood after the mid-1970s, reveal the continued complexity of actual emotional interactions, even for Americans who like to believe themselves near the forefront of sophisticated enlightenment.

Emotionology Revisited:
What Did Americans Think About Jealousy?

If exuberant baby boomers were still burdened with jealousy, it is hardly surprising that most Americans were still further from internalizing the dominant emotionology without important reservations and qualifications. Widely preached standards did have an impact, but they did not win the day outright. The resultant product, representing a real but incomplete change away from nineteenth-century beliefs, was predictably complex and typically challenging.

A philandering evangelist, in 1987, explained that his seduction of a secretary occurred at a time when his wife was in love with another man; he "merely wanted to make her jealous." The assumption, obviously, was that making a spouse or suitor jealous remained a semirespectable motive and preferable at least in born-again Christian circles to an outright admission of sexual desire. A psychological survey indicates that jealousy continues to be accepted as a legitimate grounds for anger and moral indignation, which otherwise might be regarded as a sign of disorder (though true to reigning official values, the poll takers quickly note that jealousy is not in fact an excuse in that it "greatly reduces one's freedom to act").[36] Studies from the 1930s onward suggest that most Americans admit that they would respond jealously if they saw their partner involved with another person. The conclusion? Jealousy, while not openly approved as in some cultures, remained accepted, and sometimes enjoyed or cheered.[37] A handful of popular articles in the later 1980s, as family values were being reasserted amid an aging population and AIDS-induced fears about promiscuity, pointed to the legitimacy of taking stock of one's jealousy and deciding what emotional pain might be too high a price to pay for a "contemporary relationship." Jealousy, never excised in American culture, might be gaining some new recognition, though not to the point of yet providing an alternative emotionology overall.[38]

Several factors encouraged continued belief in jealousy's validity, despite almost unanimous expert disapproval of the emotion from the 1920s onward. Sheer tradition doubtless played the dominant role. The credit given jealousy in Western culture for many centuries would not easily be dislodged, for here as often actual values about an emotion yielded stubbornly if at all to new approaches. The new emphasis on love as the basis for marriage relationships and even, for many Americans, sex, could actually heighten jealousy's legitimacy amid official insistence on the unpossessive qualities of true affection. That is, to the extent that many people continued to associate jealousy with legitimate defense of love, perhaps with a few new hesitations, increased acceptance of love tended to heighten tacit approval of jealousy, partially offsetting the attacks on the emotion when discussed in its own right. Thus, Americans could vigorously disapprove when asked about jealousy yet seemingly contradict themselves with approaching the same subject through the eyes of love. Here, even advice manuals firmly set against jealousy might occasionally slip in contradictions in noting that jealousy could cement or spice romance in an aside sandwiched among fulminations against selfishness and immaturity. And changes in love emphasis continued even in the later twentieth-century, complicating reactions to jealousy and the still more obvious impulses toward sexual experimentation. Americans from the 1960s onward not only maintained their official belief in marital stability (behavior often to the contrary) but also increasingly judged family and marriage on the basis of relationship to spouse alone. Children declined in importance, and as focus fixed on contacts between partners, jealousy might seem increasingly understandable if not legitimate. Tradition, then, heightened by modern emphasis on love, furthered in turn by contemporary conversion of marriage into a relationship between adult partners above all else, provided the framework within which jealousy reactions could still be validated.[39]

Yet the dominant emotionology concerning jealousy, though more complicated than many of its proponents officially allowed, had not been without impact. The linkage between jealousy and love, not removed, had been shaken. From the middle decades of the twentieth-century, many middle-class Americans had come to accept the idea that sexual jealousy was proof not of affection but of personal insecurity and a lack of faith in one's partner.[40] Even more revealing was evidence from the 1930s onward that teenagers made a concerted effort to demonstrate their mastery of jealousy as an unacceptably childish emotion—evidence, in other words, that American youth had learned and accepted the association between maturity and freedom from jealousy that emotional experts were preaching. By age fourteen, said the standard manual on the adolescent, most young people were eager to proclaim that they were "not really jealous," and by age sixteen the typical teenager would thoughtfully say that he or she was never jealous at all.[41] Insistence here extended from sibling settings, from which children were, as we have seen, specifically trained to shake free, to the new uncertainties of dating and romance. It was important to claim freedom from jealousy. This evaluation should not of course be taken at face value: experts could be blinded by their desire to see jealousy conquered, and teenagers doubtless harbored emotions that they were loath to admit. Even concealment, however, showed the impact of the emotionological campaign. Both adolescents and married adults had become less willing to express open jealousy than their nineteenth-century predecessors had been. The comparison is admittedly difficult, given the absence of comparable polling and experimental data from the past, yet the probability is high, and it gains further support from the vigor of the attacks directed against jealousy for many decades.

The result, obviously, was a dilemma, not unprecedented but greater than in previous periods. Many Americans really did scorn jealousy, regarding it as an emotion at once juvenile and outdated; yet, save for some unusual experimenters, they could still be susceptible and might even on occasion justify their feeling, even against their normal standards. And many traditional institutional limitations of jealousy-provoking situations, such as the domestic sequestration of women, had collapsed, adding another volatile ingredient to the mix. Jealousy was a growing emotional problem in the twentieth-century because so many people disapproved of it yet it did not disappear. That a campaign against romantic jealousy was sustained over many decades suggests the emotional tension that refused fully to abate.

Nineteenth-century Americans had admittedly faced a first version of the tension, but at a point when quietly discussing jealousy was less painful because the campaign against the emotion was less advanced and because accommodations within a courtship or marriage came easier. Compromise at this point meant an attempt to avoid provocation of the emotion and to provide reassurance when it had been provoked.

Twentieth-century adjustments were more strained, probably less successful on average, precisely because the polarization between belief and impulse was starker. Declining tolerance of jealousy in a spouse or lover was another vital ingredient. Reactions varied, to be sure, and it is possible that the campaign against jealousy had actually increased diversity particularly in swelling the number of people able to downplay the emotion in most circumstances.[42] For many, however, a number of stratagems might be combined when jealousy flared against one's best judgment.

One ploy, not surprisingly, involved a split between general belief and personal judgment. Thus many people who claimed that jealousy resulted from insecurity failed to apply this standard to their own case, finding their own emotion justifiable in terms of objective romantic threat and possibly even useful in supporting the romantic relationship.[43] Denial or concealment was another common response. Americans were unusually likely not only to disapprove of jealousy but also to wish to hide it; this was a result of sibling training that translated reality to adult romance.[44] College students, sometimes aware of their jealousy but eager to maintain a cool, tolerant facade,[45] could also be oblivious to the emotion as one of several unpleasant sensations that should be ignored.[46] Keeping up appearances and not probing too deeply, or labeling too precisely, thus characterized many Americans who professed sincere concern about being emotionally "in touch" with themselves.

If jealousy did emerge—if denial failed to function—a more obvious dilemma ensued. Apology became essential. Whereas in the nineteenth-century, an expression of jealousy would normally elicit a partner's concern, in the twentieth century the same expression was most often regarded as injurious. Reigning emotionology, while not triumphant, had resulted in moving the jealous person from the status of victim to that of offender. Thus, a collegian who could not ignore or conceal jealousy about a past relationship owed his lover amends.[47]

Even apology, of course, might leave a person face to face with the disparity between belief and sentiment. Many studies caught Americans saying one thing and feeling another, like the woman who vigorously asserted that jealousy should be no part of marriage while reporting rooted jealousy of her husband's former girlfriends. This tension might of course be concealed, but if not relieved it could eat away at secure love.[48]

And if this tension was further heightened by ongoing provocation, the remedy, lacking mutual recognition that jealousy was, if unpleasant, an emotion legitimately warranting response, might require a mixture of obfuscation and dramatic action. A moderately popular 1983 novel captured the dilemma here. A proudly independent career woman finds her husband playing around with a younger, prettier colleague. Unwilling to use the word *jealousy* (a reluctance shared by the novelist, eager to champion her heroine) lest it remove the last shred of dignity, the protagonist does admit to a host of "demeaning" and "petty" feelings that cannot be fully articulated and certainly cannot be acted upon. As a result, rather than harboring a legitimate emotion with which the errant husband can be confronted, the wife sulks, nursing a self-esteem damaged not only by her spouse's infidelity but by her own reactions, until the only possible solution occurs: she leaves the marriage, thus shaking off the feelings that had laid her low, and soon becomes her proudly careerist self once again.[49] Jealousy's existence, in other words, exacerbates a bad situation, its negative appraisal reducing confidence, its expression virtually impossible lest one's dignity be overtly shattered and one's spouse be driven further away by this childish, selfish outburst. The rules on jealousy do not suffice to prevent the emotion, though they do discourage precise labeling, but they have gained sufficient ground to make circumvention and flight, rather than righteous confrontation, the most obvious ploy of a self-respecting person. Jealousy, once criticized as a cause of violent retribution, becomes more an inner cancer, its virulence enhanced by the guilt and dismay its appearance promotes.

An important part of the emotional life of many Americans since the 1920s has thus involved at least periodic battle between pangs of jealousy that cannot entirely be denied and the desire to present a cool exterior, to hide, to disapprove. Just as the situations that might provoke romantic jealousy became more numerous, confidence in handling the emotion began to erode save for the lucky minority that could live up to the dominant emotionology or another group that managed to ignore it altogether. A love life, eagerly sought, that was supposed to be jealousy-free too often brought a green-eyed monster close to the surface, yet the means of dealing with this emotional surge had become murkier than ever before. Small wonder that comments on jealousy, if sometimes oblique or confused, so greatly exceeded nineteenth-century levels.

Bridging the Gap: How to Combat Jealousy

Twentieth-century Americans did, of course, have a strategy to bring the reality of jealousy in line with dominant values. The key was the process of socialization in early childhood, that was meant to recognize jealousy's inevitable outcropping but to nip it in its infant bud, creating jealousy-free adults.[50] Fierce concentration on socialization efforts was more than illustrative of adult concern about their own emotions as well as those of their children. It also helps explain the vagueness both of expert advice and of many jealous adults in knowing what to do with jealousy when socialization failed and the emotion loomed in later romance. It was not supposed to be there. If stern reminders of its childishness did not suffice in aiding an adult to bring it under rational control, therapy or workshops were the only theoretical recourse, escape sometimes the only practical recourse, in dealing with an emotion that was useless, unpleasant and—now—a reminder of a basic inadequacy in personality development.

The socialization effort also helps explain why the dominant emotionology that urged against jealousy was so widely known and at least partially accepted. Advice manuals on courtship and marriage, and popular articles that carried the battle against jealousy to a still wider audience, undoubtedly persuaded people that jealousy should not be linked with love, at least in theory. It was the attack on the emotion in childhood, however, that taught even more generally that jealousy should be put behind as part of maturity. Emotionology's impact on common socialization was then reinforced by adult reminders, including pressures from peers zealous in enforcing at least surface freedom from undue possessiveness. The readiness of teenagers, thus, to play jealousy down owed most to lessons learned from parents, promoted by friends; dating manuals expressed the common values but need not be given great credit for their currency.

Efforts to inhibit and deflect childhood jealousy were not, of course, uniformly successful. Jealous adults emerged, and even some covert approval of love-linked jealousy persisted, as we have seen. The intensity of socialization varied, in part by social class; it might founder on actual family tensions and complexities; and it was not designed fully to dissociate jealousy and love in any event. Thus a loving maternal reassurance, in theory designed to prevent a festering of emotion that would burst forth in adult romance or work life, carried the potential that an individual might associate a feeling of jealousy with a legitimate need for affectionate compensation. Socialization was thus the expert-urged response that most generally sought to reconcile the new emotionology with actual emotional experience, and its role could be considerable. Its limitations, however, help explain why other devices were tossed up, by the 1930s, as Americans grappled with an emotional issue that, though not supposed to exist, remained extremely troubling.

One of the most interesting responses to the gap between emotional standards and actual jealousy constituted an attempt to invent a new institutional barrier to the provocation of the emotion in the first place. This impulse was in some ways traditional, as against primary reliance on emotional control, and it did not endure. It showed the strains of emotional reality at a key point, however, as antijealousy emotionology gained ground.

Adolescence represented an almost inevitable locus for tensions over jealousy after 1920. Adolescents were taught about jealousy's evils, and they learned at least some of the lessons. At the same time, growing emphasis on romance and freedom to date and court opened new possibilities for the experience of jealousy.

After an experimental period, a growing response to this heightened dilemma for teenagers was the introduction of that form of romantic insurance known as steady dating. It must be noted that, such was the adult bias against admitting widespread jealousy in real life, that this emotional motive was never directly addressed in the many (and often anguished) studies of this innovation, and the emotional motivation was indeed only one of several causes of the going-steady phenomenon. Despite some tentativeness about the priority of jealousy reduction as a cause, the pattern merits brief inquiry from this vantage point —precisely because the realization that is now possible of potentially acute tension between new values and old impulses where romance and jealousy were concerned opens new insight on seemingly familiar interactions in love and family life over the past half century.

When dating began to spread from about 1920 onward, differing from courtship in its removal from the home and combination with other leisure activities, it initially took, and maintained through the 1930s, what some observers dubbed a "polygamous" form.[51] Daters were supposed to play the field, and the ability to date, or be dated by, a number of individuals became an important badge of popularity, first on college campuses and then increasingly in high schools. This system placed a number of burdens on adolescents, including jealousy if a favorite date insisted on continuing to enjoy the social whirl with many rivals, plus jealousy or envy of same-sex daters who excelled at the "dating and (popularity) rating" game. Not surprisingly, given the advice givers' concern about controlling jealousy, dating manuals emerged to provide appropriate emotional etiquette for this new social practice. Recommendations were directed at reducing jealous manifestations while admitting that dating frequently provoked the unpleasant emotion. Teenagers were to understand that a date's interest in someone else was not necessarily a final loss—many adolescents felt rejected too readily. It was vital to avoid "unsportsmanlike" tactics (like showing jealousy too obviously), for others must be free, while trust and self-confidence were fundamental to any successful relationship.[52] Positive reactions, through keeping a date interested, rather than jealous pouts were urged, particularly on girls who were still assumed to be jealousy-prone in their driving interest in converting dating into a more durable relationship.[53]

By the 1940s, and especially after World War II, adolescent dating patterns moved from an emphasis on playing the field to a growing preoccupation with finding a steady dating partner (or, particularly for the college-bound, a sequence of steady dating partners). By 1948, 42 percent of American high-school students had been or were involved in steady dating, and the percentage rose for another decade thereafter.[54]

A number of factors were involved in this important behavioral change. Steady dating could save money, and allow a wider range of casual activities than the earlier, entertainment-focused system had encouraged. It promoted greater sexual intimacy. Steady dating may also have responded to larger changes in culture and politics. One recent explanation, building on some contemporary surveys, has emphasized the tensions of the postwar world, to which steady dating provided an antidote through greater personal security, along with the demography of the World War II era when a scarcity of men prompted new anxieties about finding marriage partners and so (presumably on the part of young women, who are implicitly given the lead role in this dating shift) a growing interest in commitment over diversity and entertainment. Some of these factors were undoubtedly involved in the rise of steady dating and particularly its timing.

Yet jealousy, almost surely, played a vital if slightly covert role as well. Teenagers, increasingly socialized to find jealousy childish, did not like the pain of jealous longing or the simple experience of finding themselves jealous despite their best intentions. Steady dating provided an institutional response which would limit the need for jealousy for prolonged periods of time, precisely because its parameters normally regulated contacts a partner would seek with other people and, indeed, contacts other teenagers would seek with a partner identified as a steady date. This motivation could readily appeal to males, despite their presumed resistance to jealousy and their demographic advantages in an ultimate marriage market, fully as much as females. Indeed, despite some bald assertions that girls preferred steady dating more than did boys,[55] the very fact that male culture now urged a particular avoidance of jealousy may have spurred males to seek steady arrangements at least as eagerly as females did (notably when jealousy avoidance could be combined with greater sexual liberties). Teenagers of both genders certainly reported the advantage of steady dating in providing greater "security" as their primary attraction, and while this meant in part a relief from popularity anxieties and assurance of escorts for key events, it also meant security from undue jealousy concerns. Many teenagers found the competitive dating system "uncomfortable," and while they rarely mentioned jealousy as a key ingredient of this discomfort—prevailing emotionology inhibited this, in discussions with peers as well as adults—there is every reason to believe that this emotion entered strongly into the sensation.[56] The pressures of peers and revised popularity ratings then added to the institution, leading more and more teenagers to seek steady arrangements in what became an important adolescent response to a complex set of causes. During the 1940s and 1950s, declining age of marriage constituted a related institutional response that could be intended to separate jealousy from early romance and sexuality.

The steady-dating regime could of course produce its own jealousy problems, in part because (as adult critics so abundantly noted) it did generate greater romantic and sexual intensity. Breaking up a steady relationship could be a painful affair. Frequent divorces among adolescent newlyweds had the same potential. Yet many steady daters, at least, recognized that these relationships could be simultaneously intense—jealously defended while in effect—and finite, using summers of more recreational dating to ease transitions. Even here, memories of previous steady relationships could intrude on subsequent courtship. A 1953 study reported that 31 percent of all men and 23 percent of all women admitted jealousy of their partner's previous involvements, reflecting what the study's authors sanctimoniously termed a "lack of adjustment" to modern dating conditions and what many teenagers and young adults might indeed find painful.[57]

The jealousy issues involved in steady dating, along with still greater exposure to socialization and emotionological preachments aimed against the emotion, may have played some role in inducing the next shift in dating patterns, which began to occur by the later 1960s. Steady dating, a first effort to combine teenage romance and jealousy standards in the twentieth-century context, fell from favor, and in the middle class early marriage did too. Again, causation was complex, and certainly included themes from a new youth culture, shifts in sexual habits that eased access to intimacy, and changes in women's values and career patterns that helped produce later ages at marriage and so made focused dating in adolescence less viable. Certainly, however, the new patterns of adolescent social activity, embracing heterosexual contact, were designed to minimize jealousy even more sweepingly than steady dating had done. More group activities limited coupling and durably intense attachments of the sort that might build on or reflect jealousy. Important remnants of dating and its emotional assumptions remained, to be sure, in what was a complex transition to new behaviors. Many college students still expected to identify partners and expected that these partners would (often in quite early stages of a relationship) give up close personal friendship with others of the opposite sex.[58] Nevertheless, the growing tendency of high school and college students to socialize in larger groups, pairing more briefly and informally (though often intimately), was widely noted. It accompanied heightened emphasis in adolescent peer groups on a cool emotional style that would avoid jealous possessiveness in matters of sex as well as romance.

What seemed an odd reversal of adolescent romantic behavior, in moving from the intensity of steady dating to the celebration of group cool, thus had some consistency in one underlying emotional ingredient. Open to a new romantic context through the advent of dating, teenagers have in the twentieth century experimented with a variety of responses that would allow them to maintain new freedom in heterosexual encounter with the need to minimize jealousy as an emotion that was not widely accepted by their peers and that made most individuals experiencing it personally uncomfortable. The first main experiment, steady dating, constituted a classic kind of semi-institutional response, which reduced the need for personal emotional control, save at transition points, by means of reasonably clear behavioral rules. Intriguingly, for a variety of reasons by no means entirely related to jealousy control, the institutional effort was jettisoned in favor of a group-oriented social system that depended more heavily on individual jealousy restraint, abetted of course by the norms and enforcement of omnipresent peers. Both principal responses demonstrated an acute adolescent awareness of jealousy issues, and an attempt to relate standards expressed in the abstract to actual romantic behavior. The effort to combine growing interest in romance and sexuality with steadily more rigorous commitment to jealousy control constitutes one of the underlying themes of adolescent history in twentieth-century America. The progression from institutional to more explicit emotional-control responses is also interesting in its analogy with patterns in the adult sphere.

For while marriage relationships in the twentieth century did not display such explicit reactions to new jealousy control needs as did adolescent dating, in part because the context was less novel, many aspects of marriage revealed similar increases in the level of concern about jealousy and reliance on individual emotional restraint.

Marriage and Jealousy: New Tensions

The problem of jealousy in twentieth-century marriage has not, of course, been unbounded. Many American couples continued to be able to talk out jealousy issues and set agreed-upon behavioral boundaries, "so as to minimize jealousy in the future."[59] Some marriages were enhanced by jealousy, as one or both spouses continued to associate the emotion with love and were thus flattered by signs of possessive concern.[60] In a probably growing number of instances, marital partners moved, whether spontaneously or in explicit agreement, toward a reduction of jealous reactions, as a result of prior socialization and a growing desire for personal freedom; several studies indicated that marital partners interested in extramarital involvements, almost certainly a growing trend after 1920, limited their own jealousy in an implicit trade-off.[61]

Yet a host of jealousy symptoms remained in twentieth-century marriage, and some probably increased. Women's jealousy of their husbands' work roles, though not a new phenomenon, continued to be reported. The baby boom produced new attention to husbands' jealousy of their wives' involvement with children, which also may have tended to increase as marriages were rated more exclusively on the basis of spouse-spouse contacts.[62]

The most obvious situational enhancements of jealousy, however, involved divorce, infidelity, and women's work. The growing involvement of wives in jobs outside the home, beginning in the 1940s and then resuming after 1950, drew little explicit assessment from the jealousy standpoint, in part because American men were already so committed to a position of officially denying jealousy as a serious emotion. Yet resentments and adjustments could be complicated by jealousy of women's new freedom and their on-the-job contacts with other men. Divorce was more overtly productive of jealousy, and the increase of divorce rates obviously augmented the opportunities for rejected spouses to experience deeper emotional resentments.[63]

Most obvious still, in generating new jealousy, was the increased potential for, and almost certainly increased incidence of, extramarital sexual affairs. More, perhaps, in the United States than elsewhere, actual sexual behavior outstripped—the word is used advisedly—attitudinal or emotional adjustments. Despite growing professed tolerance for extramarital involvement and a related claim of substantial immunity from jealousy, American husbands and wives typically responded to an errant spouse with considerable anxiety and resentment. Only a small minority of marriages remained happy amid infidelity,[64] according to a variety of post–World War II studies. With growing sexual tolerance and still more pressure to restrain jealousy, the damage of infidelity many have diminished somewhat by the 1960s and 1970s, even aside from deliberate open-marriage experiments, but even by this point the majority of spouses continued to report intense jealous reactions. Thus marriage advisors, some of whom briefly seized on new sexual trends to urge that discreet affairs might help a deadened marriage, retained or rediscovered caution, arguing that given ongoing jealousy even mild affairs might never be forgiven. As one put it, "It does not appear possible, within our cultural setting, to maintain a marriage where extramarital sex is condoned and permitted."[65] Yet affairs, and opportunities to suspect affairs because of office parties, women's work or organizational contacts, or sheer personal insecurity, increased fairly steadily, making jealousy a recurrent ingredient of many marriages.

The results of an emotional response that lagged behind sexual behavior showed in the spate of jealousy-provoked tensions that fell into the laps of marriage counselors, from the 1940s onward, where, treated as examples of childhood insecurity, they might or might not be alleviated.[66] They showed in some popular music, particularly "country" versions linking to a Southern tradition of jealous lament. The results showed also in many episodes of jealousy-induced marital violence. Expert claims varied, and of course expert testimony was itself sometimes colored by the prevailing hostility to jealousy as a valid emotion. Nevertheless, it remains valid to note that research suggested that a minimum of 25 percent and possibly as much as 95 percent of all marital assault, including wife-battering, occurred as a result of overpowering jealousy, particularly of course when men responded to real or imagined offenses on the part of their wives.[67]

Jealousy problems in marriage, including emotionally generated violence, were not, of course, twentieth-century inventions, and we will see in chapter 6 that beliefs in crimes of jealousy may well have exaggerated reality. Knowledge of the issues increased because of more family research and because of the emotionology experts themselves applied in their evaluations. To the extent that new issues and incidences were involved, they reflected in large part shifts in behavior— particularly but not exclusively sexual behavior—played against a backdrop of continuity in jealousy. Jealousy-induced violence, in other words, if it increased in twentieth-century marriage, resulted in large part from new gender roles and a pattern of extramarital affairs that would have elicited much the same response in the nineteenth century had they been current then; the emotional base was little changed, and indeed crimes deriving from infidelity were far from uncommon in the nineteenth century itself.

Yet shifts in jealousy standards played a role in twentieth-century marriage as well, even aside from the growing minority of tolerant couples and the disapproval with which the new breed of marriage experts reacted to most signs of the emotion. Antijealousy emotionology, even when qualified in real life by ongoing ambivalence, showed in several overlapping ways—including, as we will see in the following chapter, some possible shifts even in violence itself.

Most obviously, the emotionology that spread after 1920 encouraged resentment by one spouse at expressions of jealousy by another. This was one of the famous complaints of surveyed California husbands against their wives, when they listed jealousy-induced nagging as their eighteenth most pressing grievance (far ahead of worries about wifely infidelity, which placed forty-fifth).[68] When couples disagreed about jealousy standards, another likely result of a period in which emotionology was shifting, the potential for mutual incomprehension was further enhanced. The less jealous partner, encouraged by knowledge of being more emotionally up to date, might deliberately attempt to establish greater independence or to give the jealous spouse "something to be jealous about."[69] Jealousy, in sum, was a growing ingredient of marital conflict because of new responses by the targeted partner.

The impact of emotionology could run deeper still, and interestingly the evidence for this second impact area comes particularly after 1950 when one would expect the results of the intensified campaign, now in its second generation, to be increasingly visible. Embarrassed by his or her own jealousy a spouse became increasingly reluctant to voice the emotion, eager instead to conceal. This embarrassment and guilt, however, merely exacerbated resentments and communication barriers, making a bad situation worse. Instead of clarifying the reactions and encouraging mutual discussion of problems, jealous spouses often internalized a sense that their feelings were somehow "pathological"; so the jealousy-producing behavior continued unchecked while a feeling of personal inferiority raised the anger level on its own account.[70]

Jealousy had not been a trivial subject in the nineteenth century. The familiar story about the book-resenting wife, cited in chapter 2, makes it clear that a jealous party could feel constraint in voicing concerns. But this constraint increased substantially as a result of the twentieth-century attack on jealousy, reduced belief that jealousy could be justified as a real sign of love, and the fair suspicion that a spouse might view articulation as infringement on personal autonomy. The emotion, which once had prompted communication even amid some difficulty, now became its own barrier, making marital tensions worse.

Possibly some jealousy-provoked violence became more common or more intense, at least in some decades, because frustration, delay and self-doubt were added to the primary emotional response; the proposition is consistent but hard to prove. More obvious still was the extent to which new reactions to jealousy encouraged abandonment of marriage. In order to "feel good about oneself," a resentful spouse, reluctant to voice emotion openly yet unable to sustain the sense of being in the wrong for feeling jealous, simply walks away, or still more commonly lets tensions build until an outburst ensues that drives the spouse away. The result might be one fewer marriage, but at least in theory the chance, as one account put it, to "feel good" about one's own emotional stance.

Jealousy, in other words, destabilized many marriages for several reasons. Most obviously, growing rates and openness of infidelity sparked more jealous reactions, based on ongoing beliefs that the response was valid or at least unavoidable, as part of the claims of true love. These might provoke remedial behavior by the parties, but it was increasingly likely to produce complaints about interference and immaturity. Finally, and more subtly, jealous reactions might themselves encourage not just attack but withdrawal on the part of the offended party, because they were so painful, felt increasingly to be inappropriate. It was often easier to flee, thus escaping both the memory of the partner's unfaithfulness and that of one's own response.

Shifts in the prevailing norms for handling adultery in many families abundantly reflected the new emotional climate. To be sure, the most venturesome experiments in open marriage often ended in jealousy-drenched failure, and without question extramarital excursions could still cause massive and jealous dismay; there was no simple evolution toward lessened jealousy. As adultery became more common and less cosmic, perhaps particularly for women, the legitimacy of jealous response nevertheless eroded to a degree. A "code of honesty" developed in many families that urged openness in sharing information about extramarital sex; the premise here was that frankness removed stigma and might even tighten marriage bonds, but the pattern assumed an ability to restrain jealousy and justified dismissal of jealous responses should they occur. The jealous response, indeed, might be seen as a greater violation than the act that provoked it. Clearly, rights of individual expression won out in this arrangement, and an emotion that might trammel it, though obstinately refusing to disappear, won diminished sanction.[71]

The main point is clear: growing belief in jealousy as a demeaning emotion might complicate marital reactions and encourage rather abrupt dissolutions, even as jealousy-producing behaviors tended to increase. Until the 1970s jealousy might further exacerbate the process of divorce outright, as one spouse nursed resentments by impeding legal dissolution.[72] But ultimately, with the advent of no-fault proceedings, the law caught up with new emotional standards by refusing to allow jealousy (or other complexities) unduly to delay the end of marriage. Small wonder that, by the 1970s, marriage counselors began to turn away from an earlier tendency simply to attack the jealous individual for immaturity, in order to spend more time encouraging communication around the jealousy issue. Because disapproval, both social and personal, blocked expression of jealousy, couples might need assistance in recognizing what the emotional source of resentment was and what behaviors provoked it. An emotion once hailed for its role in defending love by promoting recognition of mutual problems now typically made matters worse, leaving the problems untended and adding self-dislike to the mix.[73]

American marriage has long been something of a battleground between beliefs in individual autonomy and expression, and beliefs in the power of love. The many successes of marriage as an institution even in the later twentieth century testify to the fact that the battle can still be fruitfully resolved.[74] Yet it is obvious that many behavioral trends during the century have tipped the balance toward the individual, save in certain subcultures, increasingly redefining love to mean an absence of significant self-sacrifice. Changes in jealousy's role and impact have played an integral part in this shifting marital equation. The emotion is decreasingly available directly to defend love, because its expression is as likely to provoke further self-assertion as to induce a rush to proclaim love's primacy. At the same time the unpleasantness and debasement jealousy may cause its victim weaken the ability to protest on love's behalf and may prompt the need for withdrawal, again for the sake of healthy self-respect. And so the scales tip still further from love as a bonding transcending the individual.

Jealousy and Gender

The efforts of married and dating couples to deal with the new confusions and resentments surrounding jealousy, and with the new behaviors that spark the emotion in the first place, must obviously be assessed in the light of changing gender cultures. Gender imagery certainly shifted as part of the twentieth-century reevaluation of jealousy, though amid partial continuity, and this combination in turn affected the actual emotional experience of men and women.

We have seen that nineteenth-century emotionology tried to deal with a disapproval of jealousy while retaining recognition of its role in love by exaggerating gender differentiation. Jealousy was bad, which was why most men weren't prey to the emotion, yet as part of love it had some merit which was why it could be specially linked, with some patronizing clucking, to women. Elements of this distinction clearly survived into the mid–twentieth century, and were even internalized by family members.

Questionnaire responses and some described behavior during the first half of the twentieth century maintained much of the differentiation sketched in the emotionology of the previous century. We have seen that men claimed increasing resentment of their wives' jealousy, while disclaiming much of their own. College students displayed a similar division, as they reacted to polls about marital expectations: "Moderate attentions to the spouse from opposite sex are not resented by the men, but they are by the women."[75] Adult women agreed that their gender was more jealous, and when they complained about their husbands in this category pleaded for more, rather than less of the emotion. Women, in other words, seemed to view jealousy as a sign of love and also a defense of a relationship arguably more important to them still, if only in economic terms, than to men. Males viewed jealousy as an infringement on autonomy, not a valid plea for greater commitment, and clearly took pride in displaying, or claiming to display, nonchalance.[76]

The distinctions over jealousy could open in courtship, with women trying to provoke jealousy from their dates as a means of winning greater involvement, while young men tried to maintain a cool exterior in order to preserve their own self-respect and freedom of action.[77] Often, it was an effort to propel this courtship ritual into married life that occasioned the more active disputes, as some wives played the coquette to revive romantic intensity while men rejoiced that the game was over, asking mainly to be left alone.

The role of jealousy in a decades-long battle of the sexes should not be minimized, precisely because it did provide an emotional backdrop to real gender differences about the role of romance and marriage. Women's greater dependence on and confinement to marriage might even have pushed some previous targets for jealousy to new levels in some instances during the decades around mid-century. Jealous resentment of a husband's devotion to his job reflected different priorities about emotional commitment to marriage, as well as the simple allocation of time and attention, but reports after 1950—impressionistic, to be sure—added some understandable new ingredients. Jealousy of the job thus could include simple longing for wider outside contacts, on the part of a suburban wife, and guilt about not being able to pursue an "ideal of personal success" now spreading more widely among women.[78]

At the same time, however, the men/cool, women/jealous equation is too simple, and it fails to capture some other aspects of contemporary change. Men's readier acceptance of the dominant emotionology—for this is what male attitudes clearly expressed—often masked greater tensions, as men struggled to live up to standards they did not fully feel. Jealous impulses showed in a variety of systematic ways. Men in the early 1950s were virtually as sensitive as women in a preference that a date not mention others; they ranked higher than women (31 percent to 23 percent) in admitting jealousy of a previous affair.[79] Expert evaluation in the same decades, moving away from nineteenth-century scientific assumptions about female preponderance in jealousy, began arguing that male jealousy was equal to women's but different in kind, reflecting deeper, more possessive instincts against women's more calculating, realistic attempt to manipulate the emotion in light of emotional and pragmatic stakes in a relationship.[80] Obviously, with women taking new work roles by mid-century, even though still limited by sexual conventions and by the blossoming pattern of early marriage, some men may have encountered more occasions for romantic jealousy than at previous points.

Men had moved more quickly than women to a commitment to antijealousy emotionology, sometimes in order to protect their own freedom of action. Some became attuned to the new standards, but others warred between a desire for a disengaged image and strong jealous tendencies. The struggle against jealousy thus became an important part of men's emotional history in the twentieth century. The absence of acceptable direct outlets for the emotion, combined with the additional intensity that might result from suppression and guilt, might contribute to the violent expressions of jealousy in which some men ultimately indulged. As opportunities for jealousy grew, efforts at control probably kept pace for most men, but with some the attempt at control, if abortive, might make matters worse.

Women moved increasingly toward similar constraints, though with less explosive, more inwardly directed results. Many women had long been able to master jealousy in certain circumstances, as when men indulged in casual sex with strangers; as one authority put it, jealousy had little role when a man indulged "the lower side of his masculine nature."[81] Occasions for jealousy about work and other women may have proliferated by the 1930s, helping to explain what seems to have been a high point of gender differentiation on the subject within marriage. As women moved toward new work goals, and in some cases acquired feminist values which enhanced self-worth, open declarations of jealousy declined in validity. Women became if anything still more sensitive to infidelities, as the acceptability of a double standard waned, but as we have seen their willingness to proclaim jealousy, or to assume it might sway a partner, decreased even more rapidly. Hence, the frequent tendency to give up a relationship rather than try to articulate jealousy and work it through. As expert opinion merged gender reactions even more fully than before, in arguing male and female equality in jealousy, they picked up on a real trend. Men and women alike moved toward a similar attempt to integrate a conviction that jealousy was inappropriate and degrading with some possessive romantic impulses that stubbornly refused to yield.[82] This involved particularly rapid, and potentially fragile, emotional adjustments on women's part, along with some ongoing self-deception by men bent on displaying a coolness many could not inwardly maintain if put to a test.

Conclusion

What was the significance of twentieth-century emotional trends in modifying and complicating the actual experience of romantic and sexual relationships through a widely-accepted condemnation of jealousy plus the accompanying efforts to deny or conceal the emotion? Most obviously, Americans did not, in the main, react to a host of new or heightened provocations to jealousy, as gender roles changed and sexual standards loosened, with as much jealous outburst as could have been predicted from the emotional responses current as the century opened. Outbursts there were, from men and women alike when confronted by infidelities or slights, but their incidence did not clearly escalate as the context changed. This in itself was no small result, though it was accompanied by considerable public discussion and even more private anguish as impulse warred against values to create actual emotional experience and response. As in other sexually-tolerant societies, American hostility to jealousy became increasingly essential, with the complexity attendant on shifting paradigms concerning sexual tolerance itself.

The effort to combat romantic jealousy clearly mirrored a number of key changes in American family and personal life. The decline of family solidarity was enhanced by growing doubts about the validity of one of the emotions that had long been used in its defense. Christopher Lasch has correctly pointed to attempts to restrain jealousy in classic situations, as in a father's response to his daughter's suitors, as a change in traditional emotions long used to regularize family relationships.[83] Shifts toward more permissive sexuality, both within and without the family context, inherently depended on reductions in the willingness to countenance jealousy in oneself and others. Trends toward more equal gender roles were reflected in the progressive equalization of jealousy standards, after an interesting nineteenth-century experiment with some emphasis on female jealousy as a cement in courtship and marriage. We have seen, finally, that the vital shift in balance between individualism and family commitment was played out against a backdrop of jealousy's evolution, as possessiveness—through the right to assert jealousy and the responsibility to answer to it— waned in favor of autonomy. Jealousy reactions here reflected declining commitment but also, as suggested in the complex role in divorce, also helped cause it.

Most of these developments, of course, were not absolute. Family values persisted, and the importance of the husband-wife bond in some ways intensified as the key to a definition of happy marriage. Americans in the main proved reluctant, despite behavioral change, to dissociate sexual values fully from romantic attachments and even a lingering hope for the one true love. Again, patterns of jealousy mirrored these hesitations, as the emotionology hostile to jealousy warred with sneaking admiration for the emotion and some ineradicable, though varied, impulses toward its use.

Declining approval for jealousy and growing complexity in its manifestations as part of actual emotional experience might seem an almost inevitable development given what we know about twentieth-century permissiveness. The motivating forces of change, in other words, were growing sexual appetites and new contexts in courtship and marriage that gave them freer play, heightened individualism and so on. Jealousy changes, in this formulation, are mere by-product, interesting but adding little to what we already know about recent historical trends. This is the flavor that informs Lasch's comments on jealousy, for example, in one of the few historical treatments that has even evoked the topic.

In fact, however, the emotional changes involving romantic jealousy run deeper than simply mirroring the obvious, in several senses.

In the first place, jealousy changes helped cause—they did not only reflect. Redefinition of jealousy, and greatly heightened concern about manifesting the emotion, were neither trivial nor inevitable developments. The background for growing belief that real love and jealousy should not be twined emerged well before 1920, in the preachments and experiments of the nineteenth century. Cultural change set in motion forces that would ultimately alter emotional experience and motivation. Only this background explains why the explosion of anti-jealousy emotionology and new socialization efforts were possible in the middle decades of our century. And only the readiness to redefine jealousy, in turn, can explain some of the new behaviors in sex, courtship and marriage. There is no need to claim a primacy for jealousy redefinitions in altering family solidity and contacts between men and women, but these redefinitions were not mere aftermath. They were intimately connected with greater permissiveness, serving as preconditions at least in part.

Furthermore, the timing of the jealousy shifts reveals some limited surprises, even when ultimate directions seem familiar enough. We know that, while new sexual intensity was evoked by the culture of the 1920s, the actual revolution in modern sexual behavior awaited the postwar years. But the changes in jealousy standards that underlay this revolution took shape earlier, at least in key groups. Barbara Ehrenreich, in her provocative feminist analysis, thus points to the 1950s as the advent of a *Playboy* culture that signaled increased hedonism and decreased family commitment on the part of many American men, ultimately triggering women's response in the form of new work roles, feminism, and wider sexual interests.[84] Yet an important part of the emotional ingredient of men's new insistence on individual freedom and pleasure seeking developed earlier, in the male culture, prepared in the nineteenth century and spreading still more visibly between the world wars, that insisted officially that jealousy was unmanly and that female jealous reactions had shifted from being endearing signs of a dependence on love to symptoms of unacceptable nagging. Changes in emotional standards here preceded and underlay "revolutionary" manifestations in outward behavior. The *Playboy* outlook certainly diverted men's attention from discussing or admitting jealousy, but it really was just adding centerfolds to an established emotional posture for the gender. Clearly, we must weight the tensions resulting from the campaign to redefine romantic jealousy as an active ingredient in furthering a number of changes, in family and sexuality and in gender relationships still more generally.[85]

Reality remained complex. In part because of new provocations, but in part because of negative self-judgments imposed on emotions felt yet disapproved, the pains accompanying jealousy increased for many people during the twentieth century, prompting a number of behaviors designed to ease the stress. It might have been simpler to yield to jealousy more fully, trying to recapture tighter family structure and more discreet behaviors that would minimize its incidence. The nineteenth-century pattern, in which jealousy brought response but required relatively little comment or apparent agony, certainly has its appeal. Possibly, the future will see an effort to reduce jealousy conflicts through a revival of firmer commitments and family institutions. Yet the forces prompting disapproval of jealousy—a demanding idealization of love, belief in individual autonomy, greater freedom from ascribed gender roles—have ongoing power as well, and they may further reduce jealousy's hold.

Tensions surrounding jealousy certainly constitute one of the key forces in twentieth-century emotional life. While they built on values sketched earlier, the full confrontation between a disapproving emotionology and ongoing impulse took full shape only over the past seven decades. This helps explain the confusion apparent in so many recent reactions. It also helps explain the volatility of measures designed to reconcile standards and reality, as in adolescent shifts from the temporary possessiveness of steady dating to more communal socializing, or women's official turn from lingering enjoyment of jealous coyness to official pride, as a 1987 comic strip put it, that "we no longer play those games."[86]

While the struggle over jealousy was in many ways a twentieth-century innovation in emotional life, it also constituted a new chapter in a longer-standing effort to substitute personal emotional control for institutional or community constraints. During the nineteenth century and, though on different bases, in more traditional society, jealousy had helped motivate institutions—family ties, community defense of honor, and sexual ethics—that had in turn made actual manifestations of the emotion relatively infrequent. Save in individual cases, there was no general problem of jealousy control, because adherence to proper courtship and family norms would prevent it and because sanctioned behaviors came into play when the emotion was provoked.

Twentieth-century life, though not totally altered, became less structured. This was the context for new concerns about romantic jealousy, and it has imposed a growing effort to inculcate jealousy control within individuals, as part of their emotional makeup. The goals mirror earlier efforts, dating back to the eighteenth century at least in upper-class life, to subsume vigorous impulse under new control and etiquette.[87] The evolution of jealousy demonstrates that this pattern of relying on individual restraint, based in turn on rigorous childhood socialization, continues and deepens. Twentieth-century Americans no longer fully countenance behaviors that express romantic jealousy, and they no longer defend the sacrosanctity of institutions that minimize provocations. The definition of "civilized" emotional control becomes still more demanding. One result, not surprisingly, is still considerable strain. Another, evoked by culture critics who prefer older jealousy ideals among other nostalgias, is a fear that, in urging such tight emotional constraint, American society also implicitly turns against emotional intensity of any sort, as a desire for cool behavior permeates what used to be more meaningful romance precisely because the consequences of loss of control now seem so dire. Ironically, if Americans move (incompletely and variably, to be sure) toward fuller realization of the ideal of jealousy-free love, they may also find that love itself has lost its passion, as relationships become more restrained and less committed, attendant sexuality more mechanical.

Some of these points require further assessment, particularly as we turn to the wider implications of shifts in romantic jealousy and the general efforts to instill new levels of internalized emotional control. The point at this juncture is to recognize the extent to which many American adults had responded, counterintuitively, to a looser context for marriage and romance by heightening their efforts to monitor their own jealousy and to shift the responsibility for the emotion away from behavioral provocation, whether that of oneself or another, and onto one's own immaturity or—still better—that of someone else.

Few individuals directly admitted a jealousy problem—despite the 1970s workshop movement, which was more symbolically interesting than widely significant. Unlike other emotional areas where new constraints arose in the twentieth century—such as anger or grief—no loud appeals to therapists or group support activities responded directly to jealousy issues. This reflected ongoing diversity: some individuals really had no overt jealousy problems while others continued, in more traditional fashion, to see their reactions to real or imagined infidelities as perfectly justifiable. Yet the absence of individual admissions of the problem also reflected the pervasive desire to conceal, which ran deeper with romantic jealousy than was true of anger.[88] Thus it was that jealousy, while only occasionally discussed as a personal problem,[89] prompted such intense concern on the part of parents and contributed to major institutional shifts in dating and to more complex scenarios of marital disruption. Growing personal intolerance of jealousy in self combined here with the still more pervasive reluctance to react sympathetically to the jealousies of others, and the experience of love was altered by the result.

Furthermore, the evaluation of responses to jealousy tended to intensify over time, in some rough correspondence to socialization efforts and effects. Young adults exposed to new parental concerns but far from completely diverted from intense sibling rivalries—the people growing up from the 1930s to the 1950s—could be content with institutionalized efforts to avoid jealousy provocation; they did not attempt full self-control. More fully socialized adults—maturing by the 1960s—though still subject to sibling tensions, had experienced more successful tactical response, as parents learned how to keep childish jealousy down. They sought more actively—though as always amid diversity—to demonstrate their freedom from jealousy in "cool" dating behaviors and in some attempts to introduce greater tolerance into marriage itself. They became even more eager (men still more commonly than women) to note and condemn jealousy in others, partners or children—a significant result of intense feelings about the emotion even aside from self-appraisals. And while the 1980s saw some behavioral return to monogamy, as the population grew older and AIDS inhibited sexual license, jealousy remained officially out of favor as emotional support: hence the new rash of popularized treatments rushed to remind of dominant emotionological values, and a sense of continued emotional detachment continued, in the eyes of many observers, to describe many apparently durable relationships. Haltingly, incompletely, amid frequent confusions in personal evaluations, the campaign to separate jealousy from love had progressively greater impact.

CHAPTER 6

Jealousy Beyond
the Family

The twentieth-century campaign against jealousy, but also the increasing provocations to the emotion from childhood onward, focused most obviously on familial and romantic relationships. Changes in these areas, however, had potential implications for broader emotional styles, of the sort that might surface outside the arena of what most Americans carefully regarded as private life. The effort to damp down jealousy could alter behavior, or at least create new discomforts, in rivalrous settings at work or elsewhere. In contrast, even incompletely successful suppression of jealousy at home could spur a need to find outlets elsewhere. An exploration of jealousy in the wider context of twentieth-century American life finds traces of both impulses: an undeniable attempt to apply sanctions against jealousy uniformly—even in law—but also an ability to find some legitimate means of being jealous without applying a clear emotional label.

To the extent the expressions of jealousy within the family, and particularly in romantic relationships, were constricted, the question of compensatory outlets arises with considerable force. Some people, because of accident or really successful socialization, may have experienced so little jealousy that meeting the new standards in adult life posed no real problem. But others, although affected by sibling management and certainly aware that jealous impulses should not be expressed too openly, might face more serious issues. The palpable inclination to conceal jealousy suggested that this pattern was not uncommon.

Were there more accepted ways of letting jealousy out? As Americans tried to limit anger in the twentieth century, particularly in the workplace but to a degree at home, opportunities to vent the emotion in accepted or at least neutral formats clearly increased: hence the role of crowd release at sports events, the importance of angry portrayals in the popular media—"make my day"—and the omnipresent fist shaking and cursing on the highways. Jealousy, precisely because it was defined as a more purely personal and romantic impulse—results of previous emotionological recastings—had less clear alternate outlets. Yet the possibility of wider roles for an emotion partially blocked within family life can be usefully explored to a point.

The basic proposition is as follows: could twentieth-century Americans, amid intense efforts to repress jealousy, manage some compensatory expressions—and were they perhaps encouraged to this end? The challenge is to see how jealousy, whose evolution was clearly significant in the area of family life and personality definition, and which was shaped in part by larger forces in American society, affected other facets of behavior in turn.

Social analysis of emotion, still tentative in many ways, too often stops short of a full exploration of effects, assuming that emotions stand on their own. And it is obviously true that attempts to fathom wider results are difficult, usually tentative at best. At the same time, critics of social historians' penchant for expanding into new topics—and emotions history certainly qualifies here—justly note a temptation to spin off in isolation, without trying to link with other facets of the past, including some familiar political staples. Thus the need to ask about broader relationships is vital, lest emotions history be yet another specialty closeted by itself, without much potential for integration with other areas of historical analysis. Without pretending, then, a dramatic passage on jealousy's role in reshaping the New Deal and causing the Cold War, designed to catch the eye of those whose historical interests are confined to mainstream topics alone, a role for jealousy in economic and cultural spheres can be suggested, along with some tentative inroads into politics.

In this chapter, the outreach of jealousy and its standards is explored

progressively, beginning with manifestations in law—where sensitivity to emotionology is often revealingly great; moving to somewhat
wider personal relationships than those explicitly addressed thus far,
but where jealousy suppression might be presumed to have direct
effects; and then turning more directly still, but also more specula-
tively, to the problem of outright compensatory expressions.

Jealousy, Crime, and Law

One connection beyond the purely personal and familial has already
been discussed for the nineteenth century; its twentieth-century patterns help launch consideration of the outreach of the new emotionology directed at jealousy. In the nineteenth century, legal treatment of
crimes motivated by jealousy served as something of a collective outlet,
at a time when attempts to attack the emotion's validity produced
tensions and backsliding. Not surprisingly, the twentieth century saw
a more positive relationship with ongoing standards and legal principles. The combination was still murky however, if only because Americans remained somewhat conflicted between opposition to jealousy
and some sense that defense of love's prerogatives was valid. Nevertheless, there was change, and legal affirmation of the dominant emotionology won through with growing clarity after 1970.

The starkest use of jealousy as an excuse for what otherwise would
be considered crime ended in most of the United States by about 1900:
it was no longer possible to invoke the unwritten law that might excuse
the slaying of a wife's lover on grounds of passion-induced insanity. A
majority of state supreme courts by the 1890s were rejecting or seriously limiting such simple usage of legal insanity. Thus the North
Carolina Supreme Court led in a denunciation of the unwritten law as
a rule that encouraged lawlessness and bloodshed:[1] passionate jealousy
could not carry so far. This was not, however, a clear-cut victory for
an emotionology that urged suppression of the emotion. Many states
deliberately replaced the unwritten law defense with formal laws against
adultery, thus in principle eliminating the need for private vengeance
but substituting the state as preventer of jealousy. Furthermore, juries,
particularly in the South, were slower than appellate courts in re-
nouncing unwritten law defense, though they gradually moved in this

direction. Thus while credence to the idea of irresistible impulse waned, jealousy was hardly robbed of validity.[2]

Modified legal outlet for jealousy was positively enshrined, in fact, during the initial decades of the twentieth century, by a new current among state legislatures and juries, toward holding that a killing committed "in the heat of passion" should be judged manslaughter, not murder. This judgment fell short of the exoneration possible in the show trials of the nineteenth century, and to this extent it constituted a step down for honor-thirsting jealousy. But as a compromise it constituted a fascinating statement that extreme jealousy, though criminal, still had some legitimacy. Principles here were oddly hedged: a husband who killed on grounds of adultery committed manslaughter, but a fiancé who killed upon sight of unfaithfulness was a murderer outright. One court also ruled that a husband who calmly planned the murder of a sexual rival, in order to prevent adultery, committed justifiable homicide, whereas an enraged killing on the spur of the moment, but otherwise in the same circumstances, remained only manslaughter. The idea that jealousy produced some excuse for crime —though now without preventing its being judged a crime—and some understandable lapse from normal controls, at least in the context of marriage, was not seriously rethought. Courts, juries, and state legislatures continued to reproduce reasoning of this sort without much careful reflection.[3] There was no new approval of jealousy here, but certainly a strong legacy of traditional reactions.

Nevertheless, a few particularly explicit openings for jealousy-induced violence were subject to change.[4] A Texas justifiable-homicide statute, dating from the nineteenth century but reconfirmed in 1925, had held that killing could be legitimate "when committed by the husband upon one taken in the act of adultery with the wife, provided the killing takes place before the parties to the act have separated."[5] Texas courts did delimit the law's scope: wives could not kill husbands; a husband could not legitimately kill wife as well as wife's lover; and there could be no advance planning—emotion must be fresh. Interestingly also, mere injury without intent to kill was not legitimate, as one husband discovered in 1922 in a castration shooting. Here, clearly, was an authorization to extreme jealousy far beyond the national norms, reflecting the old southern commitment to an honor-based emotional code. Georgia, slightly less blatantly, offered a similar statute, where a killing to prevent infidelity could be ranked as self-defense, though here a vengeance slaughter after the fact was murder or manslaughter depending on heat of passion. Georgia gallantly extended privileges to wives as well as husbands—as one judge put it, "what's sauce for the gander is sauce for the goose," and it could extend legitimation for protection of provably chaste daughters or fiancées. Georgia courts thus frequently spoke of a "righteous and justifiable indignation which is a natural concomitant of those holy feelings upon which love of home and the protection of its purity must of necessity rest"; or "the human cur who has invaded the domestic fold and who is likely to invade it further, may be killed."[6]

Important as these state enactments are, in reflecting the ongoing power of traditional views of jealousy in defense of love and honor, and especially male love and honor, it is also vital to note that they were finally repealed. Texas withdrew its sanction for vengeance in 1974, while the Georgia statute was struck down in 1977. The Georgia ruling was particularly interesting, in its retraction of support for jealous reactions aroused by infidelity:

In this day of no-fault, on-demand divorce, when adultery is merely a misde-meanor, . . . any idea that a spouse is ever justified in taking the life of another —adulterous spouse *or* illicit lover—to prevent adultery is uncivilized. This is murder; and hence forth, nothing more appearing, an instruction on justifiable homicide may not be given.[7]

In the 1970s also, statutes in New Mexico and Utah, which had authorized vengeance killings in more limited circumstances, were also withdrawn.

There were of course many reasons for the 1970s shift in legal climate; just as jealousy had not alone motivated unwritten-law de-fenses, so retreat was not based only on new disapproval. Women's rights issues, wider reconsideration of sexual propriety, and new un-certainties about the death penalty even for court-verdict murders all entered in. Nevertheless, the clear reduction of public support for violence motivated by jealousy reflected the belated but genuine im-pact of ongoing emotionology. Its crystallization in the 1970s followed in part from the generational impact of socialization efforts, which as we have seen took fuller dimensions after several decades than during the most ardent initial period of the 1920s and 1930s.

Even here, the idea of change must not be pressed too far, for just as many Americans continued to harbor some sense of legitimate jealousy, so juries might lag behind legislatures in turning away from the idea of justifiable passion. Acquittals of husbands charged even with mere manslaughter of a marital interloper continued, despite clear state laws directing a conviction. Oklahoma was thus notorious for the leniency of juries in this area, despite repeated directives for judges that no unwritten law existed. A lawyer in 1952 explained a common view:

The unwritten law . . . does not exist in Oklahoma, but we can perceive where a man of good moral character . . . , highly respected in his community, having regard for his duties as a husband and the virtue of women, upon learning of the immorality of his wife, might be shocked, or such knowledge might prey upon his mind and cause temporary insanity. In fact, it would appear that such would be the most likely consequence of obtaining such information.[8]

Even here, however, if only because of repeated hammerings by higher courts, jury flexibility had declined by the 1970s, at least to the point of countenancing verdicts of manslaughter. And in most regions of the country, such rulings had become increasingly standard some time before.

Accompanying the progressive eclipse of jealousy-based defenses was a withdrawal of legal punishments for adultery itself, progressively decriminalized in most states from the 1950s onward. Here, obviously, a new sexual culture and greater permissiveness depended tacitly on recognition that neither state nor individual had the right to punish either to express or to prevent jealousy. Actions might still be taken, but they had to depend on a certain amount of impulse control.

Increasingly, Americans were able to respond to unacceptable infidelity through divorce. Here, as with jury findings, there can be no claim that American legal principles insisted on absolute self-restraint. In this case also, however, shifts in legal approach reflected the growing impact of antijealousy emotionology. Divorce continued to be a vital recourse for jealous marital partners, providing far more abundant outlet than had existed during the nineteenth century; but it became harder to state one's jealousy outright.

Two legal shifts in the later nineteenth century set a basis for particularly explicit use of divorce and related legal action to express emotions of jealousy. The catch-all divorce grounds of mental cruelty, introduced widely by the 1890s, gave many spouses—particularly wives—the opportunity to express jealous anguish at infidelity, without having to prove adultery outright. Obviously the wave of mental-cruelty actions had many sources, including convenient fictions but also many unpleasant experiences besides provoked jealousy. Jealousy was nevertheless a common ingredient. Here the key change came at the end of the 1960s, with the spread of no-fault divorce, and while this in one sense made jealous responses easier it mitigated against any formal expression of the emotion. As in the criminal area, jealousy and law, though still linked, moved further apart.[9]

Evaluation is admittedly complex, since rising divorce rates and lessened stigma did facilitate dissolution of marriage on grounds of jealousy and its provocation; in this sense outlets improved. But the no-fault idea reduced the opportunity to vent a punitive approach to jealousy—one might leave, but sticking it to the cause of jealous discomfort now had to be less public and overt.

The second change in marriage law was even more direct and explicit. Toward the middle of the nineteenth century, American jurisprudence, building on a vaguer English precedent, developed a new version of a civil suit, directed against alienation of affections. Here was an ideal means of expressing jealousy and possessiveness through the law, with some hope of monetary compensation. Targeted on someone who purposefully alienated the affections of a spouse, it also required explicit reference to the mental anguish caused by the loss of a spouse's love.[10] Alienation of affections suits, or their threat, thus expressed older ideas of jealous possessiveness—the loss of consortium—with the newer attachment to romantic marital love. And the action became relatively common in the United States (not, interestingly, in Britain) by the late nineteenth century. Here was a means of articulating a restrained form of jealousy in defense of the marital tie—not exactly in keeping with the most up-to-date emotionology, but consistent with a more popular compromise between this emotionology and ongoing attachment to jealousy. Alienation of affections actions constituted in fact something of a legal articulation of the kind of accommodation many couples sought, between antijealousy emotionology and possessive love, during the later nineteenth century, in providing recourse to law when one partner was lured away from the proper responsiveness to a spouse's jealousy.

By the early twentieth century, the frequency of alienation of affections actions increased, with some bringing substantial money awards. A successful plaintiff was entitled to his actual economic loss, such as a share of a wife's inheritance, plus punitive damages. Because the cases were heard before juries, common opinions about fidelity and the legitimacy of jealous outrage fed many lucrative compensation verdicts. Primary attention, indeed, was devoted to soothing injured honor and mental distress—the symptoms, old and new, of jealousy. A 1923 case thus specifically stated that "The degradations which necessarily follow, are the real causes of recovery."[11] Alienation of affections and related breach of promise suits reached a high point of popularity in the 1920s, in the earliest stage of the renewed emotionological campaign against jealousy. They reflected the continued power of jealousy as a legitimate emotion in response to the new challenges rising against sexual fidelity during the same period—another sign of the lag between preached emotional standards and the actual jealousy values most Americans still applied in a crunch. Known as "Heart Balm" actions by this point, the suits initially drew approving public attention.

But popular support soon ebbed. By the 1930s an anti–Heart Balm movement took shape, with support from many legal quarters. The new campaign pointed to fears that suits could extort money from innocent defendants who simply shunned publicity, while people who were willing to publicize their intimate disgraces were viewed with suspicion. In fact it was not clear that the Heart-Balm actions were abused any more than other tort suits, though there were certainly some eye-catching awards ranging up to $150,000.[12] What was clear was that the emotional basis for alienation of affections suits was beginning to erode, as the antijealousy emotionology began to place new burdens of justification of the jealous spouse. This is why jealousy as translated to legal action now seemed tawdry and embarrassing, and why the rights of the targets of suits received new respect. The rate of alienation of affections actions began to plummet, a process then encouraged, during the 1970s, by state legislation or state supreme court actions that abolished the procedures outright or tightly limited their exercise. Only in a few states, such as Minnesota, did a lively alienation of affections litigation continue into the 1980s.[13] Generally, the rise and fall of the alienation of affections gambit neatly illustrated how the dominant emotionology toward jealousy—first shaded toward a complex accommodation that infidelity violated, but then insistent on due restraint of jealousy in favor of individual freedom of action— won expression in law.

The relationship between antijealousy standards and relevant American law is certainly not a simple one. Emotionology might be actively preached for some time before it gained any impact on law. Many Americans continued to see facets of the law as ways to provide some outlet for jealousy feelings in defense of love and marriage, and some regional variations, mostly predictable on grounds of prior emotional culture, added to the complex brew. Nevertheless, there was a clear tendency, particularly by the 1970s but in some cases with important antecedents even earlier, to limit use of jealousy as a justification in law, either as an excuse for what otherwise would be seen as a crime, or as a basis for the state to prohibit certain kinds of behavior, or finally as a reason to seek redress through the means of court action. Haltingly and incompletely, the law moved away from providing any clear support for jealousy or activities motivated by jealousy. Thus, in an important area of American public life, did new emotionology gradually reshape legal dictates.

The quiet if belated triumph of antijealousy emotionology in law is in many ways the least surprising and most readily documented outgrowth of the upheavals surrounding the emotion over the past century, for law readily translates public beliefs, as these solidify, whatever the complexity of actual emotional behaviors and experiences. Yet legal change itself interacts with experience. While most Americans were never heat-of-passion slayers or bringers of alienation suits, they could view legal support as a useful addendum to their own efforts to qualify the rising emotionology in their personal lives; even the splash of a show trial, in which jealousy served as a mitigating circumstance, or a well-publicized alienation suit in which a rich paramour was socked with heavy damages, might be a balm for people who felt uncomfortable with jealousy but were unable to renounce it entirely. Progressively, the law as an outlet either real or symbolic was withdrawn, adding to the circumscription of jealousy in actual emotional life.

And there was one other tantalizing sign of change, at least by the 1970s, when antijealousy standards seemed to have attained particularly effective outreach, on the borderline between law and actual emotional motivation: not only legal support for jealousy-induced crimes, but the rate of such crimes, may have dropped.

Murders and manslaughters attributed to jealousy and a romantic triangle demonstrated some fairly consistent features during the later twentieth century (unfortunately, statistics on crime causes of this sort were kept only from 1962 onward). The majority involved attacks on "acquaintances," with strangers, friends, and girlfriends alternating as next-most-common victims (each category ranging from 8 to 11 percent). Men were three times more likely to commit such murders than women were. Regional variations were predictable and steady: murders stemming from this kind of passion were most common in the South, the only region with consistently above average rates; other regions clustered at rates about two-thirds those of the South. Emotional culture, clearly, left a lingering mark.

But what was fascinating above all was a clear tendency, after a highpoint in 1964, for the rates of murders due to jealousy to decline, both on a per capita basis and as a percent of all murders. This was true both when the overall murder rate was rising, and again when it declined in the 1980s. From the mid-1970s, indeed, murders rated as jealousy-inspired dropped down to negligible proportions.[14]

Percentage of All Known Murders Arising from Romantic Triangle

1962	8.3%	1970	7.1%	1980	2.3%
1963	8.7%	1971	6.3%	1981	2.5%
1964	10.7%	1972	7.1%	1982	2.4%
1965	10.0%	1973	7.5%	1983	2.6%
1966	8.5%	1974	6.2%	1984	2.4%
1967	8.6%	1975	7.3%	1985	2.3%
1968	7.2%	1976	2.8%	1986	2.1%
1969	7.0%	1977	2.8%	1987	2.0%
		1978	2.7%		
		1979	2.4%		

Source: "Crime in the United States," *Uniform Crime Reports, 1962–1987* (Washington, D.C.)

What could cause such a dramatic proportionate and, ultimately absolute decline in jealousy-inspired mayhem? Labeling may well have shifted, particularly for the abrupt drop-off in the mid-1970s as the increasing separation of jealousy from legal support reached something like completion. Criminals and/or law-enforcement agencies may now have internalized prevailing standards sufficiently to look for more respectable motivations, like greed, drugs or drink. Even this change is interesting, in suggesting the power of the antijealousy emotionology to reshape public presentations. But it is also possible (instead of or in addition to labeling changes) that after decades of socialization against romantic jealousy, the force of the emotional spur really did decline, at least in prompting greater constraints on spontaneous physical expression. This might be enhanced, of course, by the realistic understanding that the likelihood of vindication in the courts, never a sure thing, had greatly declined as well.

Certainly the rate of provocations to jealousy hardly decreased, as infidelity if anything continued to climb at least into the 1980s. Controlled expressions of jealousy, particularly through divorce action, surely took up some of the slack. And it is always possible that other categories of domestic violence reflected a more unchanging rate of jealous outburst than the official romantic triangle category, inherently imprecise, could encompass; with a full quarter of all murder involving family members, jealousy surely played a greater role than formal categorizations could encompass. Even here, however, it was interesting that the rate of violence due to domestic arguments, as opposed to other causes, also went down.

The point here is not to build too much on a shaky statistical structure, over a relatively short time period—attractive as the rare opportunity for quantitative precision is, in dealing with emotions history. It does seem clear that crime, or at least crime labeling, as well as key categories of law reflected gains of the antijealousy emotionology, and it is possible that some emotion-produced behaviors shifted as a result. At the least it is doubtful that rates of the most extreme violence rose in response to frustrations induced by the new emotionology juxtaposed with new standards of gender and sexual conduct.

It remained true that crimes engendered by jealousy continued to attract more than usual attention. Some serious analysts pointed to jealousy as a cause of violence without regard to available evidence— as expert statements cited in the previous chapter suggest. Jealousy still drew attention, and this could feed ongoing efforts to attack the emotion by linking it to crimes most foul. Even aside from expert glibness, elevating jealousy to the status of crime problem in a time-honored but by now highly imprecise fashion, the American public undoubtedly believed that jealousy was a more frequent cause of violent crime than was demonstrably the case. Famous jealousy-in-spired murders, like the slaying of a diet guru by the head of a fashionable girls' school, unquestionably commanded more popular interest than otherwise comparable crimes. It is possible that the lingering hesitations many Americans felt about internalizing a separation between sexual or romantic love and jealousy fed this fascination, and even that the fascination itself provided a bit of outlet still for people constricted in expressing jealousy in their own lives.[15]

Americans certainly were not fully aware of the extent of change, in law and possibly in crime rates, that the antijealousy emotionology had produced from the 1930s onward. The trend was as vivid as it was unnoticed by evaluators of the national emotional life: by the 1970s it had become immeasurably harder to bring jealousy to court than it had been a mere half century before. The pattern fit the evolution of emotionology itself, in urging greater emotional control or at least concealment, but it reached well beyond the personal relationships that had inspired the new standards in the first place.

Jealousy Outside the Home: The Realm of Experience

Socialization and Friendship. It has only recently become common to see law as an expression of emotional standards (among many other things), but the connection once made has an unsurprising quality. Where law relates to emotion, and where standards change, it would be disconcerting if there were no link.

When one moves beyond the law, to emotion-touched activities beyond the purely personal realm but where actual experience as well as standards are in play, connections become inherently trickier. Tempting as it is to say that socialization plus changing family relationships add up to a larger pattern—for example, calling for suppression of jealousy across the board—it is necessary to be cautious.

Yet, before seeking evidence that is scattered at best, it is possible to suggest a scenario, that will begin with what is known and then move progressively to less definite areas of emotional life that reflect plausible links. The result will fall short of a full survey of jealousy's outreach in an age of suppression, but it will produce some good questions and a few empirical probabilities.

We return to the pattern of jealousy control developed from the 1920s onward. Amid rising levels of tension among young siblings, including newly severe jealousy directed from older child to recently arrived baby, parents tried to teach that sibling tensions were understandable but childish. We have seen that their efforts paid off to some degree, in teaching older children and young adults that jealousy should be a source of discomfort, avoided if possible and concealed if not. Yet the parental message had some secondary ramifications, precisely because it was not frontally directed toward repression, but toward prevention of jealousy-producing situations plus an emotional mastery supported by loving reassurance. The new socialization practices could produce children who learned that jealousy, while clearly a word to be avoided, constituted an emotion that deserved attention from a loving partner, a mother-surrogate who rushed in to say that she loved as much as ever. It could certainly produce children who learned that jealousy could be legitimately directed toward certain compensations: "I feel jealous of Willy's toys and look, mom bought me a toy just like that for my very own." Or: "I know I should not attack Willy out of jealousy, but look, when I do better in school I get attention that makes me feel rewarded in an ongoing, if silent, rivalry." Jealousy suppression, in other words, even in the most up-to-date strategies, was not unambiguous, and of course it might be further complicated by parents who occasionally switched signals toward a more directly motivational use of the emotion.

An additional result of the combination of heightened sibling rivalry plus new adult attention was a keen awareness, from early age, of the fact of jealousy and its label. American children learned how to say that they were jealous—this was part of the ventilationist tactic, urging that bad emotions be talked away—and they also learned that the emotion could cover a wide variety of situations. Most directly, they learned to call certain rivalries jealous when strictly speaking they might have meant envious. Because children were now being raised with an active sense of their rights to affection and attention, at least in the middle classes and to some degree beyond, they might come to judge that attributes they saw in others really constituted deprivations of themselves, and not simply attributes they enviously wished that they had. The child who lamented the love devoted to a new baby keenly felt that he or she was being robbed of a due, and hence could talk about the resultant feelings in terms of jealousy. This vocabulary would persist in other settings, as another part of the ambiguous but far-reaching socialization process. Elements of this extension may, to be sure, have begun in the nineteenth century. The Hills sisters, cited in chapter 2, talked of jealousy about each other's perquisites when they might have spoken of envy, but the feeling of deprivation was too intense for such niceties when competition for affection was involved. Heightened tensions in the twentieth century only increased the childish propensity to cast a jealousy net widely, a trend also encouraged by experts who similarly used the term broadly where children's rivalries were concerned. Envy, as a separate category, dropped from view save on the part of emotions researchers justifiably—if perhaps now anachronistically—concerned with precise distinctions.

Ambiguities in socialization were, again in the twentieth century but to an extent in the prior century as well, heightened by some tensions in the signals children received when they left a strictly domesticated environment for school. Classrooms in the twentieth century, and particularly after the 1950s, picked up the antijealousy emotionology to some degree. Efforts to damp down competition among children by keeping grades private (rather than posting), by reducing the amount of outright flunking and in general escalating grade levels so that the majority of school students and collegians began to receive honors marks, reveal an awareness among educators that jealousy should not be pressed too far as a motivational tool. To this extent, there was consistency in adult approaches to jealousy. It is also true that the emotional environment and impact of schooling have been too little studied, particularly over time, to permit of detailed conclusions. Nevertheless, it is obvious that school did not move as far or as fast as did many middle-class households, with the result that many children, shielded from overt expression of rivalry at home to the extent possible, found that more overt competition was encouraged, indeed was basic to successful survival at school. To be sure, this competition was carefully not called jealousy, and progressive educators were told to be at pains to find good in virtually every performance, to mask criticism by accentuating the positive. Nevertheless, children knew full well that they often felt jealous of their peers at school.

School contacts, indeed, provide the first framework by which the wider experiential ramifications of jealousy can be explored. Many children researched from the 1930s onward reported jealous feelings about colleagues at school. They were jealous of scholastic abilities, hair color, popularity, and while girls tended to be a bit more open about their feelings the sentiments were widely shared. For many these jealousies for several years took pride of place over any lingering sibling tensions, most of which had been reduced in salience if not patched over. Obviously, school jealousies, to some extent deliberately provoked by the environment, reflected the widening of the term already suggested. One could be jealous of Pam's long blond hair because—trained to think of oneself as a beloved beauty at home— her good looks seemed to some extent a deprivation of oneself, a target therefore for jealous discomfort rather than mere envy.

School jealousies were, however, hard to tolerate past the primary years. Because they involved direct and personal interactions, they inevitably recalled lessons learned about jealousies at home: they were symptoms of childishness, and therefore too painful overtly to sustain. By age eleven, children began reporting a fairly explicit effort to overcome these feelings as unworthy. There is no claim that jealousy ended in fact, only that its open expression was veiled, certainly in talking with any outsider and quite possibly in self-judgments as well. Jealousy and friendship did not mix, and while rival peer groups formed, relationships within each group were supposed to be free from green-eyed tensions. Steady dating and its later replacement in group social activities in theory and to an extent in fact reduced jealous outbursts within the group even over romantic or sexual targets.[16]

This pattern continued in later life. Friends in the twentieth-century middle class were less likely to admit jealousies of each other, or of competitors such as spouses, than had been the case in the nineteenth century. A nineteenth-century pattern visible among men, in their willingness to surrender close male friends to marriage without reference to jealousy, now spread more widely, at least in the terms used to admit or describe emotional reactions. Whether friendship was diluted in the process, as friends tried to prevent jealous potential by holding back a bit from full commitment or surrounding any given friendship by a larger group of suburban housewives or work colleagues, cannot be determined with certainty. But the possibility of an inverse relationship between jealousy and deep emotional commitment is possible in this area too, distinguishing much twentieth-century friendship, on average, from earlier forms.

Ironically, the effort to deny jealousy in friendship could proceed to such a degree that the emotion went unmentioned in scholarly assessments of the relationship by the 1980s. A host of tensions were covered, such as reactions to a friend's marriage, under broader adjustment categories, but neither the researchers nor the respondents were willing to call a jealous spade green.[17]

Friendship, then, from later school years onward, constitutes an area where the dominant antijealousy emotionology had some impact, but there were other fields where the patterns were less clearcut, where jealousy's malleability and the ambiguities of childhood socialization could produce more open results.

Jealousy and Work. One cause of the twentieth-century intensification of concern about jealousy, and particularly the extension to childhood socialization, rested in shifts in the American economic structure toward more occupations in the service and corporate hierarchy sectors. Work here in principle demanded a new ability to be pleasant and/or to cooperate, and with these requirements overt jealousy was not compatible. Not surprisingly, then, twentieth-century personnel literature emphasized personable, superficially friendly traits in which jealousy had no place.

Thus Dale Carnegie endlessly urged his salesmen clientele to make people like them, by showing interest in others, encouraging them to talk about themselves and feel important.[18] Industrial psychologists, urging appropriate management styles, stressed group cohesiveness, in which individual egos would be subsumed under larger harmonies. Undue zeal was specifically counterindicated. Competition should give way, or at least be sufficiently masked, to permit bureaucrats to fit in with each other, and training programs, bent in the 1920s and 1930s toward survival of the fittest, were adapted to downplay direct rivalry. Teamwork was all.[19] Fascination with Japanese cooperativeness and selfless group spirit, in the 1980s, was another indication of the desire to extend jealousy control to work—though it also reminded of ongoing American limitations in achieving long-sought corporate harmonies. Overall, new standards at work did not eliminate jealous rivalries, but they modified their acceptability and, as in other areas of life, pushed toward some concealment.

Experts admitted, of course, that some individuals might be obstreperous, but the hope was that a combination of appropriate (implicitly, jealousy-free) personalities and rational organization would minimize emotional distractions.[20] Problems of resentment could be noted: promotion of younger employees might rouse criticism from older workers stressing seniority. But jealousy need not be invoked in this situation, which should respond to a clear organizational structure, rational job descriptions attached, plus promotion of a cooperative mood.[21]

In all this, however, there was no specific mention of jealousy as an issue. Americans were schooled by this point to think of the emotion in rather confined if vivid settings, linked to family attachments and romance, so the absence of comment is in one sense unsurprising. It is also true that failure to discuss jealousy complicates any assignment designed to explore its role in work settings. Nevertheless, it is possible to suggest that the absence of discussion, the assumption that people would be trained to control their jealousy as part of proper middle-class upbringing, and that no further emotional management was needed beyond the cooperative atmosphere, left some important loopholes. The absence of labels for jealousy in public settings when it clearly would have been possible to apply a detailed vocabulary carried over from childhood strictures on rivalry, may have authorized work-based jealousy in fact, whatever the cooperative veneer. This result of lack of labeling has applied to other emotions in the past—possibly even to sibling rivalry itself in the nineteenth century, and certainly fit a work situation where vagueness contrasted so vividly with the antijealousy precision applied to other relationships. An interesting example of the resultant complexity showed in the astonished critical response directed toward autobiographics that admitted intense professional jealousies, as in scientific research. Reactions ranged from shock at the pettiness involved to astonishment at the frankness, suggesting a clear sense that work jealousies should not usually be acknowledged but some ongoing confusion as to their incidence in fact.[22]

Some observers claimed, to be sure, that the corporate environment was unusually free from backbiting and the kinds of personal resentments that jealousy might engender. They contrasted this setting with the more harshly competitive world of entrepreneurs and also with academe, where jealousy was far more active and blatant. Perhaps, by the 1950s, middle-class Americans were sorting themselves out to a degree in their job choices, with those with more urgent jealousy choosing channels were the emotion had somewhat freer rein—as in reviews of each other's work, or contemptuous references about colleagues to scandal-mongering graduate students—while new-model jealousy-restrainers flocked to management ranks. Even in management, however, jealousy, while of necessity somewhat covert, could be vented. Worries about professional futures, when some individuals were promoted out of middle ranks toward the top slots, had a jealousy ingredient which it was hard to play down amid protestations of group loyalty. Indeed the whole phenomenon of white-collar alienation, as a sense of failure surfacing in one's forties when one realized a permanent slotting into middle management as others surged ahead—when one realized, in effect, that ambitious goals were doomed to disappointment—was heightened by the jolt embedded in facing up openly to career jealousies. Reasons for jealousy were serious in themselves, but the discomfort of recognizing one's own jealousy, given accepted emotionology, could heighten bitterness and frustration. Similar tensions touched subsequent work experiments. In the later 1980s, for example, corporate and government attempts to introduce merit pay incentives from blue collar to managerial levels were impeded by widespread colleague jealousy—in a setting in which 80 percent of all personnel regarded themselves as better than the norm. Thus jealousy, heightened by careful childhood nurturance of feelings of individual worth and related envies, but complicated by distaste for the emotion, extended into the workplace as into family life and participated strongly in work reactions and their emotional repercussions.[23]

Even the successful, earlier in their corporate or sales life, might reflect jealousy lessons in important ways. They had learned as siblings, after all, that jealousy must be concealed under superficial friendliness, in order to demonstrate maturity. But they had also learned unusual sensitivity to the activities of rivals and the legitimacy of promoting self-interest as a means of avoiding the pain of jealous feelings. Open aggressiveness was out, but maneuvering amid corporate hierarchies gave jealousy a vital if carefully unacknowledged role. The emotional complexity of corporate team play was thus prepared by the lessons learned about jealousy: both the need to hide it and the need to avoid pain from it by gaining attention and approval. Jealousy management, in sum, could prepare for management.

Work standards thus increasingly, from the 1920s onward, reflected elements of the dominant emotionology, which could make many types of workers uncomfortable with jealousy when they recognized it in themselves and which contributed to corporate bonhomie. Yet, precisely because jealousy could be redefined as appropriate motivation for competitiveness, work could serve as an outlet for emotional needs which jealousy fed. While explicit discussions of jealousy at work were rare before the 1980s—when they interestingly increased—the extension of the emotion to envy may well have undergirded important emotional reactions in the workplace.

Jealousy and Consumer Rivalry. Concern about preventing unduly forthright manifestations of jealousy, or provocations thereto, extended to the behavior of American consumers as the antijealousy emotionology took hold by mid-century. Suburban consumer culture stressed open and democratic mixing, not a maximization of individual display.[24] It was not appropriate to seem to want undue affluence.

Advertising played to similar nuance. It was not suitable to solicit consumers blatantly on the basis of inspiring jealousy. American advertisers conveyed a world in which all could inspire to improve their standards, a democracy of key products such as fashionable cars. Not only dominant emotionology, which cautioned against making Americans aware that they might be jealous, but also capitalist good sense urged against inciting direct envy of the rich. Nevertheless, a theme of consumer rivalry remained fundamental. Images, if not words, could urge a sense of jealous resentment or a belief that one's worth compelled a certain level of acquisition because others, no better, had already attained it. As at work, a tension was built into the consumer environment, in which jealousy discomfort was both recognized and utilized—recognized by avoidance of blatancy, of direct promptings to feel jealous and act accordingly; utilized, in that privileged lifestyles were shown and Americans urged to want, from deep emotion, the attributes that accompanied them.[25]

This message had particular resonance given the lessons many Americans had given to their children, that jealousy might be avoided or assuaged by access to one's own material goods. So long as a commercial appeal did not evoke jealousy directly, it would be easy to feel a sense of rivalry appeased in emulating a neighbor's new purchase or even in responding to the appeal of that downhome television star whose looks one could not match but whose car could be paid for in just three years.

Jealousy's Outreach: A Summary

The impact of antijealousy standards ran through a number of facets of American public life in the twentieth century. Discomfort with overt jealousy grew. Jealousy that intruded into relationships such as friendship, while not as dire as more intimate forms, was a subject for concern, and many Americans preferred group activities to more intense friendly bonding into which jealousy could intrude.

Less personal environments such as neighborhood or workplace were another matter, though always with the caveat that jealousy could not comfortably be labeled as such. As with nineteenth-century parental appeals to siblings, pleas for cooperativeness or democracy, while quite real, were vaguer than identification and reproval of the equally real jealousy that could crop up as competitiveness or consumerism. Some of the jealousy manifested on the job or in the mall may indeed have been displaced—that is, produced in part by personal relationships in which it could not be directly expressed. Office rivalries or shopping sprees springing from domestic emotional tensions, and relieving these tensions by feeding a need for attention and self-indulgence, were not merely fictional devices. The tensions springing from the campaign to restrict familial and romantic jealousy must be assessed as an active ingredient in furthering a number of other changes, in a wide sphere of endeavor. Here, it is revealing that popularized comment on jealousy in the later 1980s occasionally rediscovered the wider ramifications of the emotion, long downplayed, since the nineteenth century, through the near-exclusive fascination with jealousy and love.[26] Whether the new, and still inconsistent, interest in discussing jealousies at work portends a legitimation or a prelude to more explicit disapproval cannot yet be determined, but it certainly brings some welcome recognition of the emotion's real scope.

For standards for jealousy were not quite as clear outside the romantic realm as they were within it, despite their definite impact in inhibiting open references. In contrast to other reproved emotions in the twentieth century, notably anger, there was little felt need for a generalized campaign against jealousy, of the sort for example that might bring the working classes into line, precisely because the emotion was seen as personal rather than social in its implications. If efforts to reduce personal jealousy, or embarrassment at jealousy that could not be shaken off, enhanced a need to seek outlets elsewhere, the need for surrogate reassurance could seize on the resultant vagueness.

Socialization approaches greased the wheels here, for example by promoting a sense that the most unattractive jealousy could be deflected by responding to envy—by promoting a sense that personal worth was enhanced by matching another's appearance or possessions. How far jealousy's outreach ran cannot by ascertained, precisely because it was so carefully not called by name. Extensions into politics are not farfetched. Thus it is not demeaning to suggest that bursts of feminism in the twentieth century responded in part to an emotion felt, first in reaction to men's freedoms and involvements outside the home and then, by the 1960s, to the growing embarrassment rivalrous women experienced in identifying jealousy in their own reactions, which could heighten the desire for alternative identifications that among many other gains helped them circumvent the need to attack the emotion directly.

Yet jealousy as spur, intensified by its new limitations, was never given free rein. In law, in work, in advertising the reach of anti-jealousy emotionology was considerable, making it difficult to feel too comfortable with any impulse that smacked too clearly of jealousy. Here for example was a clear limitation on too much overt competitiveness, one of the fascinating will-of-the-wisps of American experience in the later twentieth century. Competitiveness was still a virtue, but when it became disruptive—and certainly if it could be identified with jealous motivation—its attractions dimmed. In school and office, concern about jealousy helped prompt new efforts to reduce competitive zeal in favor of more harmonious group relations. The emotional rules were less rigid than in family life, but they could have impact.

Competitiveness and envy indeed frame an interim summary of jealousy's outreach, beyond directly personal relationships. Socialization experiences and enhanced sense of personal rights encouraged many Americans to seek new extensions of jealousy, not to be sure into the old realm of honor but into rivalries that once were envious, but which now could seem to threaten deprivation. Childhood rivalry taught new sensitivities to personal slights, new needs to find compensation. Matching a possession, for example, could now seem a deep emotional need, because it had all the trappings of jealousy and might indeed be enhanced by the limitations on expressing romantic insecurities directly. In these senses, jealousy's outreach expanded in the twentieth century, though Americans remained unaware of the expansion save insofar as they could recognize a childish vocabulary range or could sense that there was some difference between serious and less serious targets for the emotion. Children, after all, were indulged when they commented on their jealousy of neighbor Susy's new dog, in a way quite different from reactions to their impolitic hostility toward a new baby. Yet there was no direct license for jealousy outside the home, as the new strictures on competition and its disruptively jealous components suggested. The impact of deeply felt standards, extending into various public spheres, battled against a need to express jealous impulses under more benign auspices, particularly in light of some of the compensations children had been taught to expect to relieve jealous discomforts.[27]

The roots of the extension of standards lay clearly in the new ingredients in the experience of childhood and socialization. Newly deepened attachments to mothers combined with diversions from direct expression of jealousy to inhibit; but children, while acquiring some impulse control, also learned that outlets for the intense feelings were available by gratifying what once had been called feelings of envy. The childhood patterns and associations could continue in adulthood, widening jealousy's sphere and altering emotional vocabulary alike.

The merger of jealousy and envy expressed the battle between control and selective expression. Envious feelings channeled a jealous intensity, in relations first with siblings, then with peers, workmates, consumers. They may have relieved some jealousy of the more traditional sort, now blocked or concealed by modern emotionology in the family or in romance. Calling envy jealousy articulated this new set of relationships. At the same time, the new vocabulary was a warning, precisely because jealousy brought discomfort and reproval. Unduly overt recognition of jealousy-envy in shopping, at school or at work limited the very license that the vocabulary implied, forcing caution and often increasing frustration through criticism—self-criticism—of one's own reactions.[28]

The full impact of new socialization styles seems to have hit only in the 1960s or 1970s. At this point, some implicit displacement of jealousy from personal to work relationships becomes more probable, and the meaning of jealousy began more predictably to extend in covering envy. This is the point at which adults, now thoroughly schooled as children to reject personal jealousy but also to expect compensatory attention or material goods, were able more fully to express their lessons both in denying romantic jealousy and in expressing partially concealed forms of the emotion in other settings.

The evolving public role of jealousy was thus complex, and unquestionably its outreach sets topics for further inquiry, from legal standards through the intensity of friendship. It is clear, however, that tensions surrounding the emotion had impact in a variety of settings, feeding into new work styles but also hard-to-label discontents, into consumer appeals and even some political battles. Jealousy and the campaign against it provided active emotional ingredients for many facets of twentieth-century life. The rift between real dislike for jealousy and appreciation for the emotional needs it expressed, launched in childhood, could spill over into a host of adult impulses.

CHAPTER 7

Conclusion: A New Style of Emotional Control

The complex impact of antijealousy emotionology and some need for jealousy outlets to score emotional points now impeded in personal relationships constitutes a significant strand in a number of facets of twentieth-century American history. The central importance of the interaction between standards and actual experience, however, rests in the emotional sphere itself. The campaign against jealousy played a role not only in family life, parenting and dating practices, but in the formation of many American personalities. This role tended to increase with time, from the 1920s onward, as new standards gained growing recognition and became to some extent internalized.

It remains difficult, of course, to pinpoint the extent of change in jealousy itself, buffeted between new strictures and new provocations and complicated by great diversity among social classes and different personality types. It is vital to recall that many Americans continued to react jealously and to claim to feel comfortable with their reactions. Yet a growing reticence and desire to conceal did increase with time, with demonstrable impact on many behaviors. The diminution of tolerance for the jealousy of others advanced even more sharply, with pronounced impact on many kinds of personal contacts. While relatively few Americans directly took their jealousy problems to thera-

pists, in contrast to other emotional issues, many, trying to deal with
conflicted marriages or other relationships, did bring their confusion
about what jealousy authorized, how it might win response, to the
couch. While an undeniable impulse to link jealousy and love persisted
in many quarters, the sheer duration of the campaign against jealousy,
and its integral role in middle-class childhood socialization, made jealousy problems hard to articulate. The problems could nevertheless be
very real, both in the embarrassment of a jealous individual and in the
annoyance of partners confronted by jealous reactions. Evaluation of
emotional trends must be nuanced. Jealousy in the twentieth century
neither continues unaltered—a human or Western constant—nor neatly
shifts from common to rare as part of a tidy then-now contrast. Ambivalence, no stranger to jealousy in the Western tradition, took on
new depth.

The best way to assess the shift in jealousy standards and their
partial impact on reactions and self-perceptions is to place change in a
wider context of emotional transformation, in which the patterns triggered around 1900, then developing more fully after 1920 constitute
part of a major shift in American emotional governance, different from
traditional and from Victorian approaches alike.

The three-stage approach to the modern history of jealousy should
now be clear, and it can be stated fairly simply. In the United States
(and Western Europe before the later eighteenth century), jealousy
was inhibited by strong community controls on the types of behavior
likely to provoke it. Emotionology embraced interesting reactions to
jealousy, including considerable approval, but this was less important
for actual emotional experience than the fact that there were few
occasions for display.

Community controls weakened by the early nineteenth century,
which was a key source of a more consistent set of standards bent on
disapproval. However for many Americans, particularly but not exclusively in the middle classes, family arrangements and gender differentiations effectively substituted. Again emotionology was by no means
irrelevant, and in this case it strongly supported the family environment, but it did not provide the only sanctions. Gender shifts reflected
women's new role as chief family guardians (and dependents), with
men moving from patriarchalism to greater individualism. The new

definition of love and hostility to jealousy constituted important emotionological innovations in their own right, designed to support the
family by sanctifying it—though this same emotionology could complicate family life through its demanding expectations.

By the early twentieth century the family itself weakened, as an
enforcer of fidelity and commitment. The resultant opening to more
frequent and uncomfortable jealousy was blocked, if imperfectly, by a
much more insistent demand for emotional self-control. Here, nineteenth-century emotionology added fuel, by channeling the self-control impulse toward blanket disapproval of emotions like jealousy.
Properly socialized, mature individuals were responsible for keeping
their jealousy under suitable command. Emotional individualism was
honored by new authorization to pursue personal pleasure and to
accept less responsibility for the emotional needs of other adults, but it
was seriously qualified by the promptings toward equally individual
restraint. In the process gender differences narrowed, for role differentiation was no longer the basis for a behavioral restraint that would
obviate the need for careful personal control. The burden was on the
individual, male or female.

A rough periodization of jealousy management thus runs: community to family responsiveness linked to an idealized definition of love,
to new pressure for individual self-control.

This periodization modifies, at least insofar as jealousy is concerned,
some important judgments about the modern history of emotional
management, though it builds on this work as well. Norbert Elias
called attention some decades ago to the development of new standards
for internalized emotional control during the eighteenth century, at
least in upper-class circles, accompanying more rigorous courtesy requirements. His work has been supplemented more recently by Gerhard Vowinckel, who emphasizes the link between these new individual standards and the rise of a strong, rationalizing central government.[1]
The decline of community control led simultaneously to new socialization procedures and a more orderly government, the link being the
rational governance of emotional impulse. This framework, clearly
partially correct, might seem to excuse emotions researchers from
doing more than tracing the intensification of a fundamentally
eighteenth-century framework, into the modern day. Yet the idea of

unidirectional trends is too simplistic even for emotions that were substantially redefined in the eighteenth century, like love and anger, and it certainly does not work for jealousy, where the most effective implementation of new standards occurred only a half century ago— at which point the greatest stresses surrounding the emotion emerged as well. The nineteenth-century interlude of middle-class family intensity requires serious attention as a separate stage, and forms as we have seen a complex chapter in the history of jealousy.

Obviously, the twentieth-century approach to jealousy touches base with earlier ideas about individual self-control. The detailed history of jealousy reminds, however, that some important emotional changes have been quite recent, even when they link to prior redefinitions. It reminds also of the central emotional importance of the nineteenth-century family, not only in harboring the well-known idealizations and visions of moral comfort, but also in effectively influencing behaviors that might provoke emotional distress. The Victorian family depended of course on a greater amount of self-control than had been true when community monitoring was more intense, but it also offered a framework for mutual debate and accommodation, allowing individual family members to present uncomfortable emotions and to expect some supportive response. Families both monitored behavior and supplemented the individual in emotional guidance. It was the twentieth century that imposed a fuller set of demands for individual emotional mastery. To be sure, this was cushioned by a new permissiveness toward pleasure seeking—part of the new division between acceptance of pleasant emotions but rigorous prescription of unpleasant ones that had previously been seen as somewhat useful motivators when properly channeled, as in the case of jealousy in defending family boundaries. Though overshadowed by new license, the suppressive strategies were equally important in shaping actual emotional goals.

The effort to win new levels of emotional self-control, which helps also to explain the twentieth-century fascination with beginning the instillation of internal standards in early childhood, formed part of a wider set of changes in the mechanisms of emotional suppression Americans emphasized. Here, shifts in the management of jealousy by no means determined whole strategies, but they entered the new strategies strongly and at an early date. Jealousy control became part of a new framework of emotional governance, and this linked in turn to important new personality goals dependent on a minimization of jealousy in close relationships. Jealousy's key role in inducing and shaping the new suppression strategies derived in turn from its early redefinition as a thoroughly antisocial emotion and the entry it seemed to compel, by the 1920s, into the process of reshaping the emotional reactions of young children.

From Guilt to Embarrassment:
Jealousy and the New Suppressions

The shift away from family-centered controls, and the related new attention to individual restraint of jealousy, fed into a redefinition of the emotional basis for emotional management, from guilt to a new kind of embarrassment. Americans had never felt tremendous guilt about jealousy, save in individual instances as in the nineteenth-century round of utopian experimentation. For guilt depended on a sense of betraying parental love, which might be withdrawn; yet jealousy was designed to attach to love, to defend it, which made a guilt-jealousy equation in practice somewhat problematic. It was not, then, entirely accidental that when a new level of mastery over jealousy was attempted, guilt was supplemented by a new spur, which antijealousy emotionology sought to develop directly and which became fundamental to a new and subtle style of emotional control.

Emotional control in the twentieth-century United States has not been easy to characterize, particularly because its architects have largely eschewed explicit advocacy of suppression, bedecking their strategies with a vocabulary of permissiveness and attacks on Victorian shibboleths from the past. As a result many commentators worry not about suppression but about lack of restraint; their specific comments may be on target, in noting areas where suppression is inadequate or unsuccessful, but their approach may wrongly conduce to a belief that suppressive norms do not exist.[2] Evaluation of suppression is also hampered by the microscopic experimental approach dominant in many branches of emotions research, which is very successful at identifying certain kinds of replicable emotional responses but less adequate in capturing larger suppressive styles that operate in social contexts. In this sense a historical overview not only usefully focuses on contemporary suppression as a process to be described and explained in terms of change, but also emphasizes the need to develop a balance between experimental and more macroscopic observational analyses as the basis for understanding how emotions actually work.[3]

A historical approach can build on a general sense, issuing from several disciplinary perspectives, that contemporary emotional styles differ importantly from their counterparts during previous periods of the American past. Indeed, examination of the origins of twentieth-century suppression largely confirms the judgment that contemporary Americans have been engaged in some fundamental emotional reevaluations. Here, however, a focused historical inquiry also imposes caution. Some prevailing models of historical change are wrong, either because they misconstrue past standards or misinterpret the present or both. Others, not wrong, are excessively vague, offering grand views that have not been pinned down through attention to particular emotions.

Most obviously, an attractively systematic modernization approach, developed in this area primarily by some sociologists, misleads more than it informs.[4] Modernization in this context has been used to argue for an increasingly liberated and individualistic emotional style, in contrast to a rather undifferentiated concern for suppression that presumably prevailed through the nineteenth century. The argument, certainly echoed in many facile popular assumptions (some moralistically critical, others blissfully enthusiastic about contemporary trends), points to a set of traditions which used guilt, shame, or some other set of mechanisms to curb people's natural sexual and emotional proclivities. The twentieth century, with its emphasis on individual personal expressiveness and freedom from constraint, gradually ate into these suppressions, yielding a spontaneity, an emotional openness, that has become fundamental in American personal life. This formulation is simply wrong. It fails to take into account the differentiation among emotions, from approved to disapproved, that has also characterized the twentieth century, often amid a rhetoric of emotional laissez-faire pitted against Victorian or Puritan hobgoblins. It mistakenly equates trends in emotions with trends in sexuality, while exaggerating liberation even in this latter area. It ignores necessary distinctions in the pre-twentieth-century past, that must be made even when one's primary interest lies in contemporary issues. The modernization model does accurately pick up some real shifts in the uses of guilt, but aside from this contribution it should, in the emotions area at least, be laid to rest.

Other implicitly historical models have greater potential. The idea of some basic alterations in modal personality styles, recurrently trumpeted in research since the 1950s, relates closely to the present subject of emotional repression. David Riesman's distinction between inner- and other-directed personalities, though mainly descriptive, bore strongly on emotional styles.[5] Americans concerned with peer relations and standards might become newly uncomfortable with certain emotions that impeded easy social interchange. In contrast the more individualistic personalities previously dominant could utilize intense emotion more readily and might be driven, as well, by guilt-induced suppressions. Christopher Lasch, dealing with a similar differentiation between nineteenth-century character and the personality types that began to develop from the 1920s onward, confronts emotion even more directly.[6] Lasch's twentieth century is marked by a decline in parental guidance and the working-through of inherent emotional tension, leaving children groping for direction from peers and media, alternating between conformity and outbursts of ungoverned rage. The more consistent styles of the nineteenth century, involving strong but regulated emotion, increasingly yield to the odd and troubling blend of vapidness and fits. Lasch's examination of the emotional styles of the American majority is somewhat indirect, as he focuses on the exemplary power of a shift from neurotic to narcissistic personality disorders (a shift which has been contested on empirical grounds).[7] Furthermore, the bleak and condemning tone of his characterization, while exhilarating reading for moral masochists, distracts from a consideration of the causes of change (a point on which Riesman is also vague) and from the probability that a twentieth-century style of emotional management, though novel, must in some ways be serviceable. Lasch does however pick up on a new reluctance to admit jealousy—his example features the reduction of tension between fathers and daughters' suitors where "natural" tension is replaced by trite friendliness, and his insight suggests the importance of jealousy management in new personality goals. The merger of jealousy and envy, sketched in the previous chapter, may also mirror a broader shift to greater narcissism and self-entitlement of the sort Lasch claims. Still, the definition of the central suppressive mechanism can be pressed further.

Forty years ago Ruth Benedict sketched the following shift in American modes of suppression:

The early Puritans who settled in the United States tried to base their entire morality on guilt, and all psychiatrists know what trouble contemporary Americans have with their consciences. But shame is an increasingly heavy burden . . . and guilt is less extremely felt than in earlier generations. In the United States this is interpreted as a relaxation of morals, because we do not expect shame to do the heavy work of morality. We do not harness the acute personal chagrin which accompanies shame to our fundamental system of morality.[8]

Benedict's judgment usefully focuses on the idea of a recent shift in suppressive stance, but also on its link to a longer-standing historical background. It errs at least by historical standards in defining shame as a twentieth-century mode, and may also misconstrue the context for personal chagrin in contrast to a guilt-based reaction. These are questions best explored, however, by taking Benedict's cue that a guilt regime has given way to something else in the twentieth century, but extending it through a historical framework more complex than this particular version of the traditional-modern contrast. For the emphasis on guilt was itself a historical product, not an inheritance of the ages, and its application to reproved emotions was not as rigid as some of our images of Victorianism might suggest. Getting the background right, in sum, is a first step toward building on Benedict's insight concerning the contemporary shift and our undeniable tendency to equate change with laxness.

Despite its religious thunder, Puritan society based emotional standards less on fear of damnation than on community control through shame.[9] In this, despite somewhat greater tendencies toward introspection,[10] it resembled most of Western society in the seventeenth and eighteenth centuries. Religious injunctions created discomfort with certain emotions such as anger, but on the whole attention to emotional discipline was relatively imprecise because of the manageability of behaviors, however emotion-driven, through community sanctions and attendant shame. Individuals were not encouraged, for example, to identify anger as a personal trait—indeed, recognition for Puritans might produce anxieties about a lack of humility. But anger could be expressed as part of appropriate social hierarchy, as against servants; or as a vessel of divine wrath, as against unbelievers; or indeed against neighbors so long as certain constraints were observed.[11] Children were thus taught how dangerous it was to become angry against certain individuals, such as parents—but not that anger was an emotion to be carefully monitored in and of itself. Villages tried to restrain violence against neighbors—with incomplete success, given relatively high murder rates; but they did not seek more direct controls over its possible emotional base. Hence angry insults and those kinds of charivaris that were directed aggressively against disapproved behavior were seen as a normal part of community life.[12] The overall point is obvious: specific emotions were judged less as bad than as having bad consequences, and in these instances behavioral controls were imposed. Children were taught to be attuned to community norms and were widely exposed to the punitive power of shame. They were not taught an elaborate agenda of personal emotional suppression. They might readily, as a result, find outlets for emotional tensions produced by their upbringing or by community constraints, by selecting suitable targets. Emotions such as anger and jealousy might even prove useful in spurring community action against unlicensed behavior.

This traditional emotional regime began clearly to change in the eighteenth century, in two related directions. In the first place, more specific labels were applied to individual emotions and a new list of suitable and unsuitable sentiments began to take shape. Heightened approval of familial love—both warm emotional ties between parents and children and romantic love as the basis of marriage formation—had as its counterpart a growing hostility to anger and, as we have seen, to jealousy.[13]

Along with the new list of good and bad emotions—the reduction of earlier ambivalence about jealousy, for example—came a growing tendency to rely on guilt rather than shame for enforcement of standards.[14] Growing movement of people, including outright urbanization, made the implementation of community norms more problematic by the early nineteenth century—clearly and menacingly in the case of sexual behavior. Emphasis on the distinctness of the family unit, and on growing individual privacy within the family, simultaneously pushed for the creation of internalized standards supported by family sanctions. This in turn meant that emotions themselves, and not simply behaviors, could be manipulated as part of a control apparatus. Hence the undeniable Victorian distrust of unbridled emotion and reliance on rational restraint, which could lead to assumptions about mastery over impulse that contemporary Americans readily find either brutal or naive: Thus an angry young child, clearly prone to ungoverned temper, is sent to his room for several days to meditate on his wicked ways, deprived of his family's love and society and made to feel the kind of guilt that would recur should any outbursts crop up again, a point driven home by the insistence on an elaborate apology when the incident ended—this from a popular early nineteenth-century American family manual.[15] Thus a more precise vocabulary was introduced to designate, and chastise, bad emotions and lack of restraint—such as the word *tantrum*, coined in the later eighteenth century. Jealousy of course was partially exempt from this new regime, as we have seen. It was redefined as bad, but since it supported the family it was not primary target of control through guilt.

The guilt regime was never entirely uniform, quite apart from new license for intensity in certain positive emotions such as love or grief. There was in the first place the heightened distinction between genders in emotional standards. In important respects, ironically given the labels of volatility often applied to them, women were held to stricter emotional standards than men though with some ambiguities where jealous defense of love was concerned. Men's impulses, though they might be subject to strong controls, were seen to be more complex.

Emotional suppression in the nineteenth century was also colored by the familiar division between public and private spheres. The family was a place for a number of deep feelings, but also the context where certain other emotions, such as anger or jealous disruption of cooperativeness, were supposed to be held in particular check. A good Victorian, particularly but not exclusively a good Victorian male, had thus to learn a rather subtle sense of emotional appropriateness quite different from across-the-board control. A great deal of attention to the targeting of emotion resulted. Even adult women, though presumably guardians of domestic emotional felicity, might find some outlets for jealousy and anger in public causes.

Victorian emotional suppression was furthermore seen as a lifelong agenda of character building. While launched in childhood, it was tempered by assumptions of childish innocence and a strong sense that self-control of specific impulses might come more readily in youth. Victorian parents, in other words, sought to establish a certain framework for self-control in childhood, but did not work as consistently toward repression of specific emotions as might be imagined. Many parents were more concerned about moderating behavior than examining its emotional undercurrents. Hence there was much more discussion of excessive fighting or disobedience to parents than of emotional excess in itself, in the middle decades of the nineteenth century. These emphases might produce emotional suppression as side effects, and would certainly discourage huge displays of anger or jealousy, but they did not produce the precise agendas for particular emotions characteristic of the treatment of children in more fully suppressive societies—or in American society a century later. Again, it was assumed that some of the chores of emotional self-governance would be picked up in youth, when character building could become more specific, based on rational instruction. Even sexual control in fact involved more explicit attention to youth than to earlier childhood, again in some contrast to the patterns of the twentieth century.

Finally, thorough suppression of reproved emotions was qualified by the regime of guilt itself. Guilt could, after all, enhance some of the emotions that underlay behaviors against which guilt was applied. A child taught to be guilty over angry disobedience of a parent, through isolation or other marked chastisement, might indeed learn that the parent must be handled with care—often indeed with unexamined respect and love[16]—but he or she might not learn that anger was bad. The discomfort caused by guilt might indeed increase anger. This could, to be sure, turn inward, producing some of the oblique emotional expressions often attributed to some Victorian women; but it could seek more direct outlet. In their greater concern for appropriateness of target than for emotion per se Victorians continued some of the preference for behavioral over emotional control characteristic of earlier centuries, even though they relied more on guilt than on shame as goad.

The Victorian approach to emotional control, then, involved more than a simple list of bad emotions to be bathed in childhood guilts.

Self-control was stressed and emotional excess punished, but restraint was qualified by distinctions of gender and locale; by a certain lack of specificity during childhood; and by a willingness to countenance some of the strong feelings which a guilt regime might generate. This was consistent with the de facto tendency to try to combine a jealousy-free love ideal with an understanding that the emotion might usefully motivate, or stimulate response.

For in dealing both with jealousy and with anger, Victorians were not convinced that disapproval must lead to a fixation on suppression. They were in this, as in other areas, comfortable with a certain amount of useful hypocrisy in which condemnation was less than absolute;[17] this followed from the emotional distinctions encouraged by private-public and gender divisions. They were also persuaded that unpleasant emotions could be useful in certain contexts; only in family life, and particularly for women, did they tend to insist that the discomfort of obtrusive emotions should be avoided. Finally, they were not convinced that children must be converted quickly into paragons of emotional maturity. Their belief in obedience and behavioral control, though resting on different bases from those current in previous centuries, obviated the need to set detailed standards for children, who were in any event, at whatever cost to the actual utility of prescriptive advice to parents, bathed in sentimental glow of innocence. It was not assumed to be an arduous task to teach children the appropriate strategy for difficult emotions, particularly since targeting, not complete suppression, was the aim. Continued efforts at emotional control would form an ongoing part of good character, based on an ability to respond to rational emotional rules.

An essentially "Victorian" approach toward managing emotions lasted in some respects well into the twentieth century, particularly in middle-class and Protestant families. In the 1920s, however, innovations in the American management of anger, taking shape from the 1920s onward, suggest, precisely because of their convergence with the new approach to jealousy, that a new framework was taking shape. The framework involved not only more unqualified disapproval of "bad" emotions, but new means of control. Thus while parents and experts joined in a new war on childish jealousy, and hoped that it would extend to adult relationships, industrial psychologists launched a new attempt to battle anger in the workplace and childrearing authorities urged that parents shift from attempts to channel children's anger to a blanket disapproval.[18] Victorian family ideals persisted nostalgically, but the real force and cohesion of the nineteenth-century middle-class family dissipated, both as cause and effect of what constituted a major shift in emotional regime.

Causation

The causes of this shift in the targets and goals of emotional control were, at base, twofold, though as we have seen in the case of jealousy additional specific factors, including previously developed cultural standards, could feed in where individual emotions were concerned. Thus while new sexual behaviors and demographic patterns spurred jealousy concerns, industrial strife helped refocus the emotionology directed against anger. Obviously also, expert advice givers focused on particular emotions for specific reasons: thus anger came to be attacked not only by industrial psychologists aspiring for roles in American business life,[19] but also by aggression theorists, while Freudian theories (never widely picked up in the aggression area) helped feed a separate sibling expertise. These specifics, however, should not obscure the fundamental dynamic.

The first basic factor, cutting across the disapproved emotions to urge a new strategy of control, involved the change in American economic structure beginning to take shape by the 1920s. Families in managerial and service work pioneered the new concerns, regarding the need for new emotional styles on the job. Creation of smooth personalities, able to sell goods and relate comfortably in bureaucratic interactions, dictated a new list of banned emotions and new means of keeping these emotions under control.

What the workplace increasing called for—and here other features of American public life contributed as well—was a superficially democratic style.[20] Dealings with customers, relations between middle managers and immediate superiors and subordinates, were meant to operate within a framework of theoretical comradery—"friendly, but impersonal" was the way one industrial relations manual put it. This in no sense meant real equality on the level of power and decision making, but it was a deliberate contrast to the class-conflict model that had developed in more traditional industrial interactions. Superficial democracy meant, in turn, an attack on anger, as an emotion that might constitute an abuse of hierarchy, and also the new concern about jealousy as an emotion suggesting friction and possessiveness in various relationships.

Functional explanations do not serve as the only basis for the new strategies for emotional control. Joining economic structure was the growing imbalance between family and individual interests, that made the family less reliable as either emotional governor or emotional refuge. This shift did not mean that families lost all functions, and certainly nostalgic imagery could—still in the 1950s, or 1980s—pretend that families should serve essentially Victorian functions. The fact was, however, that just as communities had earlier lapsed in enforcing behavior, requiring a new system of emotional management during the nineteenth century, so families began to decline in force as well. This change followed in part from measurable institutional shifts. It became harder, for example, to count on adolescence as a time of family-controlled character building when, by the 1920s, secondary education now regularly took middle-class children outside the home, and into the orbit of teachers and peers. The jealousy evidence suggests, however, that adults began to pull away from Victorian-style family commitments even apart from institutional change as men, for example, became newly vociferous about their discomfort with too much wifely jealousy and related moral supervision. Smaller family size, as interpreted by American parents, also encouraged more individualistic identities. New consumer interests and appeals abetted this process, allowing individual expression through acquisition and reducing the validity of guilt-based restraints. Family obligation, and guilts relating to this obligation, by no means disappeared, but they became less sweeping and reliable as emotional guideposts. These changes occurred at the same time as new provocations to jealousy, and possibly to anger, emerged in the larger environment. Jealous lovers or frustrated middle-managers became aware of impulses of which they did not approve, that conflicted with the images they wanted to have of their own personalities—an additional spur to new control strategies.

These changes, then, joined with shifts in work personality criteria in urging a new look at the emotional rating list and at the best means to enforce it. The familiar division between unpleasant and pleasant emotions, with utility judgments attached, was thus due not only to the desire to create smooth, first-name-dropping service personnel but to a new commitment to individual expression and consumer enjoyments. Guilt, clearly unpleasant, became less functional in this arrangement. The interest in emotional socialization of young children followed from a concern about shaping job traits early on, but even more from the concern that after the tender years it would be harder to rely on family management.

While changes in economic organizations and in family cohesion— this last the product of a number of forces including individualistic consumerism—explain the need for a shift to a new control strategy, and away from guilt, it is important to remember that they built on a new emotionology developed in the nineteenth century—in other words, on a powerful preexisting emotional culture already eager, for example, to dissociate jealousy and love. One other general factor may have entered into the twentieth-century shifts, though it relates to earlier changes in emotional culture as well: the decline of deeply felt religion in the bulk of the American middle class. God was no longer as intensely felt force whose presence could be invoked to smooth over difficult or demanding emotions. The jealous or angry individual was on his own, with no ability to seek a higher forgiveness or to claim emotions in service to a divine force. This shift could further the need to develop individual emotional control, and even to downplay the potentially searing qualities of guilt. It may also explain, along with economic functionalism, the real fear Americans began to manifest of socially disruptive emotions such as jealousy. Here, nineteenth-century emotionology had already begun the work of pinpointing unpleasant emotions, just as religion had begun its decline, but it was the twentieth century that saw the full flowering not only of a new emotional hit list but also of a new strategy designed to spare the American majority, now alone in an effectively godless world, the pain of dealing with emotional intensity.

The Embarrassment Strategy

New causation, in turn, gradually produced a new set of general strategies for emotional management, that went well beyond simply applying older devices to younger children. The close parallels that emerged in approaches to anger and to jealousy, though arising from different sets of advice givers dealing with somewhat different settings, bring the new style into clearer focus. In both cases innovations began to emerge in the 1920s but took full root, with measurable effects on emotional behavior, more definitely by the 1950s.

Thus anger control, from the 1920s onward, involved first a growing effort to avoid situations that might provoke emotional response—hence a new-model foreman, who listened instead of shouting. Second, they involved a ventilation tactic when, despite best efforts, anger boiled up: have an aggrieved worker repeat his angry complaint several times, so that the emotion would wear off and be replaced, hopefully, by an embarrassed willingness to drop the whole affair. Certainly wrath could be talked away, even if occasionally a valid issue remained.

The interest in anger-free work suggested a third implementation technique, which entered mainstream family emotionology by the 1940s: stress, in first socializing children, a ventilationist parental response that would prevent anger from becoming a durable personality feature. Parents were urged of course to avoid anger-provoking situations, but they were implored even more strongly to guard against the festering qualities of childish wrath. Let children talk it out, label it, but in the process defuse the whole emotion. Gone was the idea that anger could be disciplined but channeled; references to the utility of anger-charged emotion disappeared in the prescriptive literature, and key channeling symbols such as boxing gloves similarly faded from the domestic arsenal of middle-class boys. Anger was unequivocably bad, though not entirely avoidable in children. The good parent would aid a child in maturing without seeing anger as anything but an unpleasant experience, to be voided without behavioral result.

Techniques for curbing sibling jealousy similarly involved a combination of avoidance and ventilation, though attention turned to childhood socialization even earlier. Procedural arrangements combined with the need to allow the child to vent emotion, verbally, with complete freedom save that the emotional target should be absent. This approach went beyond mere ventilation of emotion, of course. Jealous children were to be lovingly reassured, and not just allowed to talk about their bad feelings in front of an adult arbiter, in contrast to the greater intolerance for anger. There were marked similarities even so. Jealousy was another of those dreadful emotions that had to be aired without finding direct behavioral expression. It had to be rendered passive, not used to motivate. And despite the sympathetic concern that a good parent should use in identifying his young child's jealous feelings, the assumption was that with proper management a child would outgrow the need for reassurance. Precisely because it could be confronted in early childhood the emotion need not persist. The same prescriptive literature that urged anxious attention to young sibling rivalry turned a cold shoulder on the jealousy problems of adults or even adolescents, who were simply immature people who had not received proper socialization when young.

The striking parallelisms in twentieth-century approaches to jealousy and to anger sketched the new overall suppressive style. Anger and jealousy both became synonymous with unacceptable childishness, emotions to be shed as part of growing up. They both demanded explicit attention during early childhood, to prevent incorporation into basic personality and to drive home the lesson that distinctions must be drawn between feeling an emotion and giving it any but verbal expression. Bad emotions could no longer be gilded with assumptions of childish innocence or entrusted to purely moral injunctions; but they could be rendered passive.

The contrasts between this new suppression style and the dominant emotionology of the nineteenth and early twentieth centuries were numerous. The new style allowed, at least in theory, for no gender distinctions. Men had no more natural right to anger than women, women no more leeway for romantic jealousy. The public-private distinction was also eroded, most obviously in the case of anger. Mid-twentieth-century emotionology urged that attention to targeting emotions be dropped in favor of across-the-board defusing. Emotional life outside the home came to be viewed increasingly as a series of interper-

sonal relationships in which more consistent levels of emotional restraint were essential; hence the extension of suppressive norms previously more exclusively directed at family life. The idea of directing
risky, in some ways unpleasant emotions toward some explicit functions, as well as earlier ambivalence about what emotions were really
unpleasant, vanished. Jealousy, which might be viewed as a reinforcer
of family unity, was now a menace; anger still more obviously lost its
entrepreneurial or reformist motivational role.

These redefinitions focused attention on the need for new strategies
for control. Neither anger nor jealousy could be wished away; both
emotions existed, and indeed their manifestations in early childhood
served as the basis for the suppressive approach. Children were to
learn from their first years a distinction between labeling a reproved
emotion and admitting it was felt, on the one hand, and experiencing
the emotion in any full sense. It was all right to say "I feel angry,"
much as one could denote a mild physical disturbance. It was not all
right to let one of the reproved emotions intensify, to act on its base,
or to express it with any pattern or frequency. These childhood lessons
well learned, emotional suppression in adulthood could then rely on
the sense of infantilization inherent in any serious, admitted recrudesc-
ence. This would be combined, of course, with normative rational
controls in the nineteenth-century sense, but the combination was
novel and many people might be more intimidated by their acute
realization that anger or jealousy were childish, rooted as this realization was in their own socialization, than by more abstract ideas that
the emotions were wrong. In this emphasis on childishness lay also the
American interest in concealing reproved emotions, rather than either
denying them or acting on them outright.

Reliance on guilt, and mechanisms to emphasize guilt, declined in
this atmosphere. Unpleasant emotions were no longer to be channeled,
for emotions themselves, and not resulting behaviors, provided the key
focus. Isolation of children and threats of loss of love, basic contituents
of the guilt regime, were now downplayed. Suppression was to be
accompanied by reassurance of affection, particularly of course in the
case of childish jealousy. Early childhood now received new attention,
as a prime target for appropriate emotional directions, and this was
why emphasis on childishness replaced injunctions toward character

building in guiding control of undesirable emotions in adolescence and adulthood. The image of festering emotions and the strategy of talking them out, rather than denying or redirecting, completed the shift away from the nineteenth-century approach. The festering model, a clear twentieth-century innovation, both motivated and guided the larger suppressive style: intensity in bad emotions must be avoided at all costs, but verbalization can dilute and expose to embarrassment even in a superficially friendly audience—and the emotional boil will be lanced.

Characteristic Victorian reliance on guilt was, to be sure, utilized in the increasing reliance on embarrassment. Guilt about certain emotions or behaviors had already extended the possibility of confusion at certain acts or feelings, in a process Norbert Elias aptly dubbed a lowering of the threshold of embarrassment.[21] Embarrassment was however less deeply internalized than guilt, more dependent on a fear of being seen as childish (though again, even in some self-judgments); because socialization in this direction had focused on ventilation amid some loving if disparaging adult reactions, it did not produce the strong internal compass that guilt-inducing isolation had done regarding, for example, sexual behavior. On the other hand, the new control system was directed as a much more thorough defanging of anger and jealousy than Victorian techniques had intended. Hence the result that the mere recognition of one's own anger or jealousy could produce a sheepish emotional retraction or desire to conceal.

Undiluted guilt, however, declined in utility just as shame once had. Changes in family life, particularly parental authority over older children, played a role here, but so did the advent of the new emphasis on consumerism by the 1920s, which played against guilt in favor of the frank recognition of pleasure.

The related shift to the notion of forming personality rather than building character denoted a move away from instilling guilt, which in turn forced a new strategy for dealing with emotions judged more thoroughly reprehensible than before.[22] This did not guarantee use of embarrassment, any more than the decline of community controls and shame earlier predicted a turn to guilt. It set the stage for innovation, however, which was then guided by the growing role embarrassment had played in middle-class emotional life and the promptings of experts about manipulating infant emotion, translated in turn into more durable, internalized strictures against infantile emotional expression.

Reliance on embarrassment—which unlike guilt does suggest an audience—followed as well from the new preoccupation with interpersonal relations. The same organizational and familial concerns that helped prompt a new suppression thus also conduced, along with expert advice on infant management, to the choice of strategies.

The unifying mechanism in this new suppressive system was the enhancement of acute embarrassment at feeling, and even more at openly expressing, a reproved emotion such as anger or jealousy. The instillation of the bases for the embarrassment reaction in early childhood reminded of a guilt regime, but unlike guilt the embarrassment mechanism was not intended to provoke strong reactions. Evisceration of intensity, not passionate judgment—even self-judgment—was the goal. In these senses the new suppressive use of embarrassment differed from both the Victorian and the more traditional systems of emotional control developed earlier in American history. Linked to the new scrutiny of early childhood, based on a newly demanding definition of emotional maturity, emotional suppression twentieth-century style coexisted misleadingly with a sense that older control devices had been relaxed in favor of a more honest venting of impulse.

For the embarrassment at seeming childish proved to be a powerful force. Partly because it was installed so early in life, with overtones of unacceptable dependency—if less starkly than Victorian guilt devices, even more pervasively—and partly because of new sensitivities to familiar peers, the desire to avoid painful childishness ran deep. It effectively pushed many Americans to avoid certain emotions or at least to conceal their expression, and it also worked against some of the emotional intensity that had been part of the guilt regime. Channeling —a key tactic to combine intensity and control—was downplayed, because childishness could not be turned on and off. And while as we will see, new outlets for reproved emotions were sought, lessons about choosing targets became more indirect and subtle than before, again because embarrassed childishness in principle knew no exception: jealousy of a little-known neighbor was in theory no more dignified than jealousy of a spouse. Finally, the embarrassment regime dictated quite a different response to the emotions of others, a greater discomfort with emotional intensity in others and a fuller authorization to turn away, than the nineteenth-century context had required. This was, in sum, a major shift in emotional framework. Its novelty explains why parents, at some point after 1920, had to innovate deliberately, as against their own parents' emotional guidelines and control strategies. It explains why so many scholars have pointed to the distance between Victorian emotional contexts and our own.

Embarrassment, to be sure, is not entirely distinguishable from shame, which recalls Ruth Benedict's judgment cited earlier. However, embarrassment differed from shame in being more internalized, not simply evoked by the judgments of others even as the importance of peer interactions rose. It involved, as we have seen, a distinctive sense of self, in some ways more finely honed and entitled, but in other ways less encouraged toward jealous possessiveness, than was true of the less differentiated personalities of the early modern era. Fewer institutional mechanisms were set to produce embarrassment, unlike the communal enforcement of shame; the force of the idea of childishness, whether invoked by an observer of emotional reactions or by oneself in judging one's own anger or jealousy, was meant to trigger the appropriate emotional response. This was thus a more directly emotional control over emotions labeled undesirable. Finally, the control itself, at least during the socialization process, was cushioned by reassurances of affection, which the starker uses of shame had not entailed.

Assessment of the impact of the new suppressive strategies, the new campaign against reproved emotions based on new use of embarrassment, is inevitably difficult, the results uneven. American society, even middle-class society, was far too diverse and far-flung to expect any general set of emotional norms to win full acceptance. Thoroughly suppressive strategies, which drive basic emotions into virtual nonexistence save in indirect displacement, depend on small, tightly knit and homogeneous settings such as those of tiny tribes or, possibly for some Victorian women, the nineteenth-century household for people confined to domesticity. Furthermore, the suppressive goals and strategies that emerged in the twentieth century were almost inherently inexact, whatever the complexity of the setting. The new emotionology that urged against anger and jealousy admitted that both emotions would appear and could legitimately be labeled and expressed. It argued that the expression should be verbal only, controlled by its very articulation and the embarrassment this would produce. The approach assumed that jealousy, at least, could largely be controlled in childhood, so that people properly raised would not have to confront the emotion very seriously. But the new suppression did not pretend to guard against all manifestations of reproved emotions, even in adulthood. Hence, even aside from continued disagreements and countercurrents, it was hardly suprising that anger and jealousy remained part of actual emotional experience for many Americans.

In the case of jealousy, furthermore, we have noted a continued disparity between the clear standards set for personal relationships, where some impact on emotional self-evaluations was clear, and the vagueness with which jealousy in work or consumer life might be identified. A regime based on personal emotional monitoring through fear of embarrassment, not supported by tight community behavioral controls, is necessarily imprecise, and this certainly applies to jealousy's ramifications.

Yet the new suppression system did have effects. We have seen evidence of a clear increase in both internalized awareness and public enforcement of new standards, after a missionary period of the anti-jealousy and antianger emotionology from the 1920s through the 1950s. Correspondingly, Americans became readier to criticize the anger or jealousy of others, and to feel excused from response to these emotions, than was the case in the early twentieth century. Actions in law or in protest that reflected jealousy or anger in some respects at least declined in incidence.[23] Many Americans learned, in sum, from the new suppressive campaigns what emotions they should claim to shun and also how in some settings these emotions might be put aside.

The impact of new suppression on overall emotional experience forms a vital agenda for further research, in which scholars concerned with contemporary emotion and those interested in processes of change over time may conjoin. Suggestions about growing uses of embarrassment and consequences in actual emotional experience invite testing by social psychologists and sociologists of emotion as well as historians; they form indeed one of the areas in which a mutual interdisciplinary agenda might take shape. Arlie Hochschild thus has persuasively argued that suppression of anger at work, particularly for many service-sector women, through new strategies of embarrassment and manipulation distorts general emotional life even off the job; but her work to date has not fully demonstrated this impact. The present analysis shows that it is possible to trace over time the development of efforts to avoid or deny anger and jealousy in certain settings but also to suggest how these efforts spill over into wider settings; clearly these connections must be expanded.

More sweeping outcomes merit inquiry. The new tactics of emotional control involved a partial redefinition of emotional maturity, defined in terms of keeping childish impulses in check. New kinds of adult supervision and emotional manipulation of children launched the process of growing up, emotionally, early on. At the same time, adulthood in some respects became more demanding, more difficult of achievement from an emotional standpoint. This might account for some interests on the part of youth to deny the imminence of adulthood—as in the 1960s hostility to those over thirty and the extension of the definition of youth. It points to the need to investigate adolescent attempts to find ways to reintroduce spontaneity into their emotional life, by stirring age-specific music or deliberate fright experiences in films or amusement parks. On another front, the new emotional gap painted between children and adults may well have contributed to growing adult intolerance for children and their antics, measurable with particular clarity from the late 1950s onward.[24] Children, after all, had by definition an unacceptable emotional makeup, which could not be ignored; innocence was gone, and automatic maturation could not be assured. Small wonder that mothers and fathers alike noted decreasing pleasure in their children. Again, the ramifications of new emotional standards and controls could run deep.

Among adults themselves the effort to control anger and jealousy alike in certain settings invites inquiry into a search for new outlets, where embarrassment was less salient than in normal circumstances. Embarrassment, after all, had a built-in flexibility, unlike guilt, in its dependence to an extent on audience setting. It encouraged a certain calculatedness, in estimating "audience" responses. Anger at sports events or in furious driving habits are two obvious candidates as settings where embarrassment need not apply, and suggest that contemporary suppression patterns raise a new set of issues concerning targeting, a need to choose relatively anonymous or symbolic settings, based on audience more than object, where outbursts cannot be prevented altogether. Channels for suppressed jealousy may also be traced, as we have seen, in consumer acquisitiveness or even the growing intensity of interest in the mechanics of sexuality, where anonymity or personal emotional neutrality obviate the need for embarrassment.

In general, the twentieth-century stance toward reported emotions increasingly produced a distinctive approach toward selecting appropriate contexts, spurred by the need for outlets though no longer directly sanctioned by emotionology itself. The emotional control regime of the nineteenth and early twentieth centuries, particularly though not exclusively where men were concerned, built on a public-private distinction, with emphasis on the emotional sanctity of the family but the need for somewhat different drives in the messier public sphere. The new suppression regime of the twentieth-century led toward a tripartite private-familiar public-strangers division. The familial sphere still called for extensive control over bad emotions but with some leeway given the need for emotional reassurance when anger or jealousy did crop up. Considerable control was now sought when dealing with a known public, at work, in neighborhood, at school, though with jealousy a distinction between intimates and colleagues still existed to a degree. Among outright strangers, occasionally encountered, a greater leeway was sought precisely because such freedom was no longer permitted, without embarrassment, either in family or at work. Angry rudeness toward strangers, then, in crowds or on the road, or jealous disparagement of an actor or public figure, or even impersonal liaisons designed to vent sexual jealousy might increase in part as unintended results of a powerful new suppressive system, as ways to escape an audience relevant to the most acute embarrassment.

The results of the twentieth-century suppressive style, while still demanding further measurement in terms of shifts in actual experience, suggest relationships to the wider efforts to sketch normative changes in the American character. Embarrassment, though partly internal, does link to new peer sensitivities and a certain other-directedness; indeed the shift to a service economy, involving more people skills, helps explain changes both in suppression and in wider personality style and is in part explained by them. The shift in emotional control differs from Lasch's invocation of narcissism, but it touches base with some of the phenomena he cites including new problems in expressing jealousy and difficulties in targeting anger.

The change in suppression demands evaluation in its own right, however, as a first step toward further understanding of the contemporary emotional framework. The very existence of a suppressive approach deeply rooted in our socialization practices and applied in essentially consistent ways to at least two reproved emotions continues to require emphasis.[25] We too often believe that suppression has been jettisoned, for good or ill, in favor of an emotional laissez-faire, whereas in fact a system has taken root that subtly, in some ways insidiously, allows Americans to believe they can express emotion freely while in fact confining certain emotions to ventilation alone—again the distinction between being allowed to say I felt angry or jealous and actually indulging in the experience of these emotions—or driving toward a limiting of the emotional range because of fear of embarrassment. Confused reaction to the adult experience of anger or jealousy, not a willingness to let either freely emerge, constitutes the real result of twentieth-century emotional norms.

This result may be good, of course. It certainly seems to fit a variety of expectations in family and sexual life and in work settings. Yet the twentieth-century campaign against jealousy and anger constitutes a serious change, not a smooth or inevitable process, and its results are thus diverse. Strategies to defuse anger and jealousy may have tended, as against more standard Victorian experience, to create some anxiety about emotional intensity in general. The relationship between the new definition of emotional maturity and the popularity of "being cool" is obvious, and not necessarily trivial. Affection may be conditioned by the worried desire not to appear possessive or jealous. Victorians claimed that intense love must exist without jealousy (though they often recognized a merger in practice), but the claim is debatable; antijealousy efforts in the twentieth century often involved wider reduction in emotional commitment. Protest loses an edge when the emotional basis for righteous indignation is curtailed. Many Americans, in sum, may have developed a blander emotional life than they realize as a result of a suppressive strategy that encourages an essentially passive stance toward key ingredients of emotional life. As embarrassment has extended its range over recent decades, it certainly affected more than a few specific, reproved emotions, as early childhood lessons and aversions were directed toward redefining what it means to be an emotional adult.[26] As control touched a range of relationships, such as friendship or dating, so it affected feelings theoretically viewed as positive but now seen as threatening embarrassed vulnerabilities. The decline in emotional intensity, though it must still be probed further, may be the most important result of the new system of emotional control, as the anxiety about jealousy-inducing or jealousy-authorizing emotional commitments has long suggested.

Spontaneity and Control

All societies impose controls on emotions, of course. There is a danger, in focusing on recently developed constraints, of implying that contemporary Americans are uniquely confined. And it is true that the suppression style developed since the 1920s can leave Americans feeling more convinced than they should be that they are free to do their own emotional thing—but some ignorance of controls is also par for the historical course. Some historians, indeed, have tried to revive a twentieth-century liberation theme, though not so crudely as self-expression modernization theory held. In this view, elite controls on popular emotional behavior began as early as the sixteenth century[27] and with steadily increasing effect to limit popular spontaneity, in leisure, roughhousing, and emotional release. But the development of new popular culture, based on the solidification of the working class, combined with new rifts in the elite approach began to reverse this pattern around 1900, with expressions of spontaneity more and more often escaping the dour control of official rationality. This is an attractive scenario, and it can be played through in some respects. But it cannot be overdrawn: the campaign against jealousy and other reproved emotions demonstrates that in some areas spontaneity—acting on jealous impulse, for example—encountered more disapproval (including dissuasion in law) and more internalized barriers in the twentieth century than had been the case in the nineteenth. And while new caution particularly described the management of unpleasant emotions, it could also spill over into redefinitions of love and friendship, where exuberant commitment may have been modified by a new circumspection designed to limit vulnerability to jealousy.

New strategies in control thus complicate any effort to see twentieth-century emotional history in simple contrast to earlier repressions. Rather, the twentieth century saw a rebalancing, with some behaviors unquestionably freer but others more circumscribed. How far the self-monitoring spilled over, into new wariness about intense romantic love for example, cannot be defined with certainty. The ramifications of the effort to control undesirable emotions need further testing, in terms of wider impact and unforeseen loopholes alike. It is safe nevertheless to point to the significance of the new suppression patterns, and the quietly central role the emotionological stance toward jealousy played in their elaboration. Americans' emotional range and their means of enforcing it have both changed over the past sixty years.

The emotional formulations that began to take shape early in the twentieth century are not of course permanent. While relatively few Americans report jealousy problems of their own—as opposed to problems of others with whom they deal—important internal tensions remain. An emotionology that insists on separation between love and jealousy has not been uniformly accepted. Women, on average, continue to disagree with men about related issues such as the emotional commitment that should accompany sexuality, and therefore about important potential for jealousy. While tensions alone do not guarantee change, accompanying shifts in context might work toward this result. The 1980s have seen much discussion, and some evidence, of a recommitment to family or equivalent fidelity. The experimental antijealousy atmosphere of the 1960s and 1970s certainly retreated in failure, though other aspects of heterosexual behavior had not greatly changed by the decade's end. A population growing older on average, with new fears about sexually transmitted disease, could conceivably find a new utility for jealousy in helping to defend committed relationships, relegitimizing an emotion for many decades on the run. All of this might happen, and if it did—if either the evaluation of jealousy or the wider suppressive style changed—it would doubtless bring another combination of advantages and drawbacks.

It would be premature, at the end of the 1980s, to suggest that a reevaluation had yet occurred. The history of jealousy and efforts toward its control suggest indeed a measurement through analogy, applicable if not infallible in trying to ascertain new trends. A new emotional style is usually heralded by a major public campaign, in which expert redefinitions and popular concerns commingle. This happened quite clearly between 1920 and the mid-1950s. Redefinitions of this sort are not normal, however, and after a missionary period one can expect a deeper rooting, and more widely ramified impact, even as the stridency of emotional crisis claims recedes. This occurred, by most measurements, from the 1960s onward. Current developments may turn out to prefigure the need for another round of emotionological redefinition—as was the case with the transitional factors that emerged around 1900; but they have not coalesced as yet, and a firm forecast of change is thus premature.

In the meantime, efforts to contain jealousy largely continue. Siblings are still recurrently seen as embattled, though more parents have confidence in an ability to keep them emotionally apart plus some awareness that hostility is not their only normal mode. Crisis has passed, but habits persist. Americans resonate to family values and a vocabulary of love, but they have often accepted a redefinition that seeks to leave jealousy out. Jealousy as constraint receives less legitimacy than was traditionally the case, because of its perceived incompatibility with mature individualism, but jealousy as cement has to a degree crumbled as well.

Notes

Preface

1. Frances Cancian, *Love in America: Gender and Self Development* (Cambridge, 1987); Carol Z. Stearns and Peter N. Stearns, *Anger: The Struggle for Emotional Control in America's History* (Chicago, 1986).

2. Gordon Clanton and Lynn G. Smith, eds., *Jealousy* (Englewood Cliffs, N.J., 1977).

3. Ayala Pines and Eliot Aronson, "Antecedents, Correlations and Consequences of Sexual Jealousy," *Journal of Personality* 51 (1983): 126–40.

4. See particularly Gordon Clanton, "Jealousy in American Culture, 1945–1985: Reflections from Popular Literature," in *The Sociology of Emotions*, ed. D. Franks and E. D. McCarthy (Greenwich, Conn., 1989); Carolyn Ellis and E. Weinstein, "Jealousy and the Social Psychology of Emotional Experience," *Journal of Social and Personal Relationships* 3 (1988): 337–57; G. White, "A Model of Romantic Jealousy," *Motivation and Emotion* 5 (1981): 295–310.

1. Introduction: Traditions of Jealousy

1. Gregory L. White, "A Model of Romantic Jealousy," *Motivation and Emotion* 5 (1981): 295–310; Lillian B. Rubin, *Worlds of Pain: Life in the Working-Class Family* (New York, 1978). On larger problems of cultural variation, see Ian D. Suttie, *The Origins of Love and Hate* (London, 1935), 130ff., who argues for a correlation between cultural differences in jealousy and whether a society is or is not matriarchal. For a claim (based largely on study of Western and modern cultures) that cross-cultural variance on romantic jealousy is slight, see Ralph B. Hupa et al., "Romantic Jealousy and Romantic Envy: A Seven-Nation Study," *Journal of Cross-Cultural Psychology* 16 (1985): 423–46. See also Kalle Achte and Tama Schaker, "Jealousy in Various Cultures in the Light of Trans-Cultural Psychiatry," *Psychiatria Fennica* 8 (1980): 33–44.

2. Judy Dunn, *Sisters and Brothers* (Cambridge, Mass., 1985), 98–99 et passim.

3. Shula Sommers, "Adults Evaluating Their Emotions: A Cross-Cultural Perspec-

tive," in *Emotion in Adult Development*, ed. Carol Zander Malatesta and Carroll E. Izard, (Beverly Hills, Calif., 1984), 319–38; Janice L. Francis, "Towards the Management of Heterosexual Jealousy," *Journal of Marriage and Family Counseling* 3 (1977): 61–69.

4. Gordon Clanton and Lynn G. Smith, eds., *Jealousy* (Englewood Cliffs, N.J., 1977).

5. Ayala Pines and Eliot Aronson, "Antecedents, Correlations and Consequences of Sexual Jealousy," *Journal of Personality* 51 (1983): 124; Nancy Friday, *Jealousy* (New York, 1983), 469; Margaret S. Clark and Harry T. Reis, "Interpersonal Processes in Close Relationships," *American Review of Psychology* 39 (1988): 609–72.

6. Kingsley Davis, "Jealousy and Sexual Property," *Social Forces* 14 (1936): 395–405.

7. David Hunt, *Parents and Children in History: The Psychology of Family Life in Early Modern France* (New York, 1970), 200.

8. Neil J. Smelser and Erik Erikson, eds., *Themes of Work and Love in Adulthood* (Cambridge, Mass., 1986), 127–49.

9. Carroll Izard, *Human Emotions* (New York, 1977), 200; see also 194–202.

10. Davis, "Jealousy and Sexual Property."

11. White, "Model of Romantic Jealousy."

12. Richard Sennett, *Families Against the City* (Cambridge, Mass., 1984); Robert N. Bellah et al., *Habits of the Heart: Individualism and Commitment in American Life* (New York, 1985).

13. Christopher Lasch, *Haven in the Heartless World: The Family Beseiged* (New York, 1977); Barbara Ehrenreich, *The Hearts of Men: American Dreams and the Flight from Commitment* (New York, 1983).

14. Lawrence Stone, *The Family, Sex and Marriage in England, 1500–1800* (New York, 1977); Carol Z. Stearns and Peter N. Stearns, eds., *Emotion and Social Change: Toward a New Psychohistory* (New York, 1988); Phillip J. Greven, Jr., *The Protestant Temperament: Patterns of Childrearing, Religious Experience and the Self in Early America* (New York, 1977); Rhys Isaac, *The Transformation of Virginia* (Chapel Hill, 1982); Peter N. Stearns, "Historical Analysis in the Study of Emotion," *Motivation and Emotion* 10 (1986): 185–93.

15. Jan Lewis, "Mother's Love: The Construction of an Emotion in Nineteenth-Century America," in *Social History and Issues in Human Consciousness: Some Interdisciplinary Connections*, ed., Andrew E. Barnes and Peter N. Stearns (New York, 1989), chap. 10; Carol Z. Stearns and Peter N. Stearns, *Anger: The Struggle for Emotional Control in America's History* (Chicago, 1986).

16. See, for example, Bernard Wishy, *The Child and the Republic* (Philadelphia, 1968); Leone Kell and Jean Aldous, "Trends in Child Care Over Three Generations," *Marriage and Family Living* 22 (1960): 176–77; Celia B. Stendler, "Sixty Years of Child Training Practices," *Journal of Pediatrics* 36 (1950): 122–34; Ellen K. Rothman, *Hands and Hearts: A History of Courtship in America* (Cambridge, Mass., 1987); Stephanie A. Shields and Beth A. Koster, "Emotional Stereotyping of Parents in Childrearing Manuals, 1915–1980" (unpublished paper, University of California, Davis, 1988); Beth Bailey, *From Front Porch to Back Seat: Courtship in Twentieth-Century America* (Baltimore, 1988); Francesca Cancian, *Love in America: Gender and Self Development* (Cambridge, 1987).

17. Margaret S. Clark, "Historical Emotionology: From a Social Psychologist's Perspective," in *Social History and Issues in Human Consciousness: Some Interdisciplinary Connections*, ed. Andrew E. Barnes and Peter N. Stearns New York, 1989), chap. 12.

18. Peter N. Stearns with Carol Z. Stearns, "Emotionology: Clarifying the History of Emotions and Emotional Standards," *American Historical Review* 90 (1985): 813–36.

19. Melanie Klein, *Envy, Gratitude and Other Works* (New York, 1977). On jealousy in

thirty-month-olds across cultures, see L. A. Stroufe, "Socioemotional Development," *Handbook of Infant Development*, ed. J. Osofsky (New York, 1979); Nancy Friday, *Jealousy* (New York, 1983). For the Darwinian approach, see Th. Ribot, *The Psychology of Emotion* (London, 1897). For a classic statement on the unvarying quality of sibling jealousy, and implicit recognition of how uninteresting this proposition can be, see Erik H. Erikson, *Childhood and Society*, 2d ed. (New York, 1963), 256.

20. Theodore D. Kemper, "How Many Emotions Are There? Wedding the Social and the Autonomic Components," *American Journal of Sociology* 93 (1987): 263–89; Helmut Schoeck, *Envy and a Theory of Social Behavior* (New York, 1988).

21. Willard Waller, *The Family: A Dynamic Interpretation* (New York, 1938), 586.

22. Suttie, *Origins of Love*, 141; Madeleine Bertrand, *La jalousie dans la littérature au temps de Louis XIII* (Geneva, 1981), 407–18; Germaine Greer, *The Female Eunuch* (New York, 1970), 149; Madeleine Chapsal, *La jalousie* (Paris, 1977).

23. Bertrand, *Jalousie*, 145; Theodor Reik, *A Psychologist Looks at Love* (New York, 1944); Friday, *Jealousy*, passim.

24. Andreas Cappellanus, *The Art of Courtly Love*, ed. F. W. Lock (New York, 1941).

25. Bertrand, *Jalousie*, passim; Edmund Leites, *The Puritan Conscience and Modern Sexuality* (New Haven, 1985), 109–10.

26. Emanuel Swedenborg, *The Delights of Wisdom Pertaining to Conjugal Love*, trans. S. M. Warren (New York, 1954; originally published 1768).

27. Bertrand, *Jalousie*, passim.

28. Barbara Harris, "Marriage Sixteenth-Century Style: Elizabeth Stafford and the Third Duke of Norfolk," *Journal of Social History* 15 (1982): 373–76. Natalie Davis has recently noted how (in contrast to men) peasant women in France used jealousy in appealing for pardons for crime, suggesting a sense of gender-appropriateness in this particular culture; *Fiction in the Archives: Pardon Tales and Their Tellers in Sixteenth-Century France* (Stanford, 1988).

29. John R. Gillis, *For Better, for Worse: British Marriages, 1600 to the Present* (New York, 1985).

30. John R. Gillis, "From Ritual to Romance: Toward an Alternative History of Love," in *Emotion and Social Change*, ed. Stearns and Stearns, 102.

31. Randolph Trumbach, *The Rise of the Egalitarian Family: Aristocratic Kinship and Domestic Relations in Eighteenth-Century England* (New York, 1978); Stone, *Family, Sex and Marriage*; Rosalind Mitchison and Leah Leneman, "Girls in Trouble: The Social and Geographical Setting of Illegitimacy in Early Modern Scotland," *Journal of Social History* 21 (1988): 493–97.

32. John Demos, "Shame and Guilt in Early America," in *Emotion and Social Change*, ed. Stearns and Stearns.

33. Dickson Bruce, Jr., *Violence and Culture in the Antebellum South* (Austin, 1979), 44–67; Daniel Blake Smith, *Inside the Great House: Planter Family Life in Eighteenth Century Chesapeake Society* (Ithaca, 1980).

34. Leites, *Puritan Conscience*; Norbert Elias, *The Civilizing Process: The History of Manners*, trans. Edmund Jephcott (New York, 1978); Bertrand, *Jalousie*.

35. Benjamin Nelson, *The Idea of Usury* (Chicago, 1969); Trumbach, *Egalitarian Family*; Nicholas Rogers, "Carnal Knowledge: Illegitimacy in Eighteenth-Century Westminster," *Journal of Social History* 22 (1989).

2. Jealousy in Nineteenth-Century Life

1. Mrs. Clarissa Packard [Caroline Howard Gilman], *Recollections of a Housekeeper* (New York, 1834), 53, 54–58.

2. Ellen K. Rothman, *Hands and Hearts: A History of Courship in America* (Cambridge, Mass., 1987).

3. Robert M. Ireland, "The Libertine Must Die: Sexual Dishonor and the Unwritten Law in the Nineteenth-Century United States," *Journal of Social History* 23 (1989).

4. David H. Flaherty, *Privacy in Colonial New England* (Charlottesville, 1972).

5. Steven Stowe, *Intimacy and Power in the Old South: Ritual in the Lives of the Planters* (Baltimore, 1987), deals best with the "deep, tense rivalry among men" (p. 21), though without treating jealousy directly. See also Bertram Wyatt-Brown, *Southern Honor* (New York, 1982), especially chs. 8 and 12; Dickson Bruce, Jr., *Violence and Culture in the Antebellum South* (Austin, 1979), 67–89; Daniel Blake Smith, *Inside the Great House: Planter Family Life in the Eighteenth Century Chesapeake Society* (Ithaca, 1980), 61–76; and, on the growing stress on romantic love, Jan Lewis, *The Pursuit of Happiness: Family and Values in Jefferson's Virginia* (New York, 1983).

6. Robert M. Ireland, "Insanity and the Unwritten Law," *American Journal of Legal History* 32 (1988): 157–72; Ireland, "Libertine."

7. *Summing Up of John Graham, Esq., to the Jury, on the Part of the Defense, on the Trial of Daniel McFarland . . . May 6th and 9th, 1870* (New York, 1870), 13.

8. John D. Lawson, ed., *American State Trials* (St. Louis, 1928), 12:731–32.

9. Max O'Rill, *Her Royal Highness Woman* (New York, 1901), 14 et passim.

10. Mrs. E. B. Duffy, *What Every Woman Should Know* (Philadelphia, 1873), 64–65.

11. Michael Ryan, *The Philosophy of Marriage in Its Social, Moral and Physical Relations* (New York, 1846), 134.

12. G. Stanley Hall, *Adolescence* (New York, 1904), 1:358.

13. Sylvester Graham, *A Lecture to Young Men* (Providence, 1837), 39.

14. John Kucich, *Repression in Victorian Fiction* (Berkeley, 1987), passim.

15. Arnold Gesell, "Jealousy," *American Journal of Psychology* 17 (1905): 484; "A proper amount of the passion is most desirable in both romantic and conjugal love," Mrs. E. B. Duffy, *The Relations of the Sexes* (New York, 1876); O'Rill, *Her Royal Highness.*

16. John Spurlock, "The Free Love Network in America, 1850 to 1860," *Journal of Social History* 21 (1988): 765–80, and *Free Love: Marriage and Middle-Class Radicalism in America, 1825–1866* (New York, 1989).

17. Hal Sears, *The Sex Radical: Free Love in High Victorian America* (Lawrence, Mass., 1977); *The Word,* 1872–74.

18. Marx E. Lazarus, *Love vs. Marriage* (New York, 1852), 24. I am extremely grateful to John Spurlock for his guidance in this area.

19. Andrew Jackson, *The Great Harmonia: Robert Owen Lectures on the Marriage and the Priesthood and the Old Immoral World* (Leeds, 1835), 7–8, 68, 162.

20. Robert D. Thomas, *The Man Who Would Be Perfect* (Philadelphia, 1977); see also Michael Fellman, *The Unbound Frame: Freedom and Community in Nineteenth Century American Utopianism* (Westport, Conn., 1973); Alice Felt Tyler, *Freedom's Ferment* (Minneapolis, 1844).

21. Louis Kern, *An Ordered Love: Sex Roles and Sexuality in Victorian Utopias* (Chapel

Hill, 1981); J. H. Noyes, *History of American Socialism* (1870; repr. New York, 1961), ch. 46.

22. Kern, *Ordered Love*, 255; Pierrepont Noyes, *My Father's House: An Oneida Boyhood* (New York, 1937).

23. Moses Hull, "A Personal Experience," *Woodhull and Claffin's Weekly*, 23 Aug. 1873.

24. Moses Hull, "Facts Are Stubborn Things," *Woodhull and Claffin's Weekly*, 6 Sept. 1873.

25. *Practical Christian*, 30 Dec. 1854, 69.

26. Hall, *Adolescence* 1:357. Hall did admit, though vaguely, that if jealousy were "broadly interpreted," men might be found as susceptible as women.

27. T. S. Arthur, *The Young Wife* (Philadelphia, 1846), passim; William A. Alcott, *The Young Husband* (Boston, 1841), 271.

28. Mary S. Hartman, *Victorian Murderesses* (New York, 1976).

29. Elements of this double-standard manipulation of jealousy had emerged in upper-class literature, as in Britain, by the late seventeenth century, when men were encouraged to play mild games with jealousy, to add spice to their relationships with women, while women were enjoined to be strictly faithful. Again, this may have described a familiar behavioral disparity between the genders, but at the level of emotionological definition it was new, a revision of gender jealousy traits that accompanied the growing emphasis on conjugal love and nuclear family ties and focused attention on women's proneness to the emotion. Edmund Leites, *The Puritan Conscience and Modern Sexuality* (New Haven, 1985).

30. Peter N. Stearns, "The Rise of Sibling Jealousy in the Twentieth Century," in *Emotion and Social Change: Toward a New Psychohistory*, ed. Carol Z. Stearns and Peter N. Stearns (New York, 1989); Daniel T. Rodgers, *The Work Ethic in Industrial America, 1850–1920* (Chicago, 1978), 146–47; Gesell, "Jealousy"; Dale Carnegie, *How to Win Friends and Influence People* (New York, 1940).

31. O'Rill, *Her Royal Highness*; Gesell, "Jealousy," 462.

32. Mary Hills to her mother, 1887–88 Hills family papers, Amherst College. Carroll Smith-Rosenberg, *Disorderly Conduct* (New York, 1985), 73; Nancy Friday, *Jealousy* (New York, 1983), 464.

33. Elizabeth Fox-Genovese, *Within the Plantation Household: Black and White Women of the Old South* (Chapel Hill, 1989), 250–51.

34. Rothman, *Hands and Hearts*; I am extremely grateful to Dr. Rothman for her further comments on the pervasive nineteenth-century silence, in a letter of 5 Aug. 1987; Stearns, "Rise of Sibling Jealousy."

35. Peter Gay, *The Bourgeois Experience: From Victoria to Freud*, vol. 1 (New York, 1984).

36. W. J. Walter, "The Jealous Lover," *Godey's Lady's Book*, Nov. 1841, 193.

37. Mary Rosemond, "Amiability vs. Jealousy," *Godey's Lady's Book*, Aug 1876, 156; see also 146–56.

38. "Editor's Table: Wedded Love," *Godey's Lady's Book*, Aug. 1861, 170.

39. "Thoughts on Married Love," *Godey's Lady's Book*, Jan. 1847, 5.

40. Ibid., 6.

41. Carol Z. Stearns and Peter N. Stearns, *Anger: The Struggle for Emotional Control in America's History* (Chicago, 1986); Gay, *Bourgeois Experience*.

42. Carol Z. Stearns, " 'Lord Let me Walk Humbly': Anger and Sadness in England

and America, 1570–1750," in *Emotion and Social Change*, ed. Stearns and Stearns, deals with the relationship between imprecise labeling and emotional experience. For another important study of the relationship between labels and emotional experience, see S. J. Yanagisako, "The Analysis of Kinship Change," in Yanagisako, *Transforming the Past: Tradition and Kinship Among Japanese Americans* (Stanford, 1985).

43. Mary Hills to her mother 6 and 23 Mar. 1887, 20 Jan., 9 Feb., and 20 Feb. 1888, Hills family papers, Amherst College. The letters concern her younger sister. I am grateful to Linda Rosenzweig for calling this material to my attention. For comparison to twentieth-century teenagers, see Arnold Gesell, Francis Ilg, and Laura Ames, *Youth: The Ages from Ten to Sixteen* (New York, 1956), passim.

44. John S. C. Abbott, *The Mother at Home* (London, 1834); Marion Harland, *Eve's Daughter; or, Common Sense for Maid, Wife and Mother* (New York, 1882), 59; Jacob Abbott, *Gentle Measures in the Management and Training of the Young* (New York, 1871), 100–21.

45. Hugh Hartsham, *Childhood and Character* (New York, 1919); see also H. Clay Trumbull, *Hints on Child Training* (Philadelphia, 1925).

46. Catharine Sedgwick, *Home* (Boston, 1841), 48, 131; Lydia Sigourney, *The Book for Girls* (New York, 1844), 72 and *The Book for Boys* (New York, 1839), 39ff.; T. S. Arthur, *The Mother's Rule* (Philiadelphia, 1856), 20, 25; Lydia Sigourney, *Letters to Mothers* (Hartford, 1838), 58; T. S. Arthur, *Advice to Young Ladies* (Boston, 1848), 108, and *Advice to Young Men* (Boston, 1848).

47. Horace Bushnell, *Views of Christian Nurtures* (Hartford, 1847); Lydia Child, *The Mother's Book* (Boston, 1831), 25; Bronson Alcott, *Record of Conversations on the Gospels* (Boston, 1837), 2:254–55.

48. Bernard Wishy, *The Child and the Republic* (Philadelphia, 1968), 47. The treatment of jealousy in *Little Women* seems archetypical, with strong emphasis on family harmony: there is little mention of jealousy or rivalry; the sisters take pride in each other's accomplishments and strengths. Jealousy emerged only concerning lovers, intruders into sisterly affection; even this young-adult jealousy is not phrased in terms of sibling rivalry. Romance, then, but not emotional relationships with parents, could stimulate thoughts of jealousy.

49. Mrs. Theodore Birney, *Childhood* (New York, 1904).

50. Hall, *Adolescence*, 1:357–82.

51. Jane S. Brossard and E. S. Boll, *The Large Family System: An Original Study in the Sociology of Family Behavior* (Philadelphia, 1956), 186–87.

52. John Demos, "Shame and Guilt in Early New England," in *Emotion and Social Change*, ed. Stearns and Stearns, 69–86.

53. Ryan, *Philosophy of Marriage*. On the condemnation of adult jealousy see also Duffy, *What Women Should Know*, 64, and Lazarus, *Love vs. Marriage*, 24.

54. Gesell, "Jealousy," 484.

55. Ruth Fedder, *A Girl Grows Up* (New York, 1939), 180.

56. For a fascinating exploration of deep male friendships, and avoidance of any recognition of jealousy, see E. Anthony Rotundo, "Romantic Friendship: Male Intimacy and Middle-Class Youth in the Northern United States, 1800-1900," *Journal of Social History* 23(1989).

57. "Thoughts on Married Love," 6.

58. *The Art of Letter Writing in Love, Courtship and Marriage* (New York, 1846).

59. Peter Filene, *Him/Her/Self: Sex Roles in Modern America* (Baltimore, 1986).

3. Jealousy Moves Front and Center: 1890–1920

1. Benjamin Nelson, *The Idea of Usury* (Chicago, 1969); Jean-Louis Flandrin, *Families in Former Times* (Cambridge, 1979); Jan Lewis, "Mother's Love: The Construction of an Emotion in Nineteenth-Century America," in *Social History and Issues in Human Consciousness: Some Interdisciplinary Connections,* ed. Andrew Barnes and Peter N. Stearns (New York, 1989), chap. 10.

2. Flandrin, *Families in Former Times.*

3. Nena O'Neill and George O'Neill, *Open Marriage: A New Life Style for Couples* (New York, 1972).

4. Arnold Gesell, "Jealousy," *American Journal of Psychology* 17(1906): 452.

5. Felix Adler, *The Moral Instruction of Children* (New York, 1893), 213–14.

6. Ernest Burgess and Paul Wallin, *Courtship, Engagement and Marriage* (New York, 1953), 207; see also Margery Wilson, *How to Make the Most of a Wife* (Philadelphia, 1947), 155.

7. Lewis Terman, *Psychological Factors in Marital Happiness* (New York, 1938), 98–106.

8. Christopher Lasch, *Haven in a Heartless World: The Family Beseiged* (New York, 1979); Jacques Donzelot, *The Policing of Families,* trans. Robert Henby (New York, 1979).

9. Sybil Foster, "A Study of the Personality Makeup and Social Setting of Fifty Jealous Children," *Mental Hygiene* 11 (1927): 533–71; Mabel Sewall, "Some Causes of Jealousy in Young Children," *Smith College Studies in Social Work* 1 (1930–31):6–22; Ruth E. Smalley, "The Influence of Differences in Age, Sex and Intelligence in Determining the Attitudes of Siblings Toward Each Other," *Smith College Studies in Social work* 1 (1930–31): 23–44; D. M. Levy, "Studies in Sibling Rivalry," *American Orthopsychiatry Research Monograph,* no. 2 (1937); D. M. Levy, "Rivalry Between Children of the Same Family," *Child Study* 22 (1934): 233–61; A. Adler "Characteristics of the First, Second and Third Child," *Children* 3, no. 5 (1938), 14–39. Only one of these studies, but an interesting one, ran counter to the pessimistic findings about jealousy, noting the diversity of reactions among children and the frequency of intense affection: M. B. Mac-Farland, "Relationship Between Young Sisters as Revealed in Their Overt Responses," *Journal of Experimental Education* 6 (1937): 73–79. But MacFarland's conclusions were ignored amid the welter of findings that jealousy was a major problem and that its resolution depended on careful parental policy, in what was almost certainly an exaggerated perception of a common (though decidely not uniform) childhood response. See Judy Dunn and Carl Kendrick, *Siblings: Love, Envy and Understanding* (Cambridge, Mass., 1982), passim.

10. Viviana Zelizer, *Pricing the Priceless Child* (New York, 1986).

11. Margaret Mead and Martha Wolfenstein, eds., *Childhood in Contemporary Culture* (Chicago, 1955), 150–62.

12. William Byron Forbush, *The Character-Training of Children* (New York, 1919), 2:179–87.

13. Judy Dunn, *Sisters and Brothers* (Cambridge, Mass., 1985), 98–99; Jane S. Brossard and F. S. Boll, *The Large Family System: An Original Study in the Sociology of Family Behavior* (Philadelphia, 1956), 186–87. I claim not that all small families are more likely to engender jealousy but that this correlation with the new demography operated in the Western context where it was combined with intense maternal affection. Not surpris-

ingly, there are signs of a similar correlation in other Western nations such as Great Britain, where children's jealousy won growing recognition in the twentieth century. For jealousy in actual nineteenth century families, perhaps increasing toward the century's end, see various studies on the James and Adams clans.

14. Note that black family manuals still do not treat sibling jealousy. See, e.g., Phyllis Harrison-Ross and Barbara Wyden, *The Black Child—A Parent's Guide* (New York, 1973).

15. Mollie S. Smart and Russell C. Smart, *Children: Development and Relationships* (New York, 1969).

16. See Claudia Lewis, *Children of the Cumberland* (New York, 1946), 69, on efforts to avoid discussing pregnancy with children.

17. David E. Sutherland, *Americans and Their Servants: Domestic Service in the United States from 1800 to 1920* (Baton Rouge, 1981); Daniel Scott Smith, "Accounting for Change in the Families of the Elderly in the United States, 1900–Present," in *Old Age in Bureaucratic Society*, ed. David Van Tassel and Peter N. Stearns (Westport, Conn., 1988), 87–105.

18. Richard Sennett, *Families Against the City* (Cambridge, Mass., 1984).

19. Dunn and Kendrick, *Siblings;* Steven C. Gordon, "The Socialization of Children's Emotions, Emotional Culture, Competence, and Exposure," in *Children's Understanding of Emotion*, ed. Carolyn Saarni and Paul Harris (Cambridge, 1989).

20. Arthur T. Jersild et al., *Joys and Problems of Childrearing* (New York, 1949), 28–30, 87, 94.

21. Robert L. Griswold, "The Evolution of the Doctrine of Mental Cruelty in Victorian American Divorce, 1790–1900," *Journal of Social History* 20 (1986): 127–48; Gerald D. Alpern, *Divorce: Rights of Passage* (Aspen, Colo., 1982), 50.

22. Dorothy Carnegie [Mrs. Dale], *Help Your Husband Get Ahead in the Social/Business Life* (New York, 1953), 73; also see 69.

23. Carl R. Rogers, *Becoming Partners* (New York, 1972), 257–61.

24. Edmund S. Conklin, *Principles of Adolescent Psychology* (New York, 1935), 258; Elizabeth Douvan and Joseph Adelson, *The Adolescent Experience* (New York, 1966), 205.

25. On jealousy and gender role assumptions, see Gary L. Hansen, "Reactions to Hypothetical Jealousy Producing Events," *Family Relations: Journal of Applied Family and Child Studies* et al., 31 (1982): 513–18; on romantic assumptions, David Lester et al., "Jealousy and Irrationality in Love," *Psychological Reports* 56 (1985): 210; Nancy Friday, *Jealousy* (New York, 1983), 469.

26. Paula Fass, *The Damned and the Beautiful: American Youth in the 1920's* (Oxford, 1978); Ellen M. Holtzman, "The Pursuit of Married Love: Women's Attitudes Toward Sexuality and Marriage in Great Britain, 1918–1939," *Journal of Social History* 18(1982): 35–52; Lois Banner, *American Beauty* (New York, 1982).

27. Conklin, *Adolescent Psychology*, 257; Ayala Pines and Eliot Aronson, "Antecedents, Correlates and Consequences of Sexual Jealousy," *Journal of Personality* 51 (1983): 126–40. John Levy and Ruth Munroe, *The Happy Family* (New York, 1962), 89.

28. Carol Z. Stearns and Peter N. Stearns, *Anger: The Struggle for Emotional Control in America's History* (Chicago, 1986), ch. 4; Fass, *Damned and the Beautiful.*

29. Neil J. Smelser and Erik Erikson, eds., *Themes of Work and Love in Adulthood* (Cambridge, Mass., 1986), 127ff.

30. Stephanie A. Shields and Beth A. Koster, "Emotional Stereotyping of Parents in Childrearing Manuals, 1915–1980" (unpublished paper, University of California, Davis, 1988).

4. The Campaign Against Sibling Jealousy

1. Stephanie A. Shields and Beth A. Koster, "Emotional Stereotyping of Parents in Childrearing Manuals, 1915–1980" (unpublished paper, Univerisity of California, Davis, 1988).

2. D. A. Thom, *Child Management* (Washington, 1925), 9–12; see also U.S. Department of Labor, Children's Bureau, *Are You Training Your Child To Be Happy?* (Washington, 1930), 31.

3. Child Study Association of America, *Guidance of Childhood and Youth* (New York, 1926), 100–101. This approach was repeated verbatim in a number of other manuals, though without attribution, perhaps because other, uncited authors might be jealous. Ada Arlitt, *The Child from One to Twelve* (New York, 1928).

4. Dorothy Canfield Fisher and Sidonie Gruenberg, *Our Children: A Handbook for Parents* (New York, 1932).

5. John B. Watson, *Psychological Care of Infant and Child* (New York, 1928).

6. Sidonie Gruenberg, ed., *Encyclopedia of Child Guidance* (New York, 1951); B. Harlock, *Child Development* (New York, 1954); Herman Vollmer, "Jealousy in Children," *American Journal of Orthopsychiatry* 16 (1946): 187.

7. Allan Fromme, *The Parents Handbook* (New York, 1956), 93; Sidonie Gruenberg, *We the Parents* (New York, 1939), 90; Dorothy Baruch, *New Ways in Discipline* (New York, 1949), 124, and *Understanding Young Children* (New York, 1949), 41; John C. Montgomery and Margaret Suydam, *America's Baby Book* (New York, 1951), 123; Daniel M. Levy, *Maternal Overprotection* (New York, 1943), 22–23.

8. Montgomery and Suydam, *Baby Book*, 123; Haim Ginnott, *Between Parent and Child* (New York, 1965).

9. Luella Cole and John J. B. Morgan, *Psychology of Childhood and Adolescence* (New York, 1947); Edmund Zilmer, *Jealousy in Children: A Guide for Parents* (New York, 1949); Mary M. Thomson, *Talk It Out with Your Child* (New York, 1953), 112; Sybil Foster, "A Study of the Personality Makeup and Social Setting of Fifty Jealous Children," *Mental Hygiene* 11 (1927): 53–77; Ruth Fedder, *You: The Person You Want To Be* (New York, 1957), 69.

10. Harold C. Anderson, *Children in the Family* (New York, 1941), 112; Mollie Smart and Russell Smart, *Living and Learning with Children* (New York, 1949), 209; Dorothy Baruch, *Parents Can Be People* (New York, 1944), 103; Gladys H. Groves, *Marriage and Family Life* (New York, 1942).

11. Benjamin Spock, *The Common Sense Book of Baby and Child Care* (New York, 1945), 272.

12. Winnifred de Kok, *Guiding Your Child Through the Formative Years* (New York, 1935), 176.

13. Zilmer, *Jealousy in Children*, 85; Baruch, *New Ways*, 122–23; Joseph Teich, *Your Child and His Problems* (Boston, 1953), 101.

14. Montgomery and Suydam, *Baby Book*, 123–25; "Family Clinic," *Parents' Magazine*, June 1955, 26 and passim, 1954–59; Spock, *Common Sense*, 272–79; Fromme, *Parents Handbook*, 251.

15. De Kok, *Guiding Your Child*, 172.

16. Groves, *Marriage and Family Life*; Leslie B. Hohman, *As the Twig Is Bent* (New York, 1944).

17. Teich, *Your Child*, 98; Margaret McFarland, *Relationships Between Young Sisters* (New York, 1938), 67.

18. Arthur T. Jersild et al., *Joys and Problems of Childrearing* (New York, 1949), 28–30, 87, 94.

19. For an earlier, more straightforward survey of the modern history of sibling jealousy, see Peter N. Stearns, "This Rise of Sibling Jealousy in the Twentieth Century," in *Emotion and Social Change: Toward a New Psychohistory*, ed. Carol Z. Stearns and Peter N. Stearns (New York, 1988).

20. Arnold Gesell, Francis Ilg, and Laura Ames, *Youth: The Ages from Ten to Sixteen* (New York, 1956), passim.

21. Shula Sommers, "Adults Evaluating Their Emotions: A Cross-Cultural Perspective," in *Emotion in Adult Development*, ed. Carol Malatesta and Carroll Izard (Beverly Hills, Calif., 1984), 324 et passim; Steven L. Gordon, "The Specialization of Children's Emotions: Emotional Culture, Competence, and Exposure," in *Children's Understanding of Emotion*, ed. Carolyn Saarni and Paul Harris (Cambridge, 1989).

22. See, for example, Frank Caplan, ed., *The Parent Advisor* (New York, 1977); Dodi Schwartz, ed., *The Toddler Years* (New York, 1986), 216–17; Seymour Fischer and Rhoda Fischer, *What We Really Know About Child Rearing* (New York, 1976).

23. Stanley Berenstain and Janice Berenstain, *Baby Makes Four* (New York, 1956), 8.

24. Benjamin Spock and Michael Rothenburg, *The Common Sense Book of Baby and Child Care* (New York, 1985), 409ff.

25. *Parents' Magazine*, 1954–85. See particularly Jan. 1961, Sept. 1961, July 1962, July 1985.

26. Frank Caplan and Theresa Caplan, *The Second Twelve Months of Life* (New York, 1977).

27. Carole Calladine and Andrew Calladine, *Raising Siblings* (New York, 1979), 31 et passim.

28. Anna W. M. Wolf and Suzanne Szasz, *Helping Your Child's Emotional Growth* (New York, 1954), 255.

29. Stephen P. Bank and Michael Kahn, *The Sibling Bond* (New York, 1982), 206–7.

30. Judy Dunn and Carl Kendrick, *Siblings: Love, Envy and Understanding* (Cambridge, Mass., 1982); Brian Sutton-Smith and B. G. Rosenberg, *The Sibling* (New York, 1979), 6, 155, et passim; Lester D. Crow and Alice Crow, *Being a Good Parent* (Boston, 1966), 136; *Better Homes and Gardens' New Baby Book* (New York, 1979), 138–39.

31. James Hymes, *The Child Under Six* (Englewood Cliffs, N.J., 1964), 81; Podolsky, *Jealous Child*, 125ff; Stella Chess et al., *Your Child as a Person* (New York, 1965), 145; T. Berry Brazelton, *Toddlers and Parents* (New York, 1974), 51ff.

32. Eleanor Verville, *Behavior Problems of Children* (Philadelphia, 1967).

33. Beverly Cleary, *Ramona Forever* (New York, 1984), 176, 182. I am grateful to Clio Stearns and Julie Wiener for guidance in this literature.

34. Judy Dunn, *Sisters and Brothers* (Cambridge, Mass., 1985), 98–99 et passim.

35. Adele Faber and Elaine Mazlish, *Siblings Without Rivalry* (New York, 1987), 15 et passim.

36. Sutton-Smith and Rosenberg, *Sibling*, 260.

37. Leila Tova Ruack, "Jealousy, Anxiety and Loss," in *Exploring Emotions*, ed. Amelia O. Rortz (Berkeley, 1980), 469.

38. Carroll Izard, *Human Emotions* (New York, 1977), 200; see also 194–202.

39. But see Richard Sennett, *Families Against the City* (Cambridge, Mass., 1984), for

some general remarks about the decreased resiliency of Americans owing to a shift toward more intense, and smaller, nuclear families.

40. This link is still to be explored. See John Modell and John Campbell, *Family Ideology and Family Values in the "Baby Boom"* (Minneapolis, 1984).

41. Lillian Breslow Rubin, *Worlds of Pain: Life in the Working-Class Family* (New York, 1976), 82–84.

42. Sennett, *Families Against the City;* Robert N. Bellah et al., *Habits of the Heart: Individualism and Commitment in American Life* (New York, 1983).

43. Joseph Veroff and others, *The Inner American: A Self-Portrait from 1957–1976* (New York, 1981); Ross D. Parke and Peter N. Stearns, "Fathers and Childrearing," *Journal of Family History*, forthcoming; John Modell, *Into One's Own: From Adolescence to Adulthood in America, 1920–1975* (Berkeley, 1989).

44. Gordon, "Socialization of Children's Emotion," while not discussing sibling jealousy directly, provides an excellent model of parents' emotional signaling and children's interpretation.

45. For a comment on how parental responses to jealousy via reassurance might heighten a dependency that might be expressed in adult jealousy, see Bram Buunk, "Anticipated Sexual Jealousy: Its Relationship to Self-Esteem, Dependency, and Reciprocity," *Personality and Social Psychology Bulletin* 8 (1982): 310–16.

46. Gordon Clanton and Lynn G. Smith, eds., *Jealousy* (Englewood Cliffs, N.J., 1977), 35.

47. Shula Sommers, "Adults Evaluating Their Emotions," 324.

48. On the depth of the immaturity and childhood-insecurity themes, and their illogic in fact, see Gordon Clanton, "Jealousy in American Culture, 1945-1985: Reflections from Popular Literature," in *The Sociology of Emotions*, ed. D. Franks and E. D. McCarthy (Greenwich, Conn., 1989).

5. Love and Jealousy in the Twentieth Century

1. Mrs. Havelock Ellis, *The New Horizon in Love and Life* (London, 1921), 27; see also Bertrand Russell, *Marriage and Morals* (New York, 1929); Mikhail Arttzybasheff, *Jealousy* (New York, 1923).

2. Ben B. Lindsay and Wainwright Evans, *The Companionate Marriage* (New York, 1927), 72.

3. Ibid., 90.

4. Ibid., 86.

5. Ibid., 72–73.

6. Arnold Gesell, "Jealousy," *American Journal of Psychology* 17 (1905): 484.

7. Emory S. Bogardus, *Fundamentals of Social Psychology* (New York, 1928), 44.

8. Gordon Clanton and Lynn G. Smith, eds., *Jealousy* (Englewood Cliffs, N.J., 1977), 126; P. A. Sorokin, ed., *Explorations in Altruistic Love Behavior* (Boston, 1970), 18; Kingsley Davis, "Jealousy and Sexual Property," *Social Forces* 14 (1936): 395–405; Theodor Reik, *A Psychologist Looks at Love* (New York, 1944).

9. Edmund S. Conklin, *Principles of Adolescent Psychology* (New York, 1935), 254; see also Jerome M. Seidman, ed., *The Adolescent* (New York, 1953), 755–61.

10. Francis S. Miller and Helen Laitern, *Personal Problems of the High School Girl* (New York, 1945), 72.

11. Elizabeth B. Hurlock, *Adolescent Development* (New York, 1949).

12. Evelyn Duvall, *Facts of Life and Love for Teenagers* (New York, 1950), 210, 231.

13. Ruth Fedder, *A Girl Grows Up* (New York, 1937), 180; see also Oliver M. Butterfield, *Love Problems of Adolescence* (New York, 1941), 77–89; Ruth Fedder, *You: The Person You Want to Be!* (New York, 1957), 63.

14. Paul Popenoe, *Marriage Is What You Make It* (New York, 1950), 17 et passim; Paul Popenoe, *Marriage: Before and After* (New York, 1943), passim.

15. *The Good Housekeeping Marriage Book: Twelve Ways to a Happy Marriage* (New York, 1938), 104.

16. John Levy and Ruth Monroe, *The Happy Family* (New York, 1962), 89.

17. Alexander Magoun, *Love and Marriage* (New York, 1956), 301, 304, 306; see also Judson T. Landis and Mary G. Landis, *A Successful Marriage* (Englewood Cliffs, N.J., 1958), 82; Evelyn M. Duvall and Dora S. Lewis, *Family Living* (New York, 1955), 19.

18. John H. Mariane, *Don't Let Your Marriage Fail* (New York, 1947), 54.

19. David R. Mace, *Success in Marriage* (New York, 1980), 113, 116; see also Marjorie Woods and Helen Flynn, *A Set of Etiquette Pointers to Help Keep Magic in Your Marriage* (Indianapolis, 1955).

20. Lear J. Saul, *Fidelity and Infidelity, and What Makes or Breaks a Marriage* (Philadelphia, 1961), 73.

21. Robert O. Blood, *Marriage* (New York, 1969); Evelyn M. Duvall and Reubin Hill, *When You Marry* (Boston, 1962).

22. Germaine Greer, *The Female Eunuch* (New York, 1970), 149–50.

23. Levy and Munroe, *Happy Family*, 89.

24. Leslie Farber, *Lying, Despair, Jealousy, Envy, Sex, Suicide and the Good life* (New York, 1976), 182, 194, 200, 202; see also Robert L. Barker, *The Green-Eyed Marriage: Surviving Jealous Relationships* (New York, 1988); Williard Gaylin, *Feelings: Our Vital Signs* (New York, 1988); David Black, "The Jealous Lover," *Mademoiselle*, July, 116.

25. Ellen Berscheid, "Emotion," in *Close Relationships*, ed. Harold Kelley et al. (New York, 1983), 162–67.

26. Verlyn Klinkenborg, "Jealousy with Dignity," *Esquire*, January 1987, 33–34; Barbara J. Ascher, "The New Jealousies," *Vogue*, September 1983, 216–17; see also Julia Cameron, "The Petty Passion," *Mademoiselle*, May 1984, 184–88.

27. Not all psychological research was evaluative, of course, particularly after 1960. But even many purely descriptive, experimental statements treated jealousy as an issue to be explained, instead of focusing on accounting for its absence.

28. Bette-Jane Raphael, "What's Green and Lives with Love? The Beast, Jealousy," *Glamour*, October 1986, 80; "Slaying the Green-Eyed Monster," *USA Today* April 14, 1986, 11.

29. Martha Wolfenstein and Nathan Leites, *Movies: A Psychological Study* (Glencoe, Ill., 1950), 47ff.

30. Nena O'Neill and George O'Neill, *Open Marriage: A New Life Style for Couples* (New York, 1972), 239, 240.

31. Ibid., 1984 ed.; Warren Mintz, review of *Open Marriage*, by Nena O'Neill and George O'Neill, *Society* 2 (1974): 291–92.

32. Carl R. Rogers, *Becoming Partners* (New York, 1972), 142, 181; Gay Talese, *Thy Neighbor's Wife* (New York, 1981); Carolyn Symonds, "Sexual Mate-Swapping: Violations of Norms and Reconciliation of Guilt," in *Studies in the Sociology of Sex*, ed. J. M. Hensher (New York, 1971), 87–88.

33. Willard Waller, *The Family* (New York, 1938), 586.

34. Clanton and Smith, *Jealousy*, 181, 195.

35. Daniel Yankelovich, *New Rules: Searching for Self-Fulfillment in a World Turned Upside Down* (New York, 1981), 50; see also Farber, *Lying, Despair, Jealousy*, 152; Grant S. McClellan, ed., *American Youth in a Changing Culture* (New York, 1972), 70; Duana Fenfeld, "Dropouts from Swinging," *Family Coordinator* 23 (1974): 45–49; Gilbert D. Bartell, "Group Sex Among the Mid-Americans," *Journal of Sex Research* 6 (1970): 113–30.

36. *Newsweek*, 13 May 1987, 62; Ayala Pines and Eliot Aronson, "Antecedents, Correlates and Consequences of Sexual Jealousy," *Journal of Personality* 51 (1983): 113.

37. April Bernard, "The Greening of America: Is Jealousy Healthy?" *Harper's Bazaar*, November 1986, 156; Klinkenborg, "Jealousy with Dignity," 33; William S. Bernard, "Student Attitudes on Marriage and the Family," *American Sociological Review* 3 (1936): 356.

38. Bernard, "Greening," 156–66.

39. John Modell, *Into One's Own: From Adolescence to Adulthood in America, 1920–1975* (Berkeley, 1989); Joseph Veroff et al., *The Inner American: A Self-Portrait from 1957–1976* (New York, 1981); Yankelovich, *New Rules*, 252.

40. Ayala Pines and Eliot Aronson, "Antecedents, Correlates and Consequences," 126–40; John Masterson, "Pretty Eyes and Green, My Love," *Psychology Today* 18(1984): 71; Gordon Clanton, "Jealousy in American Culture, 1945–1985: Reflections from Popular Literature," in *The Sociology of Emotions*, ed. D. Franks and E. D. McCarthy (Greenwich, Conn., 1989).

41. Arnold Gesell, Frances L. Ilg, and Louise Bates, *American Youth: The Years from Ten to Sixteen* (New York, 1956).

42. See, for example, the diversity among collegians in 1930 on the subject of sexual fidelity, with about a third claiming considerable, another third very little, tolerance for freedom during betrothal (with women more rigorous than men): Bernard: "Student Attitudes," 356.

43. Pines and Aronson, "Antecedents, Correlates and Consequences."

44. Shula Somers, "Adults Evaluating Their Emotions: A Cross-Cultural Perspective," in *Emotions in Adult Development*, ed. Carol Zander Malalesta and Carroll E. Izard (Beverly Hills, Calif., 1984), 319–38; G. V. Hamilton, *A Research on Marriage* (New York, 1948), 485–86.

45. Gary Schwartz and Don Merton, *Love and Commitment* (Beverly Hills, Calif., 1980), passim.

46. Shula Somers, "Reported Emotions and Conventions of Emotionality Among College Students," *Journal of Personality and Social Psychology* 46 (1984): 214.

47. Schwartz and Merton, *Love*, 80.

48. Phyllis Kronhauser and Eberhard Kronhauser, *The Sexually Responsive Woman* (New York, 1964).

49. Joy Fielding, *The Other Woman* (New York, 1983).

50. Peter N. Stearns, "The Rise of Sibling Jealousy," in *Emotion and Social Change: Toward a New Psychohistory*, ed. Carol Z. Stearns and Peter N. Stearns (New York, 1988).

51. E. E. Le Masters, *Modern Courtship and Marriage* (New York, 1957), 132–33; Maureen Daly, *Profile of Youth* (New York, 1949); Ernest A. Smith, *American Youth Culture* (Glencoe, Ill., 1962).

52. Ellen K. Rothman, *Hands and Hearts: A History of Courtship in America* (Cambridge,

Mass., 1987); Willard Waller, "The Rating and Dating Complex," *American Sociological Review* 2 (1937): 727–34. See also two important recent histories: Beth L. Bailey, *From Front Porch to Back Seat: Courtship in Twentieth-Century America* (Baltimore, 1988), and especially Modell, *Into One's Own*.

53. Butterfield, *Love Problems;* Bailey, *Front Porch to Back Seat*, 26ff.

54. Landis and Landis, *Successful Marriage*.

55. Grace Hechinger and Fred M. Hechinger, *Teen-Age Tyranny* (New York, 1963).

56. Robert D. Herman, "The 'Going Steady' Complex: A Re-Examination," *Marriage and Family Living*, Feb. 1955, 36–40.

57. Ernest Burgess and Paul Wallin, *Courtship, Engagement and Marriage* (New York, 1953), 142–51.

58. Gary L. Hanson, "Dating Jealousy Among College Students," *Sex Roles* 12(1985): 713–21.

59. Clanton and Smith, *Jealousy*, 232.

60. Gary L. Hanson, "Marital Satisfaction and Jealousy Among Men," *Psychological Report* 52 (1983): 363–66.

61. Bram Buunk, "Anticipated Sexual Jealousy: Its Relationship to Self-Esteem, Dependency and Reciprocity," *Personality and Social Psychology Bulletin* 8 (1982): 310–16; some American reports continued, however, to suggest that unfaithful partners might project on others and so feel more jealousy than usual: Pines and Aronson, "Antecedents, Correlates and Consequences," 126.

62. Louis H. Burks, *With This Ring* (New York, 1958), 97; Dorothy Baruch and Hyman Miller, *Sex in Marriage: New Understanding* (New York, 1962), 170–71.

63. Gerald V. Alpern, *Divorce: Rights of Passage* (Aspen, Colo., 1982), 50; Paul Popenoe, *Can This Marriage Be Saved?* (New York, 1960), 237.

64. Hornell Hart and Ellen Hart, *Personality and the Family* (Baltimore, 1941), 314; Lillian L. Giester, William Griffiths, and O. Pearce, *Units in Personal Health and Human Relations* (Minneapolis, 1947), 222; for a contrast between European and American attitudes, see Robert G. Blood, *The Family* (New York, 1972), 552; Yankelovich, *New Rules*, 77; Popenoe, *Can This Marriage*, 196, 237.

65. Gerhard Neubeck, ed., *Extramarital Relations* (Englewood Cliffs, N.J., 1969), 188; see also Joyce Brothers, *What Every Woman Ought to Know About Love and Marriage* (New York, 1984); R. N. Whitehurst, "Violence Potential in Extramarital Sexual Responses," *Journal of Marriage and the Family* 33 (1971): 683–90.

66. Popenoe, *Can This Marriage*, 142, 263.

67. Barker, *Green-Eyed Marriage;* Janet Sayers, *Sexual Contradictions: Psychology, Psychoanalysis and Feminism* (London, 1986), 151; Jan Pahl, *Private Violence and Public Policy* (London, 1985).

68. Lewis Terman, *Psychological Factors in Marital Happiness* (New York, 1938), 98–101.

69. Popenoe, *Marriage Is What You Make It*, 17.

70. Clanton and Smith, *Jealousy*, viii; Harriet G. Lerner, *The Dance of Anger* (New York, 1985), 104–6.

71. Lerner, *Dance of Anger*, 106. On the "code of honor" management of adultery disclosure in 1980s marriages, see a recent British study: Annette Lawson, *Adultery: An Analysis of Love and Betrayal* (New York, 1989).

72. Clanton and Smith, *Jealousy*, 28; Mariane, *Don't Let Your Marriage Fail*, 54; Lindsay and Evans, *Companionate Marriage*, 72, 80.

73. Francis, "Toward the Management," 61–69.

74. Robert N. Bellah et al., *Habits of the Heart: Individualism and Commitment in American Life* (New York, 1983).

75. Bernard, "Student Attitudes," 360.

76. Terman, *Psychological Factors*, 106.

77. Popenoe, *Marriage Is What You Make It*, 17; Duvall, *Facts of Life*, 119, 210.

78. Levy and Munroe, *Happy Family*, 227; see also Hannah Lees, *Help Your Husband Stay Alive* (New York, 1962), 227.

79. Burgess and Wallin, *Courtship, Engagement and Marriage*, 37, 142.

80. Theodor Reik, *Of Love and Lust* (New York, 1941); for a more recent version, with an intriguing oedipal twist, see Leila Tova Ruack, "Jealousy, Anxiety and Loss," in *Exploring Emotions*, ed. Amalie O. Rortz (Berkeley, 1980), 482–84.

81. Margery Wilson, *How to Make the Most of a Wife* (Philadelphia, 1947), 155.

82. Susan Dworkin, "Sexual Betrayal," *Cosmopolitan*, June 1987, 200–203; according to a 1985 *Psychology Today* survey, men and women were (or, more accurately, had become) equally afraid of betrayal, though their specific fears still varied — women dreading a beautiful rival, men a rich and powerful one. Peter Salovey and Judith Rodin, "The Heart of Jealousy," *Psychology Today* 19 (1988): 22–29.

83. Christopher Lasch, *Haven in a Heartless World: The Family Beseiged* (New York, 1979).

84. Barbara Ehrenreich, *The Hearts of Men: American Dreams and the Flight from Commitment* (New York, 1983). Note also that the changes in jealousy also influenced new women's responses in marriage, again with particular force from the 1960s onward but with clear preparation in earlier injunctions against jealousy. The leading change in women's marital norms thus involved a movement from self-sacrifice to self-assertion, as women were urged to join men in redefining intimacy. While a number of factors fed this transition, the desire to avoid the intensities and vulnerabilities of jealous love played a key role. See Francesca M. Cancian and Steven L. Gordon, "Changing Emotion Norms in Marriage: Love and Anger in U. S. Women's Magazines Since 1900," *Gender and Society* 2 (1988): 303–42.

85. Interestingly, some recent comment on jealousy, even at the popular levels, has rediscovered wider potential ramifications of the emotion, beyond romance, with particular emphasis on the workplace. See Bernard, "Greening"; see also chapter 6.

86. Cathy Gulsewitz, "Cathy," Pittsburgh *Post-Gazette,* 13 Aug. 1987.

87. Norbert Elias, *The Civilizing Process: The History of Manners*, trans. E. Jephcott (New York, 1978). While the campaign against jealousy, as it reached popular reactions more fully, built on earlier attempts to replace traditional institutional constraints with internalized emotional controls, it is important to reemphasize that the effective results for the experience of jealousy were quite new. Some earlier historians of emotion have attempted to place twentieth-century norms in a framework effectively established two centuries earlier. This idea of unidirectional trends is too simplistic even for some emotions that were substantially redefined in the eighteenth century, like love and anger, and it certainly does not work for jealousy, where it is our century that proves particularly innovative (and stressful). The distinctive manifestations and causation that must be traced for recent romantic jealousy follow from this understanding of relatively recent yet fundamental periodization.

88. Carol Z. Stearns and Peter N. Stearns, *Anger: The Struggle for Emotional Control in America's History* (Chicago, 1986).

89. Nancy Friday, *Jealousy* (New York, 1983), is of course an interesting if wordy exception.

6. Jealousy Beyond the Family

1. State v. John, 30 North Carolina 330 (1848); State v. Samuel, 38 North Carolina 424 (1859); State v. Avery, 64 North Carolina 608 (1870); State v. Harman, 78 North Carolina 515 (1878). For examples of other supreme courts' affirming convictions of outraged husbands and brothers and endorsing the English common law of provocation, see Commonwealth v. Lynch, 77 Pennsylvania 205 (1874); State v. France, 76 Missouri 681 (1882); State v. Hockett, 70 Iowa 442 (1886); State v. Peffers, 80 Iowa 580 (1890); Bugg v. Commonwealth, 38 S. W. 684 (Kentucky, 1897); Brunson v. State, 212 Alabama 571 (1925); Collins v. State, 88 Florida 578 (1925); State v. Agnesi, 92 New Jersey Law 53, 638 (1918).

2. For the deterioration of the doctrine of irrestible impulse and a general summary of historical developments of the American law of insanity, see Jerome Hall, *General Principles of Criminal Law*, 2d ed. (Indianapolis, 1960), 485–500; Henry Weihofen, *Mental Disorder as a Criminal Defense* (Buffalo, 1954), 52–173. By the early twentieth century, writers of the leading teatise on American criminal law described state statures penalizing adultery and seduction as commonplace. See Joel Prentiss Bishop, *Commentaries on the Law of Statutory Crime. . .* , 3d ed. (Chicago, 1901), secs. 630, 654a; Francis Wharton, *A Treatise on Criminal Law*, 11th ed., 3 vols. (San Francisco and Rochester, N.Y., 1912), 3:secs. 2065, 2103. See also Stanley Coben, "The Assault on Victorianism in the Twentieth Century," *American Quarterly* 27 (1975): 604–25.

3. Joshua Dressler, "Rethinking Heat of Passion: A Defense in Search of a Rationale," *Journal of Criminal Law and Criminology* 73 (1982): 421–34; Rex v. Greening (1913) 23 Cox Crim. C. 601, 603; Scroggs v. State, 94 Ga. App. 28, 93 S.E. 2d 583 (1956).

4. Jeremy D. Weinstein, "Adultery, Law and the State: A History," *Hastings Law Journal* (November 1986): 219–38.

5. Texas Penal Code art. 1220 (1925).

6. Coart v. State, 156 Ga. 536, 556, 119 S.E. 723, 733 (1923); Richardson v. State, 70 Ga. 825, 830–31 (1883) (adopting the rationale of Jackson's concurrence in Stewart v. State, 66 Ga. 90 [1880]); Lassiter v. State, 61 Ga. App. 203, 208, 6 S.E. 2d 102, 104 (1939); Gibson v. State, 44 Ga. App. 264, 161 S.E. 158 (1931); see also Miller v. State, 63 S.E. 71, 573 (Ga. 1909).

7. Burger v. State, 238 Ga. 171, 172, 231 S.E. 2d 769, 771 (1977).

8. January v. State, 16 Okla. Crim. 166, 175, 181 P. 514, 517 (1919); Neece v. State, 70 Okla. Crim. 60, 67, 104 P.2d 568, 571-2 (1940); Hamilton v. State, 95 Okla. Crim. 262, 244 P.2d 328 (1952).

9. Weinstein, "Adultery, Law," 222–23; William O'Neill, *Divorce in the Progressive Era* (New Haven, 1967); Lawrence M. Friedman and Robert V. Percival, "Who Sues for Divorce? From Fault Through Fiction to Freedom," *Journal of Legal Studies* (1981): 61–82.

10. Samuel Brown, "The Action for Alienation of Affections," *University of Pennsylvania Law Review* 82 (1934): 472 et passim.

11. Botwinick v. Annenberg, 204 A.D. 436, 439, 198 N.Y.S. 151, 153 (1923), quoting an Illinois case of 1866.

12. Fundermann v. Mickelson, 304 N.W. 2d 790, 791–94 (Iowa 1981); Cannon v.

Miller, 322 S.E.2d 780, 788–804 (N.C. Ct. App. 1984), *vacated*, 313 N.C. 324, 327 S.E.2d 888 (1985); "Heartbalm Statutes and Deceit Actions," *Michigan Law Review* 83 (1985): 1770.

13. Weinstein, "Adultery, Law," passim.

14. *Uniform Crime Reports*, 1962–87 Washington, D.C. For some related observations on unexpected twists in the rates of family murders, see Elizabeth Pleck, *Domestic Tyranny: The Making of Social Policy Against Family Violence From Colonial Times to the Present* (New York, 1987). The notion of declining jealousy-induced violence is, of course, uncertain. Such violence continues to occur, a major pretext for, if not cause of, wife battering. The unacceptability of milder expressions of jealousy and lack of training in their targeting, possible results of the twentieth-century trends discussed in chapters 4 and 5, could for a minority conduce toward this end. However, growing restraint may have occurred, despite present, highly visible problems. In this and other areas, the past may have been still more productive of violence. It is inaccurate, from a historical perspective, to be so enmeshed in current symptoms that real sources of greater self-control are ignored. Elements of some strictures about violence-producing emotions, while products of sincere revulsion, serve also as part of the ongoing campaign for jealousy control, whether precisely accurate or not.

15. Dressler, "Rethinking Heat of Passion," 421–22; Jean Harris, *Stranger in Two Worlds* (New York, 1986).

16. Arnold Gesell, Francis Ilg, and Laura Ames, *Youth: The Ages from Ten to Sixteen* (New York, 1956). For some evidence on jealousy in the wider reaches of adult friendships, see Lillian B. Rubin, *Just Friends: The Role of Friendship in Our Lives* (New York, 1986).

17. V. J. Derloga and B. A. Winstead, eds., *Friendship and Social Interaction* (New York, 1986).

18. Dale Carnegie, *How to Win Friends and Influence People* (New York, 1952), 103.

19. William H. Whyte Jr., *The Organization Man* (New York, 1956), 124, 153, 359.

20. George Fisk, ed., *The Frontiers of Management Psychology* (New York, 1964), 428; William H. Leffingwell and E. M. Robinson, *Textbook of Office Management* (New York, 1950); Henry L. Niles et al., *The Office Supervisor* (New York, 1959).

21. J. Massie and John Douglas, *Managing: A Contemporary Introduction* (Englewood Cliffs, N. J., 1973), 264–65.

22. Carol Z. Stearns, " 'Lord Help Me Walk Humbly': Anger and Sadness in England and America, 1570–1750," in *Emotion and Social Change: Toward a New Psychohistory*, ed. Carol Z. Stearns and Peter N. Stearns (New York, 1988), 39ff., on the labeling issue. On actual work jealousies, whose accounting occasionally bemused public response, see James D. Watson, *Double Helix: Being a Personal Account of the Discovery of the Structures of DNA* (Boston, 1968), and Norman Podhoretz, *Making It* (New York, 1969).

23. Whyte, *Organization Man*, 158.

24. Ibid., 312.

25. Roland Marchand, *Advertising the American Dream: Making Way for Modernity* (Berkeley, 1985), 217ff., 228–37.

26. April Bernard, "The Greening of America: Is Jealousy Healthy?" *Harper's Bazaar*, April 1986, 156 et passim.

27. Leila Tova Ruack, "Jealousy, Anxiety and Loss," in *Exploring Emotions* ed. Amelia O. Rortz (Berkeley, 1980).

28. A historically based venture into emotional labeling and related theory is poten-

tially risky, given still-tenuous links between historical findings and mainstream emotions research. The blending of envy and jealousy, however, though derived from an understanding of jealousy's growing sweep, gains confirmation from recent social-psychological research, which similarly finds an extended use of jealousy almost interchangeable with envy. Envy, to be sure, retains precise meaning when used at all, but jealousy covers the waterfront—in contrast to traditional psychological dicta, theoretical and experimental alike. The new research, becoming available only after my historical findings had been completed, focuses on interview schedules with much-tested American collegians. What the historian can add, besides pleased acceptance of congruent results and a modest suggestion that deliberately planned interdisciplilnary research programs including a strong historical component will be even more fruitful in future, involves two points. First, the contrast with traditional findings suggests a real change over time, not flaws in earlier experimental models. Envy and jealousy were more discrete terms and experiences in the relatively recent past than they have become in the later twentieth century. Second, the sweeping use of jealousy is not a matter of terminological sloppiness; rather, it suggests a real extension of a sense of personal rights and deserts; it corresponds to an important broadening of jealousy's range and legitimacy outside love relationships, while also extending a new set of constraints and ambiguities. Richard H. Smith, Sung Hee Kim, and W. Gerrod Parrott, "Envy and Jealousy: Semantic Problems and Experimental Distinctions," *Personality and Social Psychology Bulletin* 14 (1988): 401–9; for the older view, R. B. Hupka et al., "Romantic Jealousy and Romantic Envy," *Journal of Cross-Cultural Psychology* 16 (1985): 423–46 and M. Silver and J. Sabini, "The Social Construction of Envy," *Journal for the Theory of Social Behavior* 8 (1978): 313–31; and especially, P. M. Spielman, "Envy and Jealousy: An Attempt at Clarification," *Psychoanalytic Quarterly* 40 (1971): 59–82.

The extension of jealous intensity into envy, finally, suggests some of the new sense of personal entitlements associated with increasing narcissism. For an introduction to this historical claim and to the psychoanalytic literature, see Christopher Lasch, *Haven in a Heartless World: The Family Beseiged* (New York, 1977).

7. Conclusion: A New Style of Emotional Control

1. Norbert Elias, *The Civilizing Process: The History of Manners*, trans. Edmund Jephcott (New York, 1978); Gerhard Vowinckel, *Von Politischen Köpfen und schönen Seelen: Ein sociologischer Versuch über die Zivilizationsformen der Affekte und ihres Ausdruck* (Hamburg, 1983).

2. Willard Gaylin and Ethel Person, eds., *Passionate Attachments: Thinking About Love* (New York, 1988).

3. Historians attuned to interdisciplinary work in the social sciences may be surprised —and, I would expect, pleased—at the finding that in the behavioral sciences area their research compass seems ambitious and broad. The practical result, aside from undeniable complexities in interdisciplinary collaboration with researchers accustomed to rather narrow but laboratory-replicable bands of data, is that historians do more agenda setting in dealing with topics in emotions research than they have in more conventional social science interactions.

4. See for example Nena O'Neill and George O'Neill, *Open Marriage: A New Life Style for Couples* (New York, 1972).

5. David Riesman et al., *The Lonely Crowd: A Study in the Changing American Character*

(New Haven, 1973). Some of Riesman's insights concerning new anxieties about anger are particularly noteworthy in this context.

6. Christopher Lasch, *Haven in a Heartless World: The Family Beseiged* (New York, 1977).

7. Jesse Battan, "New Narcissism in Twentieth-Century America: The Shadow and Substance of Social Change," *Journal of Social History* 17 (1983): 199–220.

8. Ruth Benedict, *The Chrysanthemum and the Sword* (Boston, 1946), 223–24. For its various insights, including several that helped guide this chapter, see also E. Goffman, "Embarrassment and Social Organization," *American Journal of Sociology* 62 (1956): 264–71.

9. John Demos, "Shame and Guilt in Early New England," in *Emotions and Social Change: Toward a New Psychohistory*, ed. Carol Z. Stearns and Peter N. Stearns (New York, 1988), 69–86.

10. Carol Z. Stearns, " 'Lord Help Me Walk Humbly': Anger and Sadness in England and America, 1570–1750," in *Emotions and Social Change*, ed. Stearns and Stearns, 39–68.

11. Lawrence Stone, *The Family, Sex and Marriage in England, 1500–1800* (New York, 1977); Demos, "Shame and Guilt"; Carol Z. Stearns and Peter N. Stearns, *Anger: The Struggle for Emotional Control in America's History* (Chicago, 1986).

12. Natalie Zemon Davis, *Society and Culture in Early Modern France* (Stanford, 1975).

13. Jean-Louis Flandrin, *Families in Former Times* (Cambridge, 1979); Randolph Trumbach, *The Rise of the Egalitarian Family: Aristocratic Kinship and Domestic Relations in Eighteenth Century England* (New York, 1978); Philip J. Greven, Jr., *The Protestant Temperament: Patterns of Childrearing, Religious Experience and the Self in Early America* (New York, 1977).

14. Demos, "Shame and Guilt."

15. Catharine Sedgwick, *Home* (Boston, 1841).

16. William G. McLoughlin, "Evangelical Child-Rearing in the Age of Jackson: Francis Wayland's Views on When and How to Subdue the Willfulness of Children," *Journal of Social History* 9 (1975): 20–39.

17. Peter Gay, *The Bourgeois Experience: Victoria to Freud*. vol. 1: *Education of the Senses* (New York, 1984).

18. Arlie Russell Hochschild, *The Managed Heart: Commerialization of Human Feeling* (Berkeley, 1983); Stearns and Stearns, *Anger*.

19. Loren Baritz, *The Servants of Power* (Middletown, Conn., 1960).

20. Abram de Swaan, "The Politics of Agoraphobia: On Changes in Emotional and Relational Management," *Theory and Society* 10 (1981): 373 et passim.

21. Elias, *Civilizing Process*.

22. Warren Susman, *Culture as History: The Transformation of American Society in the Twentieth Century* (New York, 1985), 271–85.

23. Barrington Moore, Jr., *Injustice: The Social Bases of Obedience and Revolt* (New York, 1978), 500–502; Gordon Clanton and Lynn G. Smith, eds., *Jealousy* (Englewood Cliffs, N.J., 1977), 35 et passim.

24. J. Veroff, E. Douvan, and R. A. Kulka, *The Inner American: A Self-Portrait from 1957–1976* (New York, 1981).

25. The need for further study of embarrassment again relates both to historical and to contemporary perspectives. Changing social relations are often productive of new forms of embarrassment, as Goffman has pointed out in suggesting that more democratic

contacts on the job created new potential embarrassments by the 1950s. I am more impressed with the new, suppressive use of embarrassment, which gives the emotion a decided new twist, deepening its personal and social impact and the discomfort it causes, and linking it to feelings less of status inferiority than of infantilization. Parallel to this, it seems to me, has been an effort to ease more minor, conventional forms of embarrassment, by making interview situations less stiff, insisting on less punctilious sexual decorum, and so on. One subordinate theme worth pursuing involves the history of blushing and reactions to it. Blushing, rather charming in Victorian context when embarrassment had few heavy duties, recedes in notice in our own age, when embarrassment is more central, and its invocation more uniform than random individual proclivity to blushing can express. Again, the strong suggestion is that embarrassment itself has an important modern history. But the nature, causes, and uses of embarrassment clearly deserve much more exploration than they have received in any kind of emotions research.

26. It is also important to extend to other emotions consideration of the twentieth-century's pattern of suppression. Grief, in the twentieth century, has been subjected to new pressures from embarrassment, and the same may hold true for certain types of fear. There is certainly an agenda item to flesh out our understanding of reproved emotions and their treatment in our own time.

27. Arthur Mitzman, "The Civilizing Offensive: Mentalities, High Culture and Individual Psyches," *Journal of Social History* 20 (1986): 663–88.

Index